Illusions of Terrorism and Counter-Terrorism

PROCEEDINGS OF THE BRITISH ACADEMY · 203

Illusions of Terrorism and Counter-Terrorism

Edited by
RICHARD ENGLISH

Published for THE BRITISH ACADEMY
by OXFORD UNIVERSITY PRESS

Oxford University Press, Great Clarendon Street, Oxford OX2 6DP

First edition published in 2015

British Library Cataloguing in Publication Data
Data available

Library of Congress Cataloging in Publication Data
Data available

Typeset by Manila Typesetting Company, Philippines
Printed and bound by CPI Group (UK) Ltd, Croydon, CR0 4YY

ISBN 978-0-19-726590-1
ISSN 0068-1202

Contents

Notes on Contributors

Alia Brahimi is a Visiting Research Fellow at the Oxford University Changing Character of War Programme at Pembroke College, Oxford. She was previously a Research Fellow at LSE and a Research Fellow at St Antony's College, Oxford. She read Philosophy at the University of Edinburgh before completing an MPhil and DPhil in International Relations at Oxford. Dr Brahimi is the author of *Jihad and Just War in the War on Terror* (2010), as well as a number of papers on al-Qaida's evolving ideology and strategy, the Islamic Just War tradition, political Islam and the politics of the Middle East.

Audrey Kurth Cronin is Distinguished Service Professor at George Mason University in Arlington, Virginia, USA. Prior to that, she was Professor and Director of the core course on military strategy at the National War College (2007–11). She came to the War College from Oxford University, where she was Director of Studies for the Changing Character of War programme (2005–07). She continues as a non-residential Senior Research Associate at Oxford. Before that, she was Specialist in Terrorism at the Congressional Research Service, advising Members of the US Congress in the aftermath of 9/11. She has served periodically in the Executive branch, including in the Office of the Secretary of Defence/Policy, where she drafted portions of the Secretary's strategic plan. Professor Cronin has written or edited four books, including *How Terrorism Ends: Understanding the Decline and Demise of Terrorist Campaigns* (2009), and dozens of articles.

Richard English is Wardlaw Professor of Politics in the School of International Relations and Director of the Handa Centre for the Study of Terrorism and Political Violence (CSTPV) at the University of St Andrews. He was born in 1963 in Belfast, where he worked at Queen's University between 1989 and 2011. His books include the award-winning studies *Armed Struggle: The History of the IRA* (2003) and *Irish Freedom: The History of Nationalism in Ireland* (2006). He is a Fellow of the British Academy, a Member of the Royal Irish Academy, a Fellow of the Royal Society of Edinburgh, a Fellow of the Royal Historical Society, and an Honorary Fellow of Keble College Oxford.

Conor Gearty is Professor of Human Rights Law at the London School of Economics, where he is also Director of the Institute of Public Affairs. He was Director of LSE's Centre for the Study of Human Rights from 2002 to 2009, and is the author of many books and articles on human rights, civil liberties, and terrorism, including *Liberty and Security* (2013). He is a practising barrister and founder member of Matrix Chambers, and a Fellow of the British Academy.

Adrian Guelke is an Emeritus Professor in the School of Politics, International Studies and Philosophy at Queen's University, Belfast and attached to the Institute for the Study of Conflict Transformation and Social Justice. Recent publications include *Politics in Deeply Divided Societies* (2012) and *The Study of Ethnicity and Politics* (co-edited with Jean Tournon, 2012). He is also the author of two works on terrorism: *The Age of Terrorism and the International Political System* (1995) and *Terrorism and Global Disorder* (2006). He is the editor of the journal, *Nationalism and Ethnic Politics*.

David A. Lake is the Jerri-Ann and Gary E. Jacobs Professor of Social Sciences, Distinguished Professor of Political Science, Associate Dean of Social Sciences, and Director of the Yankelovich Center for Social Science Research at the University of California, San Diego. He has published widely in international relations theory and international political economy. His most recent books are *Hierarchy in International Relations* (2009) and *The Statebuilder's Dilemma: Legitimacy, Loyalty, and the Limits of External Intervention* (forthcoming). Past President of the International Studies Association (2010–11), Lake is the recipient of UCSD Chancellor's Associates Awards for Excellence in Graduate Education (2005) and Excellence in Research in Humanities and Social Sciences (2013). He was elected to the American Academy of Arts and Sciences in 2006 and was a Fellow at the Center for Advanced Study in the Behavioral Sciences in 2008–09.

Sir David Omand is a Cambridge University graduate in economics, and a Visiting Professor at King's College London. He was the first UK Security and Intelligence Coordinator, responsible to the Prime Minister for the professional health of the intelligence community, national counter-terrorism strategy, and 'homeland security'. He served for seven years on the Joint Intelligence Committee. He was Permanent Secretary of the Home Office from 1997 to 2000, and before that Director of GCHQ (the UK Sigint Agency). Previously, in the Ministry of Defence as Deputy Under Secretary of State for Policy, he was particularly concerned with long-term strategy, with the British military contribution in restoring peace in the former Yugoslavia, and the recasting of British nuclear deterrence policy at the end of the Cold War. He was Principal Private Secretary to the Defence Secretary during the Falklands conflict, and served for three years in NATO Brussels as the UK Defence Counsellor.

Rashmi Singh is Lecturer in Terrorism Studies at the Handa Centre for the Study of Terrorism and Political Violence (CSTPV) at the University of St Andrews. She holds an MA inHistory from the Jawaharlal Nehru University, and a PhD in InternationalRelations from the London School of Economics and Political Science. She has regional expertise in both the Middle East and South Asia and her primary areas of interest include the role of nationalism, culture and religion (especially political Islam) in the promulgation of political violence and terrorism, most particularly suicide terrorism. Dr Singh's book *Hamas and Suicide Terrorism: A Multi-Causal and Multi-Level Approach* (2011) examined the rise and disappearance of suicide attacks in the Israeli–Palestinian conflict. She was the primary investigator on a START-funded project, In the Eyes of the Beholder, which developed metrics of success and failure in the Global War on Terror and the Global Jihad. She is currently also serving as a member of the World Economic Forum's Global Agenda Council on Terrorism.

Acknowledgements

Some of the arguments published in this volume were first adumbrated at a joint British Academy/University of St Andrews Symposium ('9/11: Ten Years On') held in London on 2 September 2011. Both the British Academy and the University of St Andrews generously contributed to the funding of that event, which was held at the Academy itself. In addition to thanking those institutions (and also those contributors to this volume who spoke on that day), I would like to express my gratitude to the following people for their invaluable help in making that Symposium and also this book a possibility: Professor Sir Adam Roberts, Professor Louise Richardson, Jason Burke, Gillian Duncan, Professor Sir Lawrence Freedman, Professor Charles Townshend, Professor John Anderson, Professor Nick Rengger, James Rivington, Brigid Hamilton-Jones and Tim Brassell. Colleagues and students at the Handa Centre for the Study of Terrorism and Political Violence (CSTPV) at the University of St Andrews have richly informed my thinking on terrorism and counter-terrorism, and to them also I express my profound thanks.

Richard English
University of St Andrews
October 2014

1

Introduction

The Enduring Illusions of Terrorism and Counter-Terrorism

RICHARD ENGLISH

TERRORISM[1] AND COUNTER-TERRORISM represent enduringly and globally important phenomena: vast numbers of lives have been and continue to be affected through direct violence and threats of aggression, or through more indirect consequences in terms of daily patterns of behaviour and societal response. More sharply, the mutually shaping relationship *between* non-state terrorism and state counter-terrorism[2] continues to determine local and international experience in complex and powerful ways. The early years of this century and of the last one painfully exemplified this phenomenon. State responses to non-state terrorist violence triggered catastrophic effects after June 1914, and generated a blood-drenched transformation of international relations also after September 2001,[3] with US-led responses to the terrorist attacks of that month prompting conflicts in Afghanistan, Iraq and elsewhere, in what Jason Burke has referred to as the 9/11 wars.[4]

The literature on terrorism has long offered glimpses of this paradoxically intimate relationship between non-state terrorists and their state enemies, and

---

[1] Terrorism famously carries with it problematic issues of definition, to which this chapter will return. But these should not be immobilising, any more than discussion on the basis of other contested terms (nationalism, the state, imperialism, fascism, colonialism, revolution) should be halted by arguments about the precise meaning of such words. My own approach involves recognition that both non-state and state actors can be judged to use terrorism. See R. English, *Terrorism: How to Respond* (Oxford, Oxford University Press, 2009, chapter 1).

[2] Clearly, state counter-terrorism is not a monolithic category. As will be reflected throughout this book, there can be great diversity between different states, and between different wings of the same state, as they engage in countering non-state terrorist opponents.

[3] R. English, *Modern War: A Very Short Introduction* (Oxford, Oxford University Press, 2013), pp. 37–41, 88–102.

[4] J. Burke, *The 9/11 Wars* (London, Penguin, 2011).

Proceedings of the British Academy **203**, 1–20. © The British Academy 2015.

of the often unanticipated, unintended ways in which that relationship has altered politics and history. So al-Qaida's 9/11 atrocity prompted a War on Terror which, among other initiatives, involved an invasion of Iraq which in turn contributed to the creation of ISIS (the Islamic State of Iraq and Syria, formerly al-Qaida in Iraq);[5] similarly, the policies of the UK state in Northern Ireland amid inter-communal violence in the late 1960s and early 1970s helped bring recruits to the ranks of the anti-state Provisional Irish Republican Army (PIRA);[6] the actions of successive twentieth-century Spanish state regimes made ETA (Euskadi Ta Askatasuna: Euskadi and Freedom, or Basque Homeland and Freedom) violence seem legitimate to a significant number of Basques for a lengthy period;[7] Israeli policies in response to Palestinian terrorism in turn seemed to many to legitimate violence by Hamas;[8] and so on throughout much of the world and enduringly through many decades of history.

The importance of this book is its focus on the relationship between terrorism and counter-terrorism in a distinctive and urgently needed manner. The volume is distinctive in three main ways. First, it assesses the relationship between terrorism and counter-terrorism through drawing simultaneously on the insights of a range of disciplines in dialogue with one another; such sustained assessment is rare in the existing literature, and multi-disciplinary discussion of the relationship is even less frequent. Second, the book is innovative in addressing the dynamics of counter-terrorism in a more interrogative and concentrated form than is common even yet. Third, this volume repeatedly highlights a theme all too rarely considered in the field: the shared and mutually echoing failings and illusions involved in the politics of terrorism and counter-terrorism alike. The book's urgency and timeliness derive from the fact that humanity's most extended, expansive, expensive attempt to extirpate non-state terrorism – the post-9/11 War on Terror – actually prompted significant *increases* in levels of terrorist incident and of terrorist-generated fatality.[9] That humbling reality should make us strive after

---

[5] P. Cockburn, *The Jihadis Return: ISIS and the New Sunni Uprising* (New York, OR Books, 2014).
[6] R. English, *Armed Struggle: The History of the IRA*, 3rd edn (London, Macmillan, 2012).
[7] C. J. Watson, *Basque Nationalism and Political Violence: The Ideological and Intellectual Origins of ETA* (Reno, Centre for Basque Studies, 2007).
[8] R. Singh, *Hamas and Suicide Terrorism: Multi-Causal and Multi-Level Approaches* (London, Routledge, 2011).
[9] E. Berman, *Radical, Religious, and Violent: The New Economics of Terrorism* (Cambridge, MIT Press, 2009), p. 1; E. Stepanova, *Terrorism in Asymmetrical Conflict: Ideological and Structural Aspects* (Oxford, Oxford University Press, 2008), pp. 3–4.

a more comprehensive and candid assessment of the ways in which terrorism and counter-terrorism operate, especially in relationship with one another, so that our understanding allows for more productive and less ossified responses in the future. The current moment is far enough on from the post-9/11 decade for us to be able to assess that experience seriously; now is also a time when we need urgently to reflect on what can be known about this vital subject, so that we can be better prepared to respond to future crises in a more effective and appropriate manner than we have reacted to those of the past.

It is not, of course, that there has been no excellent scholarly work done on terrorism already. Pre-9/11 scholarship in the field grew in late-twentieth-century reaction to a series of terrorist challenges to existing political arrangements and structures of power, and saw the emergence of a small but influential group of distinguished experts in the field.[10] The work of such scholars offered extremely valuable insights into the definition, causation, organisational dynamics and political effects of non-state terrorist activity.[11] That pioneering scholarship was then complemented by a vast explosion of research and publication after 9/11, and in particular following the growth in scholarly interest in the field in the United States of America. This has produced extremely valuable analyses of (among other subjects) the dynamics of suicide terrorism, the reframing of some religious communities in response to terroristic violence, the complex processes by means of which terrorist campaigns come to an end, the distinctive moral problems involved with terrorist action, the intricacies of relevant ideologies and the economic roots and effects of the broader terrorist phenomenon.[12] Together with a range of

---

[10] For discussion and analysis, see L. Stampnitzky, *Disciplining Terror: How Experts Invented 'Terrorism'* (Cambridge, Cambridge University Press, 2013).

[11] A. P. Schmid and A. J. Jongman (eds), *Political Terrorism* (Amsterdam, North Holland Publishing, 1988); P. Wilkinson, *Political Terrorism* (London, Macmillan, 1974); P. Wilkinson, *Terrorism and the Liberal State* (Basingstoke, Macmillan, 1986); B. Hoffman, *Inside Terrorism*, 2nd edn (New York, Columbia University Press, 2006); M. Crenshaw, *Explaining Terrorism: Causes, Processes and Consequences* (London, Routledge, 2011); M. Crenshaw (ed.), *Terrorism, Legitimacy, and Power: The Consequences of Political Violence* (Middletown, Wesleyan University Press, 1983).

[12] R. A. Pape, *Dying to Win: Why Suicide Terrorists Do It* (London, Gibson Square Books, 2006); R. A. Pape and J. K. Feldman, *Cutting the Fuse: The Explosion of Global Suicide Terrorism and How to Stop It* (Chicago, University of Chicago Press, 2010); S. Croft, *Securitising Islam: Identity and the Search for Security* (Cambridge, Cambridge University Press, 2012); A. K. Cronin, *How Terrorism Ends: Understanding the Decline and Demise of Terrorist Campaigns* (Princeton, Princeton University Press, 2009); R. E. Goodin, *What's Wrong with Terrorism?* (Cambridge, Polity Press, 2006); M. R. Habeck, *Knowing the Enemy: Jihadist Ideology and the War on Terror* (New Haven, Yale University Press, 2006); A. B. Krueger, *What Makes a Terrorist: Economics and the Roots of Terrorism* (Princeton, Princeton University Press, 2007).

monographic studies based on particular organisations,[13] there has therefore grown an impressive library of work on various aspects of terrorism and on varied kinds of approach to studying the subject.

Crucial within these debates have been the issues of definition, of terrorist efficacy, of appropriate state response, of non-state terrorist organisational development, and of the most fruitful hermeneutical framework within which to analyse terrorism and terrorists. So let us consider each of these important questions in turn.

Scholars have long reflected on the extensive problems involved in defining terrorism. These difficulties include the vast range of competing attempts that there have been to define it, and the ensuing problem that the phenomenon has become (in one eminent scholar's words) rather 'shrouded in terminological confusion';[14] as another expert has put it, 'Few words are plagued by so much indeterminacy, subjectivity and political disagreement as "terror", "terrorise", "terrorism" and "terrorist".'[15] There is also the problem of whether terror itself is more central to what we commonly consider to be terrorism than it is to other forms of activity (such as organised crime or orthodox warfare) to which the term is not normally applied. Derived from the Latin 'terrere' (to terrify, frighten, deter or scare away), the word has been conceived by some scholars centrally and distinctively to involve such dynamics: 'What makes an act terrorism is that it terrifies';[16] 'This is the essence of terrorism: the breaking of an enemy's will through the exploitation of fear'.[17] With terror centrally involved in other kinds of activity, however, some have argued that the word terrorism should also be applied (for example) to much that happens during war.[18]

This relates to another definitional problem: that of whether states as well as non-state actors deserve the term to be applied to their violence. Some scholars have argued strongly that non-state, non-governmental individuals and groups

---

[13] T. Whitfield, *Endgame for ETA: Elusive Peace in the Basque Country* (London, Hurst and Company, 2014); Singh, *Hamas and Suicide Terrorism*; English, *Armed Struggle*; G. Kassimeris, *Inside Greek Terrorism* (London, Hurst and Company, 2013); A. R. Norton, *Hezbollah: A Short History* (Princeton, Princeton University Press, 2007); B. Riedel, *The Search for al-Qaida: Its Leadership, Ideology, and Future* (Washington, Brookings Institution Press, 2008).

[14] C. Gearty, 'Introduction', in C. Gearty (ed.), *Terrorism* (Aldershot, Dartmouth, 1996), p. xi.

[15] B. Saul, *Defining Terrorism in International Law* (Oxford, Oxford University Press, 2006), p. 1.

[16] M. Juergensmeyer, *Terror in the Mind of God: The Global Rise of Religious Violence*, 2nd edn (Berkeley: CA, University of California Press, 2001), p. 139.

[17] J. Gearson, 'The Nature of Modern Terrorism', *Political Quarterly*, 73 (2002), p. 8.

[18] M. Fellman, *In the Name of God and Country: Reconsidering Terrorism in American History* (New Haven, Yale University Press, 2010).

alone deserve the application of the T word,[19] while others have taken the view that states also practise and threaten violence which merits the term terrorism.[20] A further area of definitional disagreement has focused on change over time: has there emerged on occasions a 'new' terrorism which is decisively different from what has preceded it? During the 1990s and even more forcibly after 9/11, some people argued that there was indeed a new form of terrorism, variously involving a more markedly religious dimension, a more transnational scope and ambition, a less hierarchically organised and looser kind of formation, and a greater zeal for large-scale casualties and destruction.[21] Others have been sceptical, stressing the strong continuities that have existed across the fault-line supposedly separating an old from a new form of terrorism. As Martha Crenshaw put it:

> the departure from the past is not as pronounced as many accounts make it out to be. Today's terrorism is not a fundamentally or qualitatively new phenomenon but grounded in an evolving historical context. Much of what we see now is familiar, and the differences are of degree rather than kind ... old and new have more in common than proponents of a new terrorism seem to think.[22]

A further definitional problem concerns the notoriously pejorative connotations of the word: as Adrian Guelke suggests, 'the word "terrorism" cannot possibly be treated as if it were a neutral, technical term for a particular category of violence. The term carries a massive emotive punch';[23] Conor Gearty observes that 'It may thus be most useful to call off the search for a coherent definition and to accept that advances will be possible only when we abandon the hope that there is a credible answer to the question – what is terrorism?'[24] It is certainly true that no consensual definition of the word is

---

[19] L. Richardson, *What Terrorists Want: Understanding the Terrorist Threat* (London, John Murray, 2006); J. Lodge, 'Introduction', in J. Lodge (ed.), *Terrorism: A Challenge to the State* (Oxford, Martin Robertson, 1981), p. 5.

[20] P. Wilkinson, *Terrorism Versus Democracy: The Liberal State Response*, 3rd edn (London, Routledge, 2011), p. 17; English, *Terrorism*, p. 9.

[21] S. Simon and D. Benjamin, 'America and the New Terrorism', *Survival*, 42/1 (2000); R. Gunaratna, *Inside al-Qaida: Global Network of Terror* (London, Hurst, 2002); D. Haubrich, 'Modern Politics in an Age of Global Terrorism: New Challenges for Domestic Public Policy', *Political Studies*, 54/2 (2006).

[22] Crenshaw, *Explaining Terrorism*, pp. 53–54. Cf. O. Lynch and C. Ryder, 'Deadliness, Organisational Change, and Suicide Attacks: Understanding the Assumptions Inherent in the Use of the Term "New Terrorism"', *Critical Studies on Terrorism*, 5/2 (2012); A. Gofas, '"Old" vs. "New" Terrorism: What's in a Name?', *Uluslararası İlişkiler*, 8/32 (2012).

[23] A. Guelke, *The Age of Terrorism and the International Political System*, 2nd edn (London, I. B. Tauris, 1998), p. 7.

[24] Gearty, 'Introduction', in Gearty (ed.), *Terrorism*, p. xiv. Cf. R. Jackson and S. J. Sinclair (eds), *Contemporary Debates on Terrorism* (London, Routledge, 2012), pp. 11–25.

likely to emerge, and scholars such as Alex Schmid have demonstrated the extent to which rival understandings of the term persist and grow in number.[25] In practice, however, the considerable overlap between definitions (so often involving the use of deliberately terrorising violence for political purpose) and regarding so many groups judged to have used terrorism, means that debate can flourish despite the disagreements and problems of terminology summarised here. As Walter Laqueur expressed it, 'a comprehensive definition of terrorism … does not exist nor will it be found in the foreseeable future'; but 'To argue that terrorism cannot be studied until such a definition exists is manifestly absurd.'[26]

Also controversial in the scholarly literature has been the question of terrorist efficacy. This is an issue on which work has expanded greatly in recent years. Some have argued very strongly that terrorism has been allowed to work far too effectively in the past. 'The real root cause of terrorism', Alan Dershowitz claims, 'is that it is successful – terrorists have consistently benefited from their terrorist acts. Terrorism will persist as long as it continues to work for those who use it, as long as the international community rewards it, as it has been doing for the past thirty-five years.' Dershowitz continues:

> Terrorism will persist because it often works, and success breeds … the 'root cause' of terrorism that must be eliminated is its success … Before September 11, terrorism worked – not in every case and not for every group, but often enough to be seen as a successful tactic for bringing about considerable change … In all, the international community responded to terrorism between 1968 and 2001 by consistently rewarding and legitimising it, rather than punishing and condemning it … Any rational terrorist group that operates according to cost–benefit calculation will, at least in theory, be inclined to opt for the tactic or tactics that hold the best prospect for furthering their goals. At the moment, that tactic is terrorism.[27]

Other scholars have also suggested that terrorism has, historically, proven to be successful, a particularly interesting aspect of which has been the claim that suicide bombing has had a particular kind of efficacy, whether in terms of securing goals against foreign occupation,[28] or in terms of allowing

[25] A. P. Schmid (ed.), *The Routledge Handbook of Terrorism Research* (London, Routledge, 2011), especially the listing of over 250 rival definitions, pp. 9–157; Schmid and Jongman (eds), *Political Terrorism*.
[26] W. Laqueur, *Terrorism* (London, Weidenfeld and Nicolson, 1977), p. 5.
[27] A. M. Dershowitz, *Why Terrorism Works: Understanding the Threat, Responding to the Challenge* (New Haven, Yale University Press, 2002), pp. 2, 6, 26, 31, 85, 167.
[28] Pape, *Dying to Win*; Pape and Feldman, *Cutting the Fuse*; R. A. Pape, 'The Strategic Logic of Suicide Terrorism', *American Political Science Review*, 97/3 (2003).

groups successfully to outbid communal rivals within their own political struggle.[29]

In stark contrast, others have reached very different assessments. David Rapoport claims that, 'By their own standards, terrorists rarely succeed';[30] in the words of others: 'campaigns of terrorism – shocking and brutal as they may seem – rarely succeed in achieving their stated objectives';[31] 'terrorist groups rarely achieve their policy objectives'; 'terrorist success rates are actually extremely low'.[32] Reinforcing such scepticism, other scholars have argued powerfully that *non*-violent methods have proved far more successful in the pursuit of political change. According to this view, civil resistance is much better than violent methods for attracting diverse, large-scale groups of activists, participants and supporters to mass-based struggle.[33]

Yet again, some scholars have interpreted the efficacy question as one that is open only to more ambivalent answer. Paul Wilkinson, for example, points out that terrorism 'has proven a low-cost, low-risk, potentially high-yield method of struggle', yet also that it has been one which 'very rarely succeeds in delivering strategic goals'.[34] Louise Richardson likewise suggested that 'Terrorist groups have been singularly unsuccessful in delivering the political change they seek, but they have enjoyed considerable success in achieving their near-term aims.'[35]

The challenge of ongoing assessment of terrorist efficacy is one taken up in this book (especially in chapters 2, 3, 8 and 9) and these assessments are decisively situated within a framework of considering terrorist success or failure as parts of a process of relationship between non-state terrorism and state action and response.

[29] M. Bloom, *Dying to Kill: The Allure of Suicide Terror* (New York, Columbia Press, 2005).
[30] D. C. Rapoport, 'The International World as Some Terrorists have Seen it: A Look at a Century of Memoirs', in D. C. Rapoport (ed.), *Inside Terrorist Organisations* (London, Frank Cass, 2001), p. 54.
[31] P. R. Neumann and M. L. R. Smith, *The Strategy of Terrorism: How it Works, and Why it Fails* (London, Routledge, 2008), p. 100.
[32] M. Abrahms, 'Why Terrorism does Not Work', *International Security*, 31/2 (2006), pp. 43–44.
[33] E. Chenoweth and M. J. Stephan, *Why Civil Resistance Works: The Strategic Logic of Nonviolent Conflict* (New York, Columbia University Press, 2011). Cf. A. Roberts and T. Garton Ash (eds), *Civil Resistance and Power Politics: The Experience of Non-Violent Action from Gandhi to the Present* (Oxford, Oxford University Press, 2009); M. E. King, *A Quiet Revolution: The First Palestinian Intifada and Non-Violent Resistance* (New York, Nation Books, 2007).
[34] P. Wilkinson, 'Politics, Diplomacy, and Peace Processes: Pathways Out of Terrorism?', in M. Taylor and J. Horgan (eds), *The Future of Terrorism* (Abingdon, Frank Cass, 2000), p. 66.
[35] Richardson, *What Terrorists Want*, pp. 105–106. Cf. D. K. Gupta, *Understanding Terrorism and Political Violence: The Life Cycle of Birth, Growth, Transformation, and Demise* (London, Routledge, 2008), p. 191.

That question of state response itself has been another major area of terrorism debate, and again there has been much disagreement. But two areas of at least some impressive measure of scholarly consensus have concerned the extraordinary importance of high-grade intelligence in countering non-state terrorism, and the ambiguous effects of a militarisation of state reaction to terrorist challenge. Scholars from various disciplines and backgrounds have reached similar conclusions here:

> The secret of winning the battle against terrorism in an open democratic society is winning the intelligence war: this will enable the security forces, using high-quality intelligence, to be proactive, thwarting terrorist conspiracies before they happen[36]

> Perhaps 95% of the important action in any campaign against terrorism consists of intelligence and police work: identifying suspects, infiltrating movements, collaborating with police forces in other countries, gathering evidence for trials and so on.[37]

Similarly, many scholarly assessments have pointed to the ambiguous and painfully counter-productive effects of over-reliance on military means in countering non-state terrorism.[38] Does killing the leader or leaders of a terrorist group work, for example? Research suggests that, quite frequently, the answer is no.[39] It is not that there can never be a valuable role for the military in deterring or containing or constraining non-state terrorists. It is rather that there frequently exist dangers that direct military intervention will backfire.[40] In trying to defeat terrorists, 'offensive military action rarely works. Although military action can disrupt a terrorist group's operations temporarily, it rarely ends the threat.'[41]

Interestingly, even some who have famously decided to use military muscle in the fight against terrorism have at times acknowledged its unanticipated costs. Regarding his post-9/11 policies, former UK prime Minister Tony Blair referred

---

[36] Wilkinson, *Terrorism Versus Democracy*, p. 76.
[37] A. Roberts, 'The "War on Terror" in Historical Perspective', *Survival*, 47/2 (2005), p. 109. Cf. M. Sageman, *Understanding Terror Networks* (Philadelphia, University of Pennsylvania Press, 2004), p. 180; M. Howard, 'What's in a Name? How to Fight Terrorism', *Foreign Affairs*, 81/1 (2002), p. 9.
[38] For a wise and recent assessment, see A. Roberts, 'Terrorism Research: Past, Present, and Future', *Studies in Conflict and Terrorism*, 38/1 (2015), pp. 67, 70–71.
[39] A. K. Cronin, *Ending Terrorism: Lessons for Defeating al-Qaida* (London, Routledge, 2008), p. 31.
[40] Berman, *Radical, Religious, and Violent*, pp. 207–208; Bloom, *Dying to Kill*, pp. 34–35, 37, 40, 42, 82, 93; Richardson, *What Terrorists Want*, p. 220; Cronin, *Ending Terrorism*, p. 8; S. G. Jones, *Counterinsurgency in Afghanistan* (Santa Monica, RAND, 2008), p. xii; English, *Terrorism*, pp. 127–131; V. Held, *How Terrorism is Wrong: Morality and Political Violence* (Oxford, Oxford University Press, 2008), p. 69.
[41] Pape, *Dying to Win*, p. 239; Cf. Cronin, *How Terrorism Ends*, pp. 190–191, 204.

to his choice to confront terrorism 'militarily. I still believe that was the right choice, but the costs, implications and consequences were far greater than any of us, and certainly me, could have grasped on that day.'[42] In this light, the reflections offered by Sir David Omand in chapter 4 regarding the UK's military response to the terrorism threat add a valuable layer to this book's contribution. If discussion on terrorism and counter-terrorism is to carry maximum weight regarding the fundamental issues involved, then multi-disciplinary academic arguments need to be complemented by the insights of people who possess senior policy experience.

The terrorist group with which Prime Minister Blair was understandably most concerned after 11 September 2001, the jihadist al-Qaida, has been the focus of another major scholarly debate with policy implications: namely, the question of how far organisational changes have emerged in this most salient of non-state terrorist groupings. Not only have al-Qaida become the most scrutinised terrorists in the literature in recent years,[43] but extensive debate and disagreement have emerged about their exact organisational nature as a group.

Some have argued that the decisive level of al-Qaida activity has moved to the grass roots. Pre-eminent here is Marc Sageman, who strongly suggests that the al-Qaida threat has dramatically changed in recent years, with jihadists embodying 'more fluid, independent and unpredictable entities than their more structured forebears, who carried out the atrocities of 9/11'; in his forcefully expressed view, al-Qaida has become 'a multitude of informal local groups trying to emulate their predecessors by conceiving and executing operations from the bottom up'.[44]

In stark contrast, others have forcibly put the case that the group's core leadership continues to play a significant role.[45] Bruce Hoffman referred

[42] T. Blair, *A Journey* (London, Hutchinson, 2010), p. 349.

[43] See, for example, D. Holbrook, *The al-Qaida Doctrine: The Framing and Evolution of the Leadership's Public Discourse* (London, Bloomsbury, 2014); P. L. Bergen, *Holy War, Inc: Inside the Secret World of Osama bin Laden* (London, Phoenix, 2002); P. L. Bergen, *The Osama bin Laden I Know* (New York, Free Press, 2006); P. L. Bergen, *The Longest War: The Enduring Conflict Between America and al-Qaida* (New York, Free Press, 2011); M. Scheuer, *Osama bin Laden* (Oxford: Oxford University Press, 2011); B. Hoffman and F. Reinares (eds), *The Evolution of the Global Terrorist Threat: From 9/11 to Osama bin Laden's Death* (New York, Columbia University Press, 2014); M. D. Silber, *The al-Qaida Factor: Plots Against the West* (Philadelphia, University of Pennsylvania Press, 2012); L. Wright, *The Looming Tower: al-Qaida's Road to 9/11* (London, Penguin, 2007); Sageman, *Understanding Terror Networks*.

[44] M. Sageman, *Leaderless Jihad: Terror Networks in the Twenty-First Century* (Philadelphia, University of Pennsylvania Press, 2008), p. vii. Cf. the exchange in M. Sageman and B. Hoffman, 'Does Osama Still Call the Shots? Debating the Containment of al-Qaida's Leadership', *Foreign Affairs*, 87/4 (2008).

[45] B. Hoffman, 'The Myth of Grass-Roots Terrorism: Why Osama bin Laden Still Matters', *Foreign Affairs*, 87/3 (2008); M. Sageman and B. Hoffman, 'Does Osama Still Call the Shots? Debating the Containment of al-Qaida's Leadership', *Foreign Affairs*, 87/4 (2008); Hoffman and Reinares (eds), *Evolution of the Global Terrorist Threat*.

to al-Qaida's 'continued resilience, resonance, and longevity',[46] and in 2014 Hoffman and Fernando Reinares argued powerfully that al-Qaida has 'remained a clearly defined and active terrorist organisation with an identifiable leadership and chain of command'; global jihadism has become 'a polymorphous phenomenon – not an amorphous one' – and al-Qaida's leadership role remained significant and lethal. According to Hoffman and Reinares, by the time of bin Laden's brutal death in 2011, his organisation had come to comprise four interlinked parts: the enduring nucleus of 'al-Qaida Central or al-Qaida Core'; the group's 'Territorial Extensions or Branches', such as al-Qaida in the Arabian Peninsula (AQAP) or al-Qaida in Iraq (AQI); 'Entities Affiliated and Associated with al-Qaida', such as the Afghan Taliban and Lashkar-e-Taiba (LeT); and 'Independent Jihadist Cells and Individuals'.[47]

Others again have stressed the importance of 'middle managers' – people who link the top of the organisation with the grass roots;[48] or have presented al-Qaida as a jihadist network rather than an organisation, as comprising adaptive systems which are self-organising from the bottom upwards, decentralised and coalescent, tactically diverse, and lacking a systematically uniform ideological philosophy.[49]

Of course, the very notion of coalescence implies some resulting unity, and I suspect that the lines dividing various scholars in these organisational debates are sometimes less stark than observers have at times assumed them to be. It is clear that the kind of al-Qaida organisation which existed immediately prior to 9/11 has been constrained and changed in key ways. But al-Qaida has now survived for nearly thirty years (no trivial achievement in itself, given the range of powerful enemies that it possesses); and their more fluid and complex identity now seems to me to comprise both a damaged core element and also a series of concentric circles of associates and supporters. So there remains an al-Qaida core: not as decisively or definitively crucial as it was before 11 September 2001, but not irrelevant either in its brand-sustaining (and at times still lethal) role.

An equally intriguing debate has also emerged in recent years regarding the most fruitful hermeneutical approach to adopt when analysing terrorism and

---

[46] Hoffman, *Inside Terrorism*, p. x.

[47] B. Hoffman and F. Reinares, 'Conclusion', in Hoffman and Reinares (eds), *Evolution of the Global Terrorist Threat*, pp. 618–622.

[48] P. Neumann, R. Evans and R. Pantucci, 'Locating al-Qaida's Centre of Gravity: The Role of Middle Managers', *Studies in Conflict and Terrorism*, 34/11 (2011); J. Jordan, 'The Evolution of the Structure of Jihadist Terrorism in Western Europe: The Case of Spain', *Studies in Conflict and Terrorism*, 37/8 (2014).

[49] A. Bousquet, 'Complexity Theory and the War on Terror: Understanding the Self-Organising Dynamics of Leaderless Jihad', *Journal of International Relations and Development*, 15/3 (2012).

terrorists. This has been prompted by the emergence of the Critical Terrorism Studies (CTS) school,[50] which has presented existing terrorism studies as exhibiting methodological and conceptual shortcomings and an overly narrow focus. Where orthodox terrorism studies have paid too little attention to state terrorism and to the negative effects of state counter-terrorism, it is argued, CTS scholarship draws richly on a variety of theoretical approaches (including discourse analysis, and Frankfurt School-style critical theory); it calls also for greater attention to state terrorism and for a widening of the range of subjects to be assessed by terrorism researchers; it questions the moral primacy of the state; it seeks to be more critical of state interests and perspectives; and it calls for a greater attention to be directed towards the need to acquire reliable primary data.

Some responses to this CTS endeavour have been deeply hostile. D. M. Jones and M. L. R. Smith, for example, attacked the journal *Critical Studies on Terrorism* for failing to demonstrate the supposed state bias within terrorism research that its contributors have frequently assumed to exist.[51] And it might be judged that the division between 'critical' and 'orthodox' scholars is not as sharply drawn as is sometimes suggested by CTS commentators themselves. The idea, for instance, that orthodox terrorism scholars consider terrorism not to be practised by states is clearly false (as has been noted above in regard to Paul Wilkinson, one of the founding fathers of the supposedly orthodox school of terrorism scholarship). Likewise, the CTS suggestion that orthodox terrorism scholars accept the legitimacy and effectiveness of force-based counter-terrorism[52] clashes with the reality that many scholars not associated with the CTS school are in fact very sceptical of such counter-terrorist methods (as demonstrated above).

So either there does not exist the assumed division between 'critical' and 'orthodox' scholarly communities, or the continua of opinion involved are actually more complex than is sometimes suggested in CTS critiques, with scholars relating variously to the supposedly dichotomous hermeneutical positions set out by CTS exponents. If the latter, then individual scholars might not fit neatly into 'critical' and 'orthodox' categories, and there will prove room for more shared argument and approach than might initially seem

[50] Much of the CTS work has appeared in the journal *Critical Studies on Terrorism*. See also R. Jackson, M. Breen Smyth and J. Gunning (eds), *Critical Terrorism Studies: A New Research Agenda* (London, Routledge, 2009); R. Jackson, L. Jarvis, J. Gunning and M. Breen Smyth, *Terrorism: A Critical Introduction* (Basingstoke, Palgrave Macmillan, 2011).
[51] D. M. Jones and M. L. R. Smith, 'We're All Terrorists Now: Critical – or Hypocritical – Studies "on" Terrorism', *Studies in Conflict and Terrorism*, 32/4 (2009).
[52] Jackson, Breen Smyth and Gunning (eds), *Critical Terrorism Studies*, p. 74.

to be the case. In itself, however, the CTS call for terrorism scholars to study an ever-wider range of subjects is surely very welcome, as is its emphasis upon acquiring fresh and direct new evidence upon which to base our assessments.

Despite the deep insights provided by much of the scholarly debate summarised above, a new framework is now required if we are more fully to understand what has been emerging in relation to terrorism, and why it has done so: that framework must look synoptically at terrorism, counter-terrorism and the relationship between them; and it must look at them through multi-disciplinary lenses with an eye to policy seriousness. So the chapters in this book take forward specific aspects of the debates summarised above (regarding the efficacy of state response to terrorism, for example, or the degree of success achieved by certain terrorist groups). This book also addresses such issues in a new manner: it brings together scholars not only from different disciplines but also from different perspectives regarding scholarly hermeneutics (for example, Adrian Guelke and Audrey Cronin have different attitudes towards CTS, so chapters 6 and 7 are complementary in their illumination of our subject); it brings these scholars together in one volume to consider *simultaneously* the dynamics of non-state terrorism and state politics, and to reflect on the relationship between the two; it draws attention repeatedly to the decisive, shared illusions on either side of that state/non-state division; and it embodies an honest effort to produce rigorous scholarly argument of high policy relevance (chapter 4 strongly reinforces this point). Taken together, this embodies an importantly new approach. If there is, as some have prominently argued, something of a stagnation in terrorism research,[53] then what is embodied in this book represents the most productive way of trying to improve the situation: the approach reflected here allows for a new understanding of one of the grandest and most persistent challenges of our period.

The majority of scholarship on terrorism and on counter-terrorism to date has analysed these two phenomena without sufficiently integrating them in terms of their antiphonal, mutually sustaining relationship with each other.[54] Not only, therefore, has there been far more research on non-state terrorists

[53] M. Sageman, 'The Stagnation in Terrorism Research', *Terrorism and Political Violence*, 26/4 (2014).
[54] This can be true even of very impressive scholarly work. Huw Bennett's excellent study of British military responses in Kenya, for example, pays less attention than necessary to the nature and effect of non-state terrorist atrocity: H. Bennett, *Fighting the Mau Mau: The British Army and Counter-Insurgency in the Kenya Emergency* (Cambridge, Cambridge University Press, 2013). Likewise, Berman's excellent *Radical, Religious, and Violent* would have been even more powerful had it attended to the dynamics of state counter-terrorism as well as non-state mobilisation.

than there has been on their counter-terrorist adversaries; there has also been far too little investigation of the ways in which each group has sustained the myths and activities of the other, or of the manner in which each has reinforced the other's sense of urgency, necessity and validity.[55] At a policy and political level, the effects of this analytical failure have arguably been pernicious, allowing for disproportionate, often wasteful, pointless and counter-productive state responses to non-state terrorism,[56] and also for the clumsy sustenance by states of the seeming validity of terrorist zealots' own interpretations.[57]

Compounding this problem is the fact that a rarely asked (and even more rarely answered) question in the scholarly literature to date has been the crucial one of how well counter-terrorism actually works. As discussed earlier, the issue of whether non-state terrorism itself works is one that has now begun to be seriously explored. But far more money, time, person-power and violence are expended on state counter-terrorism than on the practising of non-state terrorism itself; and state responses to non-state terrorists are historically much more likely to change history than are the acts of anti-state terrorist individuals or groups. Nonetheless, systematic reflection on the efficacy of counter-terrorism remains largely absent in the scholarly realm. Despite the extraordinary growth in scholarship in the field of terrorism studies since 9/11,[58] there remains less systematic, practically applicable assessment of the effectiveness of counter-terrorism than would be ideal. The definition, causes, dynamics and demise of terrorism have now been scrutinised rather thoroughly.[59] But, despite some outstanding occasional contributions,[60] there has not been an equivalent level of interrogation into the extent to which state *counter*-terrorism (much of it very violent indeed) has actually been effective, despite the billions of dollars spent on it and the high-level political commitment devoted to countering terrorism globally.

---

[55] There are fascinating partial exceptions, of course, including J. Zulaika, *Terrorism: The Self-Fulfilling Prophecy* (Chicago, University of Chicago Press, 2009).
[56] For sharp argument regarding exactly how much has been overspent and misspent on countering terrorism since 9/11, see J. Mueller and M. G. Stewart, *Terror, Security, and Money: Balancing the Risks, Benefits, and Costs of Homeland Security* (Oxford, Oxford University Press, 2011).
[57] A. Brahimi, *Jihad and Just War in the War on Terror* (Oxford, Oxford University Press, 2010).
[58] For interesting reflections on this expansion, see Jackson, Breen Smyth, Gunning (eds), *Critical Terrorism Studies*.
[59] Wilkinson, *Terrorism Versus Democracy*; Cronin, *How Terrorism Ends*; Crenshaw, *Explaining Terrorism*; Richardson, *What Terrorists Want*; English, *Terrorism: How to Respond*; Roberts, 'The "War on Terror" in Historical Perspective'.
[60] J. Lyall, 'Are Co-Ethnics more Effective Counter-Insurgents? Evidence from the Second Chechen War', *American Political Science Review*, 104/1 (2010); J. Argomaniz, *The EU and Counter-Terrorism: Politics, Polity, and Policies after 9/11* (London, Routledge, 2011).

As suggested, central to this book is something too infrequently addressed to date: the extent to which non-state terrorists and their counter-terrorist state opponents share the misleading illusion that their acts of violence will transform politics in ways deeply favourable to their respective causes. Are there repeated patterns across such cases, elements of the relationship between non-state terrorism and state action which might valuably inform our understanding and direct our thinking? Some recent scholarly research here does occasionally suggest possible themes, including (for example) the ways in which terrorists' control over the spending of money or the choosing of targets makes them more vulnerable to state counter-terrorism.[61] And there does often seem to be a striking contrast (on the part of both non-state terrorists and state counter-terrorists) between people's technical proficiency and tactical ingenuity on the one hand, and their lack of political understanding and sometimes crass strategic misjudgements on the other.[62] In this, the 9/11 hijackers and al-Qaida have at times been echoed by their post-9/11 Western enemies, with both sides in the 9/11 wars displaying greater technical sophistication than political wisdom and historical or cultural understanding, often with mutually reinforcing and bloodily disastrous consequences. But such themes remain under-scrutinised even in what is now a vast literature on terrorism.

One important strand running through this (in itself, one could argue, evidence of a vital shared illusion) is the fact that terrorist and counter-terrorist violence very often lead to an undermining of support for the causes in whose name they have respectively been practised, especially if that brutal, unmerciful violence is directed against civilians. The experience of al-Qaida in the period from 9/11 onwards, but also of the United States and its allies in their wars in Afghanistan and Iraq, reflects this process. So the illusion of military efficacy is one, it seems, which transcends the line dividing the state from its non-state opponents.

How do the chapters in this book work within this new framework, and what do they contribute towards new collective understanding? They derive from a range of disciplinary backgrounds, with the authors between them having trained or worked across many parts of the academic world (Political Science, Law, International Relations, History, Philosophy) and also in the high-level policy world itself. As such, they bring complementary lenses

---

[61] J. N. Shapiro, *The Terrorist's Dilemma: Managing Violent Covert Organizations* (Princeton, Princeton University Press, 2013).
[62] This struck me again on reading the impressive B. S. Zellen, *State of Recovery: The Quest to Restore American Security After 9/11* (London, Bloomsbury, 2013).

through which to read a geographically, organisationally and conceptually wide range of questions around our theme.

The chapters discuss the ways in which state policy and action affect levels of terrorist violence and activity. Viewed through the lens of the political historian, this has (as in the case of the Irish republican terrorism discussed in chapter 8) variously involved harsh state responses prompting higher levels of PIRA and other violence; more restrained state policy making it more difficult for (contemporary dissident republican) violence to be sustained; and intelligence-led counter-terrorism constraining terrorist groups during ongoing campaigns. A similar pattern is suggested in chapter 3, which concludes that successes against al-Qaida and its affiliates have been rare, and that the militarisation of counter-terrorist response has partly been the cause of this failure. Complementing this, and on the basis of the author's experience at high policy level in the United Kingdom, chapter 4 suggests that the most contentiously military aspect of post-9/11 counter-terrorist response, the Iraq venture, now looks to have been an ill-judged over-reaction, and that it actually seems to have made anti-Western jihadism worse. This theme is echoed in chapter 6, while chapter 5 points to the disproportionate effect that comparatively trivial late-twentieth-century terrorism in Western liberal democracies actually had upon those states and upon their policies and their thinking.

Central here, therefore, is subtle consideration of the lasting dangers inherent in the illusion of military efficacy, an illusion arguably evident among non-state terrorists and their state counter-terrorist opponents alike. In relation to non-state terrorism, chapter 2 points out that most victims of post-9/11 al-Qaida-related violence were Muslims, a fact which has done serious damage to that group's popularity and brand within the Muslim world; and this echoes the doubts articulated in other chapters, regarding the plausibility of arguing for militarily based counter-terrorist success from various disciplinary perspectives.

Clearly, different kinds of state regime possess varied inheritances and possibilities in terms of their response to non-state terrorist violence. The kind of brutal policy eventually adopted by Sri Lanka against the Liberation Tigers of Tamil Eelam (LTTE)[63] would be unthinkable for the UK in its dealings with twenty-first-century dissident Irish republican terrorists, for example. But chapter 4's argument that state response to terrorist assailants must be proportionate remains an immensely important one across many different contexts.

---

[63] P. Staniland, *Networks of Rebellion: Explaining Insurgent Cohesion and Collapse* (Ithaca, Cornell University Press, 2014), pp. 141–177.

Relatedly, regarding the efficacy of military methods, the illusions of terrorism and counter-terrorism have at times colluded to turn history in unfortunate directions. As noted, there are stark disagreements in the scholarly literature regarding the nature and extent of the efficacy of non-state terrorism. But, as pointed out in chapter 7, terrorism has only comparatively rarely fructuated in the achievement of groups' central, strategic goals (a point echoed also in chapters 2 and 8). Recognition of this reality – the fact that non-state terrorists frequently have illusions about how successful their violence will prove – should affect states' responses. For if states recognise that terrorist hopes of strategic victory are probably illusory, then calmer and more patient state reaction (more proportionate in its scale, more realistic in its own counter-terrorist objectives) might ensue. This could then limit the frequency of state over-reaction, of the exaggeration of threat, and of the setting of over-ambitious objectives (the post-9/11 goal of extirpating international terrorism, for example). In this sense, acknowledging the existence of one set of illusions might make the other set less attractive, plausible and sustainable.

For what we sometimes see here is a sequence of unfortunate and responsive illusions. Non-state terrorists act out of an exaggerated confidence in the effectiveness of their violent methods, with states then misdiagnosing the threat and over-reacting, and thereby making the situation far worse. Chapter 7 shows that, while ISIS is clearly very different from al-Qaida, the West's failure to understand the nature of and respond properly to al-Qaida terrorism seems now to have produced opportunities for much more extensive anti-Western jihadism in the form of the ISIS challenge. Chapter 3 similarly demonstrates that al-Qaida has had far from the greatest success (having exaggerated the efficacy of its own political violence), but that new opportunities for radical jihadists have arisen out of the transformative chain of events prompted by 9/11 and by ill-judged Western responses to the brutal assaults of that day.

Another element of the work contained in this book involves the complex effects of non-state terrorism upon the nature of states themselves – again, something understood properly only if we draw on numerous disciplines and look simultaneously and synoptically at terrorism and at counter-terrorism (and also at the policy implications of the relationship between them). So chapter 6 forcibly shows that states' maintenance of fundamental human rights has often been greatly undermined by their counter-terrorist responses, despite the things so often claimed by states about the principles to which they supposedly adhere. It suggests that a culture of secrecy and misinformation can be delineated here, a point reinforced in chapter 5 which argues that state responses to terrorism have frequently witnessed the use of laws to stifle diverse kinds of dissent, accompanied by the deployment of counter-terrorist rhetoric and of claims regarding a terroristic threat as the means for justifying this behaviour; the result is that states maintain the appearance of democracy while reducing its egalitarian impact in practice.

Chapters 5 and 6 both point out the degree to which there has evolved a tension between (on the one hand) countering terrorism and (on the other hand) maintaining human rights and civil liberties within targeted societies. One of the central legacies of al-Qaida's 9/11 attacks (along with the ironic achievement of Americanising the study of terrorism and of making US-based scholarship now the decisive centre of gravity within that literature), has been the degrading of aspects of US and other Western civil liberties. Al-Qaida (like so many terrorist groups throughout history) has therefore produced a dual degradation of human rights: first, through their killing and maiming of so many people through violence; second, through prompting states to react in ways that have further denied people's human rights and civil freedoms.

Beyond this, the relationship between non-state terrorism and state counter-terrorism has seen sequences of response between the two phenomena deeply affect politics at world-historical level. Chapter 9 demonstrates that what states do has profound implications for the costs that they pay in terms of non-state terrorist reaction. Sometimes, indeed, non-state terrorists are looking to further this cycle by deliberately trying to provoke states into self-damaging over-reaction. More broadly still, chapter 9 argues that when the United States responded to terrorist assault with state-building endeavours, its work had paradoxical implications. In order to sustain these newly fashioned states, the US has supported some local, pro-American rulers whose autocratic politics have in turn produced a violent, terroristic backlash. When seen synoptically, therefore, each side's aggressively founded hopes can seem illusory, and can be recognised as having produced a chain of frequently dispiriting political outcomes as a result.

In part, this is because responding to non-state terrorism is so difficult in practice. As suggested in chapter 7, it is true that terrorism scholarship can have some significant policy implications: scholarly reflection and the making of policy decisions are not coextensive realms, but they should probably overlap to some degree if either is to become sharp-sighted. Yet even the best explanatory clarification by scholars will not provide easy answers for those involved in the labyrinthine, fast-paced and complex world of policy response to terrorist challenge. The author of chapter 7 also says it is very difficult for governments to be strategic in their responses to terrorism, a difficulty made more stark by the jagged unpredictability of the future, as terrorism and its national and international contexts evolve in complex and unexpected ways (a broad, global theme addressed in chapter 9). Part of this wider process concerns the role repeatedly played by small numbers of actors who initiate terrorist violence confident that they will thereby change the world in a particular direction, only to find that they have indeed altered the direction of the train of events but in ways very different from those that were anticipated. Again, therefore, the terrorism process turns out to be haunted by illusion. Moreover, counter-terrorism can be about far more than merely countering terrorism, since other imperatives (political authority, individual careers, economic benefits, the aggrandisement of national interest and the like) can also be involved. In reflecting on such issues, chapter 4 identifies the central problematic challenge for governments of protecting their population from terrorist attack while still sustaining democratic politics, civic harmony and the appropriate rule of law.

Another difficulty identified here is the illusion entertained by some, that terrorist atrocity straightforwardly prompts the addressing of underlying issues. As chapter 5 demonstrates, terroristic violence tends in fact to make it more difficult to discuss the genuine nature of the threat which terrorism embodies. It also makes the addressing of underlying problems more famous and urgent, yet simultaneously much more difficult to achieve in practice, because it creates a climate of increased polarisation, panic and short-term reaction.

Here again, ironically, state and non-state actors can collude in sustaining the illusion. Repeatedly, non-state terrorists claim that only their violence will achieve redress of grievances. In Algerian National Liberation Front (NLF) member Saadi Yacef's words: 'It's our only way of expressing ourselves';[64] or there is the claim from one Tamil Tiger leader that 'The Tamil people have been expressing their grievances in parliament for more than three decades. Their voices went unheard like cries in the wilderness';[65] again, in the words of one Hamas activist, 'When all channels are closed to us, we use violence.'[66] But chapter 7 shows that states then often compound the problem, first, by not realising that terrorist violence rarely achieves the intended redress in practice and, second, by failing to attend to the real causes behind the terrorism promptly or honestly.

Relatedly, one methodological priority respected across the disciplines reflected in this book is the importance of acquiring and interrogating

---

[64] Quoted in Crenshaw, *Explaining Terrorism*, p. 31.
[65] Quoted in Richardson, *What Terrorists Want*, p. 71.
[66] Quoted in M. Perry, *Talking to Terrorists: Why America Must Engage with its Enemies* (New York, Basic Books, 2010), p. 133.

first-hand evidence regarding terrorism and the causes of terrorism. This need not involve scholars interviewing non-state terrorists themselves (though that remains, in my view, one valuable route towards understanding, as demonstrated in chapter 8). But there is a wide range of first-hand materials emerging from non-state terrorists and these should be analysed closely if we want truly to understand terrorist causation. As chapter 7 suggests, scholars and policy-makers alike have often failed to look carefully enough at what terrorists actually say. Inattention to such material can sustain what might be termed a failure of intimacy of understanding, and that failure represents one of the great flaws within much post-9/11 analysis of this Protean subject. Knowing intimately what terrorists say that they want, and what the wider causes behind their violence actually are, will facilitate more shrewd responses by states than the over-reaction often generated by misdiagnosis and exaggerated anxiety.

State tendencies towards such over-reaction are sometimes reinforced by a failure to root terrorism and counter-terrorism within their appropriate geographical (and therefore historical and cultural) contexts when we try to understand these phenomena. Attention to such contextualisation is stressed particularly in chapter 3 in its consideration of the War on Terror, but it is also evident in chapter 7 in reflecting on the avoidable transformation of al-Qaida jihadism into the ISIS threat, and in the arguments in chapter 8 about contemporary Irish republican terrorism and its relationship to a particular form of nationalism. For the situating of non-state terrorism within its relationship to the state must also be complemented by seeing the organic connections between terrorism and other world-historical forces. These can include terrorism's roots in powerful nationalist movements (see chapter 8 on dissident Irish republicans and the understanding of nationalism); or its effects on the nature of democracy (see chapters 4, 5 and 6 for different perspectives); or its complex relationship to a major religious faith (see chapter 2); or its consequences for the international state system (see chapter 9). The central reason for thinking that all academic disciplines should simultaneously engage in the study of terrorism, therefore, is that this will (as here) more firmly root our understanding of the phenomenon within what we systematically know about law, about religion, about history, about international relations, about the politics of states and so forth. Consequently, one key aim of this book is to bring together the complementary insights of leading scholars deeply grounded in the professional study of these phenomena themselves: people who are in a position collectively to analyse terrorism as something to be studied through the hermeneutical processes appropriate to understanding those broader issues.

For if, as the scholarly literature overwhelmingly suggests, terrorists tend to be psychologically normal and recognisably rational,[67] then their experiences and motivations (and their illusions and mistakes) will be explicable within normal explanatory and analytical frameworks. As pointed out in chapter 2, for example, al-Qaida itself has experienced difficult leadership struggles of exactly the kind that we witness in much less violent careers and organisations than those associated with terrorism. Likewise, chapter 8 argues of the latest wave of Irish republican terrorism that it will only be understandable (and that we can only respond sensibly to it) if we see those involved as explicable within recognisable frameworks of nationalist explanation.

In all of this, there will be little likelihood of finding neat patterns which can easily be applied to the wide variety of cases with which we all – as scholars, citizens, policy-makers, societies, states – have to deal. It is emphatically terrorism*s* and counter-terrorism*s* in the plural that we are considering, and the emergent picture will necessarily therefore be complex. The chapters in this book offer expert scholarly reflection from varied and complementary intellectual perspectives on major issues concerning: the evolution of jihadist and other forms of non-state terrorism (chapters 2 and 8); the efficacy and development and complicated nature of contemporary counter-terrorism (chapters 3 and 4); the damaging effects of some counter-terrorist policies upon the nature of states and societies (chapters 5 and 6); the ending of some (but the durability of other) terrorist campaigns (chapters 7 and 8); and the wider global and political and intellectual frameworks within which terrorism and counter-terrorism alike continue to dwell (chapter 9). Quite properly, there are differences of emphasis and approach, and I recognise that no single book can resolve all dilemmas in a field as complex as this one. But the authors' multi-disciplinary reflections on counter-terrorism and terrorism (and crucially on the relations between those two phenomena) will, it is hoped, move the debate forward in an erudite, original and rewarding fashion.

---

[67] J. Horgan, *The Psychology of Terrorism* (London, Routledge, 2005), pp. 50, 53, 62–65; Hoffman, *Inside Terrorism*, p. xv; Richardson, *What Terrorists Want*, pp. 7, 148–149; Sageman, *Understanding Terror Networks*, pp. 80–83, 97; Sageman, *Leaderless Jihad*, pp. 17, 62–64; Pape, *Dying to Win*, pp. 23, 27.

2

Al-Qaida and the 9/11 Decade

ALIA BRAHIMI

Introduction

AL-QAIDA'S EMISSARY was found dead.

In February 2014, five masked men opened fire on a gathering of militants in Aleppo, Syria, and then one of their number detonated a suicide bomb.[1] A dozen men were killed, including the target of the assault, Abu Khalid al-Suri, a colleague and longtime friend of al-Qaida's leader, Ayman al-Zawahiri. Al-Suri had been appointed by Zawahiri to mediate a violent dispute between the al-Nusra front, al-Qaida's official affiliate in Syria, and an increasingly aggressive group calling itself the Islamic State of Iraq and the Levant (ISIL). On the battleground of Syria's intractable civil war, the leader of ISIL, an Iraqi upstart known as Abu Bakr al-Baghdadi, had tried to subsume al-Nusra under his command. The move was resisted by the al-Nusra leadership and the global head of al-Qaida, who ordered al-Baghdadi to return to Iraq. When al-Baghdadi refused to fall in line, al-Zawahiri publicly disassociated al-Qaida from ISIL and its 'seditious' actions.[2] Soon after, al-Suri was killed.

Pushing out of Syrian and some Iraqi territories already under its control, ISIL went on to seize major towns and cities in northern and Western Iraq in June 2014, and to declare an 'Islamic State' with al-Baghdadi as Caliph. Decreeing that, henceforth, his lands and estimated 50,000 fighters[3] would be known simply as the 'Islamic State', Baghdadi called on all Muslims to pay obeisance to him.[4] However, while the announcement of a Caliphate by

[1] See Aryn Baker, 'Al-Qaeda's Top Envoy Killed in Syria by Rival Rebel Group', *Time*, 24 February 2014.
[2] Zawahiri uses the word 'fitna'. See al-Qaida General Command, 'Bayan Bishan Alaqat Jama'at Qaidat al-Jihad Bi-Jama'at Daeesh', 3 February 2014, available at http://www.hanein.info/vb/showthread.php?t=349952 [accessed 10 February 2014].
[3] 'Jihadist Islamic State has 50,000 Members in Syria: NGO', *Daily Star* (Lebanon), 19 August 2014.
[4] Al-Furqan Foundation, 'Tagtiya Khasa Li-khutbat wa Salat al-Juma' fi al-Jamaa' al-Kabir bi Madinat al-Mosul', 4 July 2014, available at https://www.youtube.com/watch?v=CXempOO7Fl4.

Proceedings of the British Academy **203**, 21–38. © The British Academy 2015.

an al-Qaida offshoot would, in itself, imply a strong element of political–religious unity, in reality the story is one of competition and deep division at the heart of radical Islam. Indeed, this chapter will argue that the 9/11 decade was, for al-Qaida, marked by the fragmentation of authority. It begins by critically assessing al-Qaida's progress on its four main objectives.

Al-Qaida's objectives

To end Western presence in Muslim lands

Al-Qaida's first objective was to end the Western military presence in the region. As bin Laden bluntly phrased it, 'pack your luggage and get out of our lands'.[5] For bin Laden, the American assault on Muslims was symbolic as US troops, who were stationed in Saudi Arabia at the invitation of the regime, were depicted as having 'defiled'[6] Islamic holy lands and 'looted'[7] Islam's sacred symbols. But, beyond this figurative harm, the assault also involved 'attacks and massacres committed against Muslims everywhere'.[8] Before 9/11, bin Laden threw together a host of global injustices, framed in Islamic terms and ranging from Burma to Western Sudan, to determine that the US was waging a war against Muslims.

In contrast to these more tenuous charges of US aggression against Muslims, the 9/11 attacks precipitated a massive Western military backlash. On the heels of al-Qaida's operation, the George W. Bush administration and its allies launched two full-scale military interventions in Iraq and Afghanistan, inaugurating a prolonged and overwhelming Western military footprint in the region. Shortly thereafter, and only slightly short of open warfare, the US initiated intensive intelligence and aerial-targeting campaigns in countries such as Pakistan and Yemen, using unmanned 'predator' drones. Alongside these new combat zones, the US established legally controversial detention practices (for example, at Guantanamo Bay in Cuba, Bagram Airbase in Afghanistan, and Abu Ghraib in Iraq) and stepped up its support

---

[5] Letter to the Americans, 6 October 2002, reprinted in Bruce Lawrence, *Messages to the World: The Statements of Osama Bin Laden* (London/New York, Verso, 2005), p. 171.

[6] Bin Laden, 'To the Islamic Umma, on the First Anniversary of the New American Crusader War', 11 September 2002, at http://www.jihadunspun.com/articles/10152002-To.The.Islamic.Ummah [accessed 25 January 2005].

[7] Interview with John Miller (ABC Television), May 1998, text available at http://www.pbs.org/wgbh/pages/frontline/shows/binladen/who/interview.html.

[8] Declaration of jihad, 23 August 1996, in Lawrence, *Messages to the World*, p. 25.

for authoritarian regimes which were able to re-invent their track records in the aftermath of the attacks and re-brand themselves as guarantors of stability and partners for the West. Any violence and instability attributable to the West pre-9/11 was eclipsed dramatically by that which followed al-Qaida's *de facto* declaration of war.

The 9/11 attacks heavily securitised the region for the United States, including its languages, traditions and dominant religion. They spawned entire industries in Afghanistan, in Iraq and in Western capitals, revolving around counter-terrorism, counter-insurgency, arms deals, security companies, state-building and humanitarian assistance projects. Al-Qaida forged a lasting link between the West and the region, which is military and political, but also partially cultural, as demonstrated on the one hand by the proliferation of Middle East Studies courses in the Western higher education sector, and on the other hand by a new generation of Westernised elites in Baghdad and Kabul. If the US had 'luggage' in the region before 9/11, far from packing its bags, it spent the ensuing decade setting up house.

However, from 2009 the Obama administration pursued a more 'narrow and constrained'[9] approach, ending combat missions in Iraq and Afghanistan, encouraging coalition partners to lead the 2011 intervention against Muammar al-Qadhafi in Libya and the 2013 intervention against militants in Northern Mali, providing only limited support to Bashar al-Assad's opposition in Syria, and committing to fighting terrorism indirectly through the 'Counterterrorism Partnership Fund'. Still, the Obama administration showed itself prepared to act militarily when US vital interests were at stake, as with the August 2014 air strikes in Northern Iraq against ISIL militants pushing toward the Kurdish capital of Irbil, in which US military advisers and diplomats were stationed. More importantly, however, the local partners empowered by Obama's indirect approach remain al-Qaida's principal *bêtes noires*.

To bring down corrupt regimes

Indeed, another key objective behind Osama bin Laden's al-Qaida was to oust the region's authoritarian regimes. In fact, most of the pioneers of the global jihad against the West had cut their teeth fighting local tyrants. The reason they threw down the gauntlet to the 'far enemy' in the first place was because

---

[9] Tamara Cofman Wittes, 'The Obama Administration's Middle East Policy', Brookings Institution *Up-Front Blog*, 8 June 2014, at http://www.brookings.edu/blogs/up-front/posts/2014/06/08-obama-middle-east-policy-wittes.

Western governments helped to prop up the godless 'near enemies' that ruled over Muslims with an iron fist.

After the 9/11 attacks, the Bush administration sought to materially support and diplomatically entrench the very regimes al-Qaida aimed to unseat, and conspired with several countries to illegally 'render' wanted individuals to the custody of foreign governments for detention and interrogation, often involving torture.[10] Having stepped away from the Bush administration's militarist approach, the Obama administration relied, at first by default and later by design, upon alliances with governments in the region as the *primary* means of battling al-Qaida. Obama's $5 billion 'Counter-terrorism Partnership Fund' envisaged a network of partnerships from South Asia to the Sahel, involving training, capacity building and the facilitation of partner countries 'on the front lines'.[11]

Of course, the Arab Spring introduced important new dimensions to al-Qaida's battle against regimes in the region. In the beginning, al-Qaida appeared imperilled by two aspects of the Arab Spring. First, the fundamental assumption underlying the global jihad strategy – that changes to the status quo 'can only be achieved through jihad'[12] – was dealt a body blow by the rainbow coalitions of peaceful protesters who, within a few months and with a largely secular discourse, claimed the scalps of four regional strongmen. Second, al-Qaida was threatened by the boon the revolutions seem to provide to political Islamists. If Islamists were able to integrate themselves into a genuine democratic process, throw off decades of political impotence, and govern with legitimacy, they would have presented a viable and effective alternative to al-Qaida when it came to the question of Islam and governance.

Instead, the breezes of the Arab Spring whistled two resounding notes of optimism for al-Qaida. In the first place, the power vacuums that developed as the result of ousted regimes afforded jihadi militants the opportunity to gain significant footholds in North Africa, Yemen and the Levant.

The overthrow of Qadhafi in Libya contributed to the spectacular military offensive launched by a jihadi coalition in Mali in 2012. Ever on the lookout for ways to needle his regional rivals, Qadhafi had been a major patron of the

---

[10] See Open Society Foundation, *Globalising Torture: CIA Secret Detention and Extraordinary Rendition* (New York, Open Society Foundations, 2013).
[11] Barack Obama, 'Remarks by the President at the United States Military Academy Commencement Ceremony', 28 May 2014, at http://www.whitehouse.gov/the-press-office/2014/05/28/-remarks-president-united-states-military-academy-commencement-ceremony.
[12] Interview with Rahimullah Yousafsai (ABC), 22 December 1998.

Tuareg people, who he declared to be 'the lions and eagles of the desert'.[13] On the heels of his downfall, heavily armed and well-trained Tuareg fighters flowed back into Mali, re-igniting a (secular) separatist rebellion there, intimidating the weak Malian army, and making significant advances that were then violently usurped by radical Islamist factions. Until they were rolled back by the French military in January 2013, these militants looked set to take over the country.

In Libya itself, a fragile central government headed by five Prime Ministers in three years struggled to exercise authority, particularly in the absence of a national army. Indeed, as anti-Qadhafi militias refused to disarm, the parliament was stormed, oil installations were seized, political assassinations and kidnappings were routinised, the police and judiciary were too fearful to operate, and most foreign nationals were evacuated, including the United Nations mission. Amid talk of a failed state, one former Prime Minister noted that 'there is no state in Libya to say if it is a failed state or not.'[14] In August 2014, the Libyan parliament passed a resolution calling for foreign intervention to halt the unrest.[15]

Against this backdrop, jihadi fighters established training camps in the northeast, northwest and southwest of the country. A hardline Salafi group, Ansar al-Sharia, wrested control of virtually the whole city of Derna and governed significant portions of other urban centres, including Benghazi and Sirte. Attacks were launched against foreign diplomatic missions, Western aid organisations and Sufi shrines. Militants were spotted brandishing heavy weaponry, including man-portable air-defence systems,[16] and overran both a US training facility for Libyan counter-terrorism forces on the outskirts of Tripoli ('Camp 27', April 2014) and a Libyan Special Forces base just outside Benghazi ('Camp Thunderbolt', July 2014). Notorious al-Qaida veteran Ibrahim Ali Abu Bakr Tantoush and former Guantanamo Bay inmate Abu Sufian bin Qamu operated openly in Libya, and combined with a new generation of leadership (Mohammed Zahawi and Ahmed Abu Khatalla) to transform post-Qadhafi Libya into an important node on the map of radical Islam. Indeed, Derna became a major training and transit point for the thousands of North African militants heading for jihad in Syria.

---

[13] Ronald Bruce St. John, *Libya: From Colony to Independence* (Oxford, Oneworld Publications, 2008), p. 231.

[14] 'Mahmoud Jebril Li al-Quds al-Arabi: Baqaa Nidaam al-Asad Khudma Li al-Israeel wa al-Mu'arida al-Suriya Adwa Nefsuha', *Al-Quds al-Arabi*, 14 April 2014, at https://www.alquds.co.uk/?p=156365.

[15] 'Libyan Parliament Asks UN for "Urgent Intervention" against Militias', *Deutsche Welle*, 13 August 2014, at http://www.dw.de/libyan-parliament-asks-un-for-urgent-intervention-against-militias/a-17852874.

[16] Mary Fitzgerald, 'Libyans are Wary of Self-Declared Saviour', *Sunday Times,* 25 May 2014.

On account of developments in Libya, Algeria militarised its 6385-km land borders, and also sent military aid to Tunisia, including fighter planes and surface-to-air missiles.[17] Indeed, though Tunis boasted a more successful political transition than Tripoli, the Tunisian authorities struggled with militancy on both the border with Algeria, where jihadis made a training ground of the Chaambi mountain range, and the border with Libya, where thousands of fighters and weapons crossed in both directions. Groups like the Uqba bin Nafi Brigade attacked the US Embassy, planted mines and IEDs and ambushed Tunisian soldiers.[18]

In Yemen, al-Qaida in the Arabian Peninsula (AQAP), made significant advances during nation-wide protests in 2011. Together with Yemen's own branch of Ansar al-Sharia, AQAP managed to seize a number of towns in the Shabwa and Abyan Provinces, where they ran a parallel government named the 'Emirate of Waqar' until they were finally dislodged a year later. From their desert strongholds AQAP militants continued to pressurise the government's presence in the south and the east with brazen attacks, and to stage jailbreaks, assassinate senior army officers, ambush paratroopers, murder foreign nationals and sabotage power lines. The Yemeni government was, moreover, side-tracked by emerging coup plots[19] as well as the advance of Houthi rebels in the northern portion of the country. In April 2014, Sana'a announced a renewed military push against AQAP with US drone support, and claimed to have killed 500 militants.[20] However, others wondered whether there was any longer term strategy behind the offensive, given that the government was not rebuilding what it took back from al-Qaida.[21]

As the political opposition movement in Syria became militarised, that violent space in turn became dominated by a number of jihadi groups,[22] of which ISIL was the most powerful, three years into the 'revolution'. Winning

---

[17] Ahmed Jum'a, 'Al-Jazair Manhat Tunis Tairaat wa Sawareekh Li Muwajihat al-Jama'at al-Irhabiya', 3 August 2014, al-Youm al-Sabi', at http://www1.youm7.com/story/2014/8/3/الإ_الجماعات_لمواجهة_وصواريخ_طائرات_تونس_منحت_الجزائر_الخبر/1802220#.U_c1_v3wtZg.

[18] 'En Tunisie, L'Armee Victime de la Plus Grave Attaque Depuis 1956', *Le Monde,* 17 July 2014, at http://www.lemonde.fr/tunisie/article/2014/07/17/tunisie-deux-soldats-tues-dans-une-attaque-terroriste_4458450_1466522.html.

[19] 'Tension in Yemen Amid Coup Fears', *Al Jazeera*, 17 June 2014.

[20] 'Yemen Says 500 Militants, 40 Soldiers Killed in Campaign', *Reuters*, 5 June 2014.

[21] Former US ambassador Barbara Bodine, in Shuaib al-Mosawa and Christopher Dickey, 'Hunting al-Qaeda: America's Epic Yemen Fail', *Daily Beast*, 15 May 2014.

[22] This development was helped along by, first, the influx of hardened fighters from the war in Iraq and, second, the Syrian regime's deliberate release of scores of jihadi prisoners. See remarks of the former head of the Syrian Military Intelligence Directorate in Phil Sands, Justin Vela and Suha Maayeh, 'Assad Regime Set Free Extremists from Prison to Fire Up Trouble During Peaceful Uprising', *The National*, 21 January 2014.

control of up to one third[23] of Syria's territory, often from the hands of other opposition groups including fellow radicals, ISIL engaged in proto-state building, with traffic police and tax collectors,[24] as well as the severe enforcement of its austere and uncompromising interpretation of the sharia. ISIL also claimed a large share[25] of the thousands of Western foreign fighters in Syria's civil war. Combining a prominent global brand with a utopian narrative and conducting its outreach in multiple languages, from English to Tamil,[26] ISIL attracted at least a dozen American nationals to its cause, including a member of the US National Guard.[27] One quarter of its foreign fighter contingent was British. Expanding into Iraq at lightning pace in June 2014, and prompting fears in Lebanon and Jordan of a similar invasion, ISIL was a major beneficiary of the rising sectarian temperature across the region, which threatened millions of civilians with wars for survival and which seemed set to continue to soar, regardless of whether the Bashar al-Assad regime remained in power or Syria experienced state collapse.

The second way in which the Arab Spring brought hope to al-Qaida was through the renewed repression of political Islamists by authoritarian regimes – thus providing a longer-term entry point for radical Islam. In 2012 a Muslim Brotherhood government came to power in Egypt, in the wake of Hosni Mubarak's demise, but the military regime which unseated the Brothers the following year carried out mass arrests, 'gunned down hundreds of unarmed demonstrators' at sit-ins,[28] handed down collective death sentences, and outlawed the Muslim Brotherhood, as part of its own 'War on Terror'.[29] Radical groups have proliferated since,[30] particularly in the underdeveloped

---

[23] 'ISIS in Control of "35 Percent" of Syrian Territory', *Al-Arabiya*, 19 July 2014, at http://english. alarabiya.net/en/News/middle-east/2014/07/19/270-Syrian-fighters-killed-in-biggest-ISIS-operation-. html.

[24] 'Life in a Jihadist Capital: Order with a Darker Side', *New York Times*, 23 July 2014.

[25] Shiraz Maher in remarks at launch of 'Greenbirds: Measuring Importance and Influence in Syrian Foreign Fighter Networks', International Centre for the Study of Radicalisation, King's College London, 15 April 2014.

[26] 'ISIS Uses Internet to Reach Indian Youths to Wage Jihad', *India Today*, 13 August 2014, at http://indiatoday.intoday.in/story/isis-uses-internet-to-reach-indians-youths-to-wage-jihad/1/376788.html.

[27] Gene Johnson, 'California Student Nicholas Teausant Allegedly Tries to Join Al-Qaeda Fighters in Syria', *Associated Press*, 18 March 2014.

[28] 'The Rab'a Massacre and Mass Killings of Protesters in Egypt', Human Rights Watch, 12 August 2014, at http://www.hrw.org/reports/2014/08/12/all-according-plan.

[29] See 'Egypt's Army Chief will Continue Protecting People's Mandate', *Al-Ahram*, 7 October 2013.

[30] Alongside relatively more established groups such as Ansar Beit al-Maqdis (est. June 2012) and Ansar al-Jihad (est. January 2012), the Hilwan Brigades announced their formation in August 2014 as a defensive and reluctant measure against the new predatory authorities: 'Our life has been full of misery and misery and misery and poverty, poverty, poverty. We can only complain to God… There has to be a group of people who seek to exact justice and respond to what these [troops] have

Sinai region. Saudi Arabia also intensified its crackdown on Islamists, declaring the Muslim Brotherhood to be a 'terrorist organisation' and going so far as to tacitly support Israel's bombardment of Gaza in 2014 because of Tel Aviv's aim to weaken Hamas, an offshoot of the Brotherhood. Given that radical Islamism was catalysed by the repression of political moderates and Islamists in the 1960s and 1970s,[31] the trend of pushing Islamism underground will likely yield an upsurge in radicalisation. Thus, after the Arab Spring, al-Qaida finds advantage in both the chokeholds of strong states and the chaos of weak states.

To signal the emergence of a new virtuous leadership

In the words of one al-Qaida military commander, one of the three objectives of the 9/11 attacks was 'to signal the emergence of a new virtuous leadership dedicated to opposing the Zionist–Anglo-Saxon–Protestant coalition'.[32] Osama bin Laden circumvented established patterns of Islamic leadership with the argument that al-Qaida gained the authority to declare jihad by default. This was as a result of the fact that both the religious establishment and ruling regimes of the Islamic world had abandoned the duty of jihad. Because the clerics were beholden to the rulers and the rulers pandered to the 'Crusaders', proper Islamic authority had vanished. It was left for the vanguard of al-Qaida, then, to protect the Muslims' interests, in the manner laid out by the Egyptian theorist Sayyid Qutb in his seminal tract, *Milestones*.[33]

In establishing new claims to Islamic authority, al-Qaida scored notable successes. Jihadi groups with global ambitions multiplied, often relying upon the political and normative arguments that bin Laden elaborated over the

---

perpetrated and what the Interior Ministry in particular have done. They have forgotten January 25 and the day of rage on January 28. They have forgotten what the people did with them. Rather than reconcile themselves with the people they took a hostile position'. See video at 'The First Appearance of the Hilwan Brigades', *Middle East Monitor*, 15 August 2014.

[31] For the case of Egypt, see Gilles Kepel, *Le Prophete et Pharaon* (Folio, Paris, 1984).

[32] Sayf al-Adil's other two aims were to retaliate against the US for its aggression in the Muslim world and to provoke the US 'out of its hole'. See Christopher M. Blanchard, 'Al-Qaeda: Statements and Evolving Ideology', *CRS Report for Congress* (code RL32759), 9 July 2007, p. 5.

[33] Sayyid Qutb, *Milestones* (New Delhi, Abdul Naeem, 2001), pp. 11–13.

years. From Ansar Eddine in Mali[34] to al-Shabaab in Somalia[35] to Boko Haram in Nigeria[36] to Lashkar-e-Taiba in Pakistan,[37] the once-nationalist mission statements of local, al-Qaida-linked groups shifted towards the Ladenese paradigm of global jihad. Indeed, the rhetorical legacy of bin Laden was even pronounced in the words of the self-proclaimed Caliph, Baghdadi, a rival to the al-Qaida leadership, who used his 2014 Ramadan address to describe the tragic state of an oppressed umma (the global community of Muslims), to redefine terrorism, to denounce Western hypocrisy, and to outline the individual duty for jihad.[38] This emerging globalist narrative will shape and be reshaped by the rising trend of foreign fighters joining the ranks of jihad, as well as the confrontation of these local groups with the 'West' and its counter-terrorism partners in the decade to come.

Another achievement for al-Qaida in this context was the spread of its cult of martyrdom. While Palestinian fighters had used suicide bombings as a tactic since 1994, 'Hamas never sought to find a theological argument for the use of suicide bombings, relying instead on popular acceptance among the Palestinians of the legitimacy of such attacks and the "martyrdom" of its perpetrators.'[39] Owing to al-Qaida's ideologists, treatises proliferated, as evidenced by the materials readily available in web forums such as 'Shumukh al-Islam' and 'Minbar Tawhid wa Jihad', and one major consequence of this was the subtle erosion of the strict Islamic principle of non-combatant immunity. No doubt, Osama bin Laden's arguments overturning that principle for Western civilians – because Western armies target our civilians, we

---

[34] Dressed in a black robe and white turban, and displaying the al-Qaida logo, Iyad Ag Ghali vowed to fight against 'the Crusade aggression' in an August 2014 video. See 'Le Chef d'Ansar Dine Reapparait dans une Video pour Menacer La France', *France 24*, 7 August 2014, at http://www.france24.com/fr/20140807-chef-ansar-dine-apparait-video-menace-france-islamisme-iyad-ag-ghali-djihadistes-mali-youtube/.

[35] See 'Press Statement by Al Shabaab Regarding the Westgate Terrorist Attack', *Kenyan Daily Post*, 26 September 2013.

[36] From 2011 onwards, Abubakar Shekau took to framing his war against the Nigerian state in terms of fighting global injustice and oppression against Muslims everywhere. See, for example, 'Boko Haram Leader Shekau Releases Video on Abduction of Chibok Girls', YouTube, https://www.youtube.com/watch?v=wrfWS_vL0D4 [accessed 12 August 2014].

[37] For the unilateral plot in Denmark, see Stephen Tankel, 'Lashkar-e-Taiba in Perspective: An Evolving Threat', New America Foundation: Counterterrorism Strategy Initiative Policy Paper, February 2010, p. 5, at http://carnegieendowment.org/files/Lashkar-e-Taiba_in_Perspective.pdf.

[38] See 'Khutabh by Abu Bakr al-Husayni al-Qurayshi al-Baghdadi on Ramadan 6th 1435 in Mosul Iraq', YouTube, https://www.youtube.com/watch?v=im6-G6q6G_k [accessed 2 August 2014].

[39] Brian Wicker, Maha Azzam and Peter Bishop, 'Martyrdom and Murder: Aspects of Suicidal Terrorism', in Brian Wicker (ed), *Witnesses to Faith? Martyrdom in Christianity and Islam* (Aldershot, Ashgate, 2006), p. 133.

can target theirs; because civilians vote for and pay taxes to their hostile governments, they are not innocent; because we don't directly intend to kill women and children, their deaths are legitimate – have gained a foothold in the jihadis' moral universe and, over decades, as these arguments are parroted[40] and elaborated, it is possible they will lead to the weakening of the principle's absolute character. Indeed, among a new generation of even Western jihadis, the heroic status of Osama bin Laden ('I love Osama bin Laden. I think he looks kinda cool'[41]), the legitimacy of 'martyrdom operations' and the existence of an *individual* duty for Muslims in the West to fight for their Sunni brethren across the seas, are often assumed.

While al-Qaida has championed a new idiom of leadership, which manifests itself in a global current that is defining the political and security landscape of the MENA region in 2014, it cannot be reasonably described as virtuous.

To defend Muslim lives and property

Al-Qaida's foundational mission was to protect Muslim lives and lands: 'we are following our Prophet's mission ... This is a defensive jihad to protect our land and people.'[42] However, most of the victims of al-Qaida-related violence since 9/11 have been Muslim civilians.[43]

All of bin Laden's legal, moral and political arguments rested on the premise that al-Qaida was defending Muslims, yet the credibility of this claim exploded alongside the scores of suicide bombers dispatched to civilian centres with the direct intention of massacring swathes of (Muslim) innocents. Moreover, as I have argued elsewhere, none of bin Laden's arguments overturning the Islamic principle of non-combatant immunity were applicable when the targets were Muslim, and civilian.[44]

---

[40] For example, the second of these arguments was used by the leader of al-Shabaab to justify the siege of the Westgate Mall in Nairobi: 'the taxes that you pay are being used to arm [Kenyan President] Uhuru Kenyatta's army that is actively killing Muslims and it is you who have supported your government's decision to go to war' (26 September 2013).

[41] Ifthekhar Jaman, see 'Our Brother Died a Martyr Fighting in Syria', *Channel 4 News*, 5 February 2014, http://www.channel4.com/news/iftikhar-jaman-syria-death-isis-jihad-british-portsmouth.

[42] Interview with Hamid Mir, 12 November 2001, in Lawrence, *Messages to the World*, p.141.

[43] Between 82% and 97% from 2006–11. See National Counterterrorism Centre, '2011 Report on Terrorism', at http://fas.org/irp/threat/nctc2011.pdf. The report also noted that Muslim majority countries bore the greatest number of attacks involving ten or more deaths.

[44] See Alia Brahimi, 'Crushed in the Shadows: Why al-Qaeda will Lose the War of Ideas', *Studies in Conflict and Terrorism* 33/2 (2010), pp. 93–110.

Certainly, bin Laden's poetic narrative of resistance once resonated even beyond the Muslim world, in particular at the height of the US-led occupation of Iraq. But that more broad-based sympathy dried up dramatically when the reality of what al-Qaida represented laid itself bare in the scenes of senseless savagery in places like Algiers, Amman and Al-Anbar. These incidents were self-evidently detrimental to al-Qaida's cause: one al-Qaida commander described the 2007 bombings of UN offices in Algiers as 'sheer idiocy';[45] after the uproar over the hotel bombings in Amman in 2005, Zarqawi's family took out full-page advertisements in newspapers severing links with him 'until doomsday';[46] and for al-Qaida's well-documented fanaticism in Iraq, Osama bin Laden himself seemed to apologise.[47]

Bin Laden's aim was to lead a popular and mainstream resistance movement yet, within his lifetime, fanatical footmen had consigned the group to the more radical margins of the umma. As bin Laden recognised before his death, the killing of Muslims resulted in 'the alienation of most of the [Islamic] nation from the mujahidin'.[48] When direct al-Qaida casualties are coupled with those which resulted from the ire of a superpower reeling from the 9/11 attacks (i.e. the 'War on Terror'), al-Qaida's claim to be the vanguard group protecting Muslim blood is called into doubt.

This reality was borne of the focus on what we might term the '*nearer enemy*' – that is, impure society. Al-Qaida 'brothers' anathematised their neighbours from other sects and religions, and those Sunnis with different interpretations of the faith. Indeed, the perverse reality of a globalised al-Qaida was an increasingly localised one. This misdirected war against the nearer enemy culminated in Iraq and Syria in 2013–14, where ISIL stoned to death 'adulterers', slaughtered or expelled religious minorities, enslaved women and girls from other faiths, beheaded children and declared war on the Shia'.

The democratisation of Islamic authority

At the root of al-Qaida's inward turn was the democratisation of Islamic authority.

---

[45] Abu Turab al-Jaza'iri in 'Al-Qaeda Commander in Northern Iraq: We are in Dire Straits', *MEMRI*, 11 March 2008, http://www.memri.org/bin/latestnews.cgi?ID=SD186608 [accessed 11 March 2008].

[46] Michael Howard, 'Zarqawi's Family Disown Him after Bombings,' *Guardian*, 21 November 2005.

[47] 'Bin Laden issues Iraq Message', *Al Jazeera*, 23 October 2007.

[48] Letter recovered at bin Laden's Abbottabad compound, believed to be from bin Laden to Atiyeh Abdulrahman, written sometime between July and October 2010. See 'Document 'SOCOM-2012-0000019', p. 9, made available by the Combating Terrorism Centre at Westpoint, at http://www.ctc.usma.edu/posts/letters-from-abbottabad-bin-ladin-sidelined.

During the 1990s, building upon arguments elaborated by Abdullah Azzam for the jihad in Afghanistan,[49] Osama bin Laden was eager to portray the concept of jihad as a popular uprising by individual Muslims. Historically, the idea behind defensive jihad was for Muslim rulers in neighbouring provinces to come to the aid of their co-religionists in other parts of the empire. The assumption was that all jihads, including defensive ones, would be led by established Muslim leaders within pre-modern states or clearly defined communities.

The architects of global jihad, however, reached out to Muslims as individuals, rather than as members of politically organised communities. In the 1990s, bin Laden called for Muslim individuals to come aboard and, quite literally, join him in the caravan of jihad. Going over the heads of the region's rulers and clerics, bin Laden democratised Islamic authority. A layman with no religious training, he formally declared a jihad of self-defence, and called upon his fellow Muslims to individually come forward for training and combat.

After 9/11 and the destruction of al-Qaida's headquarters in Afghanistan, al-Qaida devolved into a global cadre of autonomous cells, a moving target which enabled it to survive the War on Terror. However, with the globalisation of his jihad, bin Laden's authority was at once far-reaching and fragmented. Bin Laden had eroded the authority of the religious establishment and opened up the arena of Islamic interpretation, but he was unable to claim a monopoly over it himself. The proliferation of al-Qaida affiliated groups arrayed against the 'nearer enemy', employing brutal tactics for largely local ends, began, as discussed above, to portend its downfall. Intercepted communications revealed that al-Qaida's central leadership was unable to halt the violence,[50] and that one of the worst offenders in this regard, the Islamic State in Iraq, was established in 2006 'without consultation from the al-Qaida leadership … [and] has caused a split in the mujahidin ranks and their supporters inside and outside Iraq'.[51] Indeed, by arguing that individuals were entitled to wage jihad independently of the political and religious establishment, bin Laden

---

[49] See Abdullah Azzam, *Join the Caravan* (London, Azzam Publications, 2001).

[50] See, for example, letter from Atiyeh Abdelrahman to Abu Mus'ab al-Zarqawi, 11 December 2005, available at www.ctc.usma.edu/harmony/CTC-AtiyahLetter.pdf [accessed 12 February 2008] and letter from Ayman al-Zawahiri to Abu Mus'ab al-Zarqawi, 11 October 2005, reprinted in Laura Mansfield, *In His Own Words* (Old Tappan NJ, TLG Publications, 2006), pp. 250–279.

[51] Letter from Adam Gadahn to unknown recipient written in late January 2011 and recovered at the Abbottabad compound. See 'Document 'SOCOM-2012-0000004', p. 8, made available by the Combating Terrorism Centre at Westpoint, at http://www.ctc.usma.edu/posts/letters-from-abbottabad-bin-ladin-sidelined.

himself planted the seeds of discord in the heart of al-Qaida, guaranteeing its fragmentation.

But if this democratisation of authority precipitated major problems, then the further fragmentation of authority was, from 2010, presented as one solution. The call for jihad, emanating principally from Yemen, altered subtly, but significantly. The aim of al-Qaida in the Arabian Peninsula – the affiliate most closely associated with Osama bin Laden and his belief that violence should be employed strategically and not wantonly – was to get back to basics. A new ideological and strategic current championed lone-wolf attacks by Muslim individuals living in the West, without prior contact with al-Qaida networks or consultation with any of its radical jurists. Thus, the democratisation of authority entered a second stage.

The English-language propaganda materials of AQAP vigorously re-imagined the landscapes of jihad and increasingly advocated 'individual terrorism'.[52] The argument was that Muslims in the West were perfectly placed to play an important and decisive role, particularly as America is awash with easily obtainable firearms.[53] Furthermore, individual operations were much harder to detect and intercept because, as AQAP's *Inspire* magazine pointed out, nobody else in the world needed to know what these lone operatives were thinking and planning.[54] The global jihad became at once universal and highly particularised.

Playing on the gritty urban glamour associated with the videogame generation, the 'knight of lone jihad' and the 'terrorist next door' were rendered, both discursively and through graphics and images, as akin to dark, perhaps reluctant, superheroes.[55] Launched in 2010, *Inspire* magazine was clearly aimed at the uninitiated Western amateur. The meanings of Arabic terms (such as 'al-Sham') were carefully explained to the reader and the lone wolf was reminded not to leave his ID cards, fingerprints or schoolbooks behind at the scene of an operation. *Inspire* was found in the possession of several foiled plotters, including the US soldier Nasser Jason Abdo, who tried to make a bomb in his motel room, four British Pakistanis from Luton who planned an attack on a British Army base using a toy car, and the Tsarnaev brothers, who used its 'Open Source Jihad' section as a manual for building the

---

[52] For example, in one letters section, an anonymous Muslim living in the West asks about the best way to reach the jihad frontiers. Stay where you are, he is advised, and focus on planning an operation in the West instead, like attacking an army recruitment centre or a nightclub (issue V).

[53] Adam Gadahn in video released early June 2011, available at http://www.youtube.com/watch?v=7fAnpHiuVoQ.

[54] Letters section, *Inspire V*, March 2011, p. 12.

[55] See especially *Inspire X*, March 2013.

pressure cooker bombs they left near the finish line of the Boston Marathon in 2013.[56] Consequently, the 2011 US Counter-terrorism Strategy was 'the first that focuses on the ability of al-Qaida and its networks to inspire people in the US to attack us from within'.[57]

Shortly after its public dispute with ISIL, 'al-Qaida central', which maintained close ties with AQAP, announced in March 2014 the launch of its own English language publication. The magazine had not been released at the time of writing, but a slick video trailer, which was posted to YouTube by al-Qaida central's media arm, al-Sahab, spliced together images of aggressive US soldiers and successful al-Qaida operations, accompanied by audio from a speech by Malcom X: 'if a man speaks the language of brute force you can't come to him in peace.'[58] The purpose was to renew the push against Western targets – by regenerating the jihadi threat with a native grasp of language, culture and environment – and, in the process, to re-assert centralised authority over the global jihad.

Al-Qaida in the near future

No doubt, it remains a priority for Zawahiri and his comrades in the al-Qaida old guard to launch a large-scale attack against a Western target, in order to re-energise the ranks and, more importantly, to silence internal critics. With the spectacular rise of Baghdadi's 'state', however temporary, and the corresponding criticism in jihadi circles that a state (ISIL) cannot take orders from an organisation (al-Qaida), it also becomes incumbent upon Zawahiri to declare or become affiliated with another Islamic Emirate. To that end, the ISAF drawdown in Afghanistan presents an opportunity, particularly in the Kunar and Nuristan provinces, where an operative by the name of Farouk al-Qahtani is likely already laying the groundwork, and where Afghan al-Qaida allies known as the 'Salafi Taliban'[59] have carved out a haven. The fall of the Taliban government in late 2001 seemed traumatic for the al-Qaida

---

[56] The recurring 'Open Source Jihad' section advises on how to make a bomb in your mum's kitchen (issue I), how to outfit a pickup truck with blades so that it can be used to mow down enemies (issue II), how to start forest fires in hospitable environments like Montana (issue IX), how to cause road accidents using cooking oil (issue X), and how to make a car bomb (issue XII).

[57] John Brennan, Obama's Counter-Terrorism Chief, in Howard LaFranchi, 'US Unveils New Counterterrorism Strategy', *Christian Science Monitor*, 19 June 2011.

[58] 'Al-Qaeda Media Arm Announces New English Language Magazine', YouTube, at https://www.youtube.com/watch?v=nJ8HFnJLDiY [accessed 12 March 2014].

[59] Author correspondence with Pakistani journalist Zia Ur Rehman, March 2014.

leadership,[60] therefore the revival of some form of Islamic state in Afghanistan would also play a cathartic role.

Leadership struggles, then, will have a hand in shaping al-Qaida's future, and Western targets, with their capacity to instil awe in the ranks, will be implicated in any score settling. It was divisions within al-Qaida in the Islamic Maghreb, for example, which led directly to the 2013 attack against the British/Norwegian gas facility at Ain Amenas in eastern Algeria. Passed over for promotion within AQIM for a second time, and castigated for his unwillingness to follow orders, refusal to submit expense reports, and 'back-biting',[61] Mokhtar Belmokhtar put into motion the Ain Amenas attack to signal the arrival of his new group, the 'Signed-in-Blood' brigade, which had been formed a few weeks earlier.[62] By-passing the AQIM leadership once and for all, Belmokhtar pledged allegiance directly to Zawahiri.

Similarly, the storming of the Westgate shopping centre in Nairobi by al-Shabaab militants was related to internal rivalries. The siege at the mall, popular with foreigners, can be understood as the end result of a push by Abu Zubayr to purge the nationalist element within al-Shabaab and direct the group towards a more transnational agenda. The schism between clan-based nationalists,[63] led by Mukhtar Robow and Hassan Dahir Aweys, and al-Qaida-linked internationalists culminated in armed clashes in June 2013, in which the latter triumphed. A few weeks after the leadership coup, in which two of the group's co-founders were killed and Robow and Aweys were chased away,[64] Abu Zubayr ordered Westgate. Al-Shabaab now recruits among impoverished and unemployed Kenyans.[65]

At a time when, in the words of Zawahiri, 'the jihadi awakening is intensifying',[66] this trend of fragmentation will only increase, particularly as feuding camps are demarcated along generational lines. One major fault

---

[60] See bin Laden, SOCOM-2012-0000019, p. 24.

[61] See letter from the AQIM Shura Council to Belmokhtar, recovered by the Associated Press in Timbuktu, Mali. 'The al-Qaida Papers: A Disciplinary Letter from al-Qaida's HR Department', *Associated Press*, 3 October 2012, at http://hosted.ap.org/interactives/2012/al-qaida /?START=al-qaida-papers#.

[62] Belmokhtar's independent efforts have come under a variety of names, including 'al-Mulathimin' and the 'Khaled Abu al-Abbas Brigade'. In August 2013, he announced that his outfit would merge with MUJAO in Mali, to form 'al-Murabitoun'.

[63] For this contingent's determination to oust the current Somali government and put their own clans in power, see Bronwyn Bruton and J. Peter Pham, 'The Splintering of al Shabaab: A Rough Road from War to Peace', *Foreign Affairs*, 2 February 2012.

[64] Hassan M. Abukar, 'Somalia: The Godane Coup and the Unravelling of al-Shabaab', *Royal African Society's African Arguments*, 2 July 2013.

[65] 'Outside Source', BBC World Service Radio, 14 August 2014, 10.29 am.

[66] Interview with al-Sahab media, 17 February 2014, available at https://www.youtube.com/ watch?v=4RhfKQF_YgA [accessed 21 August 2014].

line will be the establishment by ISIL of its 'Islamic state', in whatever form it endures, which has rocked the jihadi community, and prompted affiliated groups to come down on one side or the other. While Zawahiri can count on the support of AQIM, AQAP and famous Salafi ideologues, lesser known jihadi groups in Southeast Asia,[67] the Sinai[68] and Mali[69] have thrown their lot in with Baghdadi hoping, no doubt, to win more attention from an alternative leadership. However, even within the pro-Zawahiri bloc, cracks appeared – a chief judge in AQIM seemed to issue a statement of support for Baghdadi,[70] and defections to ISIL by AQAP foot soldiers were also reported.[71]

Countless questions of authority are central to these debates, with supporters of ISIL claiming that there never was an allegiance to Zawahiri or al-Qaida central, because ISIL was formed out of the remnants of the Islamic State of Iraq, whose fighters had sworn an oath of allegiance to its (now dead) Emir.[72] Baghdadi himself claimed to be a descendent of the Prophet Mohammed. His critics accused him and his followers of being Khawarij,[73] a deviant sect from the early days of Islam, which repudiated the rightful succession of the Caliphs and was infamous for its slaughtering of women and children.[74] These intensifying leadership disputes will give a lift to the global jihad, as teams of rivals compete to lead the charge against 'Islam's enemies', and thereby establish independent authority.

The identification of those enemies will be crucial to defining the nature of al-Qaida in the decade to come. Osama bin Laden targeted the 'far enemy' as a means to weakening the dreaded 'near enemy' but, as discussed, the 9/11 decade brought an ever-increasing (and, from bin Laden's perspective, foolish) fixation on the 'nearer enemy'. Indeed, the principal illusion of terrorism was

---

[67] For example, the Abu Sayyaf group in the Philippines and Abu Bakir Bashir's group, Jema'a Anshour Atawhid, in Indonesia.

[68] For example, Ansar Beit al-Maqdis and Majlis Shura al-Mujahidin.

[69] For example, Ansar Eddine led by Iyad Ag Ghali.

[70] Message from Abu Abdullah Othman al-Assimi, Qadi of AQIM Central Regions, June 2014, posted to YouTube at https://www.youtube.com/watch?v=klLZPezL-Cw [accessed 30 June 2014].

[71] Greg Miller, 'Fighters Abandoning al-Qaeda Affiliates to Join Islamic State, US Officials Say', *Washington Post*, 9 August 2014. Indeed, 'disagreements' within AQAP were reported. See Ali Ibrahim al-Moshki, 'AQAP Announces Support for ISIL', *Yemen Times*, 19 August 2014.

[72] See Aymenn Jawad al-Tamimi, 'ISIS and al-Qaeda Compete for Supremacy in Global Jihad', *Al-Monitor*, 11 February 2014.

[73] Abu Qatadah, for example, argued that ISIL were Khawarij and 'dogs of the hellfire' – see 'Al-Salafi Abu Qatadah al-Filastini Yasaf Daish Bilkhawarij Wa Ahl al-Nar', *Al-Watan News*, 29 April 2014.

[74] For more on the Khawarij see Jeffrey T. Kenney, *Muslim Rebels: Kharijites and the Politics of Extremism in Egypt* (Oxford, Oxford University Press, 2006).

the belief, held by bin Laden, that terror could somehow be tamed, limited or transcended.

At first glance, there is a spectrum. At one end, AQAP remains devoted to bin Laden's cause, insisting that the US and its allies are the principal enemy,[75] committing considerable resources to radicalising Western Muslims, developing cell-phone bombs that can circumvent airport security,[76] and urging al-Qaida fighters to go easy on enforcing the sharia.[77] At the other end of the spectrum are groups like ISIL, born in sectarian killing fields in Iraq and Syria, and Boko Haram in Nigeria which, despite its new globalist rhetoric, concentrated on slaughtering Nigerian Christians, blowing up World Cup screenings and abducting and seemingly enslaving 276 schoolgirls for having received 'non-Islamic' education (Osama bin Laden was, by contrast, well known for personally educating his daughters, particularly in maths and science).[78]

However, in reality, there is ample scope for these different preoccupations to come together under one umbrella, particularly with the rise of ISIL, which, having honed its fighting skills against the 'near enemies' in Baghdad and Damascus, and having earned an unrivalled reputation for brutality against civilians deemed the 'nearer enemy', will almost certainly branch out into 'far enemy' jihad. Over the coming months, Baghdadi can be expected to direct some of his Westernised foot soldiers and part of his group's billion-dollar fortune (amassed through seizing oil fields,[79] selling off antiquities and extorting the population), towards a campaign against the West – and he will perhaps relish in straying onto Zawahiri's home ground. Boko Haram also appears interested in forging a three-pronged focus, merging a virulent sectarian agenda and its war against the authorities in Abuja with new threats against world leaders.[80] In North Africa, too, extreme Salafi organisations like

---

[75] See, for example, a video which surfaced on an Islamist website showing Nasser al-Wuhayshi speaking to an open-air gathering of militants. Available at https://www.youtube.com/watch?v=b934hBtZFfc [accessed 15 April 2014].

[76] Briant Bennett and Richard A. Serrano, 'More Western Fighters Joining Militants in Iraq and Syria, *Los Angeles Times*, 19 July 2014.

[77] See letter from Nasir al-Wuhayshi to the Emir of AQIM, recovered by the Associated Press in Timbuktu, Mali. 'The al-Qaida Papers: How to Win Friends and Govern People', *Associated Press*, 21 May 2012, at http://hosted.ap.org/interactives/2012/al-qaida/?START=al-qaida-papers#.

[78] See Lawrence Wright, *The Looming Tower: Al-Qaeda's Road to 9/11* (London, Penguin, 2006), p. 252.

[79] Oil smuggling alone earned the group $1 million a day in 2014. See Vivienne Walt, 'How Guns and Oil Net ISIS $1 Million a Day', *Fortune*, 11 August 2014.

[80] For example, 'Ban Ki Moon you are in trouble, Benyamin Netanyahu you are in trouble, Queen Elizabeth you are in trouble'. See 'Boko Haram Leader Shekau Speaks: Vows to Attack Nigerian Refineries, Buhari, Babangida, Others', *Premium Times* (Abuja), 20 February 2014. A month later,

Ansar al-Sharia may well deepen their links to established global jihadis from AQIM, particularly in Libya, thus posing a combined menace to society, state and the West.

In terms of counter-terrorism, the temptation remains for a coercive solution, though now less directly, through 'partner' governments. Beyond questions about competence – illustrated starkly by the capitulation of the US-trained Iraqi army in the face of the ISIL advance on Mosul in June 2014 – many of the West's 'partners' perpetuate the violent binary between repressive 'secular' regimes and radical Sunni Islam. The Egyptian authorities, suspected by human rights monitors of 'crimes against humanity',[81] benefitted from the resumption of US military aid in 2014, including $575 million and 10 Apache attack helicopters to combat militants in the Sinai,[82] while Kenya's Anti-Terrorism Police Unit, funded by the US and the UK, was accused of carrying out extrajudicial killings and forced disappearances.[83] In fact, the spectacular rise of ISIL can be attributed to the misguided militarisation of two political issues: the Assad regime's iron-fisted response to the Syrian opposition and the Iraqi government's violent crackdown on the Sunni protest movement in al-Anbar province.

Moreover, at a time when al-Qaida is resurgent in Egypt's impoverished Sinai regions, in eastern and southern Libya's marginalised enclaves, on Iraq and Syria's sectarian battlefields, in northern Mali's separatist strongholds, in the Sahel's ungoverned spaces, in Nigeria's chronically underdeveloped north, in Somalia's fragile state, and in refugee camps from Dadaab to Peshawar, many of the West's 'partners' are by their exclusionary nature unable to open the file on governance issues. Yet if the principal illusion of terrorism was that terror could be tempered, the 9/11 decade, with its 'War on Terror', war in Iraq, war in Afghanistan and drone wars, suggested that the illusion of counter-terrorism was the possibility of a military solution. Large populations in the Middle East, Africa and South Asia remain suspended between these dangerous fantasies.

Shekau again underlined Boko Haram's global mission: 'Let me make it crystal clear to you because you are taking a lot of pains making analyses in the newspapers and the radio. We are not fighting the North, we are fighting the world. And you will see us fighting the world'. See 'Boko Haram Leader, Abubakar Shekau's Message in New Video', *Nigerian Times*, 28 March 2014.

[81] 'Egypt: Rab'a Killings Likely Crimes Against Humanity', Human Rights Watch, 12 August 2014, at http://www.hrw.org/news/2014/08/12/egypt-rab-killings-likely-crimes-against-humanity.

[82] 'US Unlocks Military Aid to Egypt, Backing President Sisi', *BBC News*, 22 June 2014.

[83] 'Kenya: Killings, Disappearances by Anti-Terror Police', Human Rights Watch, 18 August 2014, at http://www.hrw.org/news/2014/08/18/kenya-killings-disappearances-anti-terror-police.

3

Counter-Terrorism in the Post-9/11 Era

Successes, Failures and Lessons Learned

RASHMI SINGH

Introduction

ON 5 NOVEMBER 2009, MAJOR NIDAL MALIK HASAN opened fire at the medical centre of Fort Hood, Texas killing thirteen and injuring over thirty individuals. At his military trial not only did he admit to killing unarmed soldiers waiting for their final medical check-ups before deploying to Iraq and Afghanistan, but he also acknowledged that he acted in response to the United States' aggressive foreign policy in both countries.[1] A few years later, on 22 May 2013, two men ran over and then hacked to death an off-duty British soldier later named as Drummer Lee Rigby of the Royal Regiment of Fusiliers, on the streets of Woolwich in southeast London. Once again, instead of fleeing the scene the men, Michael Adebolajo and Michael Adebowale, remained at the site and justified their actions to eyewitnesses as a response to the killing of thousands of Muslims in Afghanistan and Iraq by the British Army as part of their role in the Global War on Terror (GWoT).[2] These incidents bring into sharp focus the numerous outcomes of counter-terrorism policies adopted after the 11 September 2001 attacks under the rubric of the GWoT.

---

[1] The Associated Press at Fort Hood, 'Fort Hood Shooter Nidal Hasan Sentenced to Death for Killing 13 Soldiers', *The Guardian*, 23 May 2013, http://www.telegraph.co.uk/news/uknews/terrorism-in-the-uk/10075488/Woolwich-attack-the-terrorists-rant.html [accessed 4 August 2014].

[2] There is a large body of news and commentary on both the Fort Hood Shootings and the Woolwich murder quite easily available online. For the Woolwich incident see, for instance, Simon Jenkins, 'The Woolwich Killers Don't Threaten the State, Yet are Treated as Warriors in a New Cold War', *The Guardian*, 19 December 2013, http://www.theguardian.com/commentisfree/2013/dec/19/woolwich-killers-new-cold-war-lee-rigby [accessed 8 September 2014]. Staff Reporter, 'Woolwich Attack: The Terrorist's Rant', *The Telegraph,* http://www.telegraph.co.uk/news/uknews/terrorism-in-the-uk/10075488/Woolwich-attack-the-terrorists-rant.html [accessed 8 September 2014].

Proceedings of the British Academy **203**, 39–55. © The British Academy 2015.

It has been thirteen years since the horrific attacks of 9/11 and over twenty years since the fall of the Berlin Wall and what was euphorically, albeit somewhat unfortunately, termed the 'End of History.'[3] In that time it has become clear that the GWoT not only represents the single most significant conflict since the end of the Cold War, but is also undoubtedly the lengthiest and most far-reaching counter-terrorism enterprise in history. At the same time, the GWoT has significantly challenged, and arguably altered, expectations regarding how liberal democratic states can and do behave in the international system. Yet in all this time, there has been very little reflection regarding the real effectiveness of this huge enterprise. Many authors take the absence or, as evidenced by the examples cited above, the minimal presence of 'terrorist' attacks on the homeland as a key benchmark of success. However, this not only reveals a somewhat simplistic understanding of the notion of success in the GWoT, it is also deeply isolationist and risks disregarding the complex long-term consequences of what is perceived by many to be an overly aggressive foreign policy abroad. In short, it is imperative to look back at the past decade of counter-terrorism policy in order not only to assess its successes and failures but also to answer some key questions, including what our post-9/11 experiences teach us about the end of terrorism and terrorist organisations. It is also imperative to address questions about the likely decline of al-Qaida and transnational terrorism, as these should also quite rightly affect our notions of success and failure. Unfortunately, in painting a picture of counter-terrorism policy since 9/11 our strategic successes, perhaps somewhat predictably, seem few and far between, whereas our failures and their consequences are amplified across the world stage with what seems to be much greater resonance.

Understanding how terrorism ends is a critical element in formulating any counter-terrorism strategy. In 1991 Martha Crenshaw forwarded what was perhaps one of the earliest models in the discipline discussing the ways in which terrorism could decline.[4] This model clearly outlined the relationship between specific government actions and the end of terrorist campaigns. Crenshaw argued that the decline of terrorism seemed to be related to the combination of three key factors: the response of the state under attack, the strategic choices made by the terrorist organisation in question, as well as its organisational resources. More significantly, Crenshaw underscored that hinging our understanding of success on the mere physical defeat of a terrorist group was too simplistic an understanding of this process. Nearly twenty years later, Audrey Cronin also identified and outlined six broad patterns in

---

[3] Francis Fukuyama, *The End of History and the Last Man* (New York, Avon Books, 1992).
[4] M. Crenshaw, 'How Terrorism Declines', *Terrorism and Political Violence*, 3/1 (1991).

how terrorist campaigns have historically ended.[5] Cronin's work reads like a deeper, historically grounded empirical engagement with Crenshaw's original thesis and attributes the decline of terrorism to: *decapitation* or the capturing and/or killing of group leaders; *negotiation* or the organisation's entry into a legitimate political process; *success* or the achievement of the group's aims; *failure* or the group's implosion and/or loss of public support; *repression* or the defeat and elimination of the group by brute force; and finally *reorientation* or the transition from terrorism to other forms of violence. Speaking about the counter-terrorism response to al-Qaida, Cronin quite rightly emphasises that recognising the ways in which the organisation is both similar to and different from previous terrorist threats is a critical first step in devising a more effective and measured strategic response to the physical and psychological challenge(s) it presents.

But if understanding how terrorism ends is an important element in formulating counter-terrorism strategy, then why have the US and its allies failed so dismally to grapple with the al-Qaida threat despite the insights provided by such models? Or perhaps, to frame it more precisely, why has strategic 'victory' against al-Qaida, its affiliates and their virulent ideology remained so elusive and indecisive? Have we achieved *any* degree of success in the GWoT? Contemporary developments suggest that the al-Qaida network, or some manifestation thereof, is going to exist and remain active for some time to come. This is despite the fact that up until September 2013 the war in Afghanistan alone had cost the United States $657.50 billion and it was spending over $17.0 billion in classified funds *each* year in fighting terrorism.[6] Add to this the huge human costs as signified by the thousands of civilian and soldier deaths around the world during the course of this campaign as well as the recent developments in Syria and Iraq, including the rise of the Islamic State, and it would appear that the GWoT has been bitterly ineffective. However, at the same time it would also be inaccurate to suggest that the US and its allies have experienced pure failure in their post-9/11 counter-terrorism efforts against al-Qaida and its affiliates. To this end, in what follows I probe some of the reasons why policies against transnational terrorism have not only resulted in infrequent, indecisive victories but also why achievements in the GWoT have been limited to short-term tactical triumphs as opposed to

---

[5] A. K. Cronin, *How Terrorism Ends: Understanding the Decline and Demise of Terrorist Campaigns* (Princeton, Princeton University Press 2009).

[6] Dylan Matthews, 'Twelve Years after 9/11, We Still have No Idea how to Fight Terrorism', *The Washington Post*, 11 September 2013, http://www.washingtonpost.com/blogs/wonkblog/wp/2013/09/11/twelve-years-after-911-we-still-have-no-idea-how-to-fight-terrorism-2/ [accessed 4 August 2014].

long-term strategic successes. I argue that counter-terrorism policies under the GWoT have failed to meet set goals for a number of reasons including, but not limited to: the shifting character of war, the unintended fallouts of the counter-terrorism policies adopted, and an inadvertent strengthening of al-Qaida's material and ideological capabilities through the US macro-securitisation of the GWoT – all of which, in combination, point to the absence of a long-term strategic vision. These reasons constitute critical lessons to be learned from the current counter-terrorism response to the al-Qaida threat and should inform future academic thinking as well as policy formulation on the matter.

Lesson I: A shift in the overall strategic character of war

Perhaps the single most relevant lesson learned over the past thirteen years from the operations conducted in Afghanistan and Iraq is that there has been a qualitative shift in the strategic character of war and conflict. Not only is it clear that new security threats have emerged but also that these threats do not readily lend themselves to a conventional military response. For similar reasons it has also become very clear that these new threats cannot be addressed by the United States alone, and nor are the old, established alliances sufficient to respond to what seems to be a much more insidious, unconventional and far-reaching menace. In other words, over the past decade or so the overall character of conflict within the international system has changed quite rapidly.

Since the 9/11 attacks, NATO countries have found their militaries deployed to places like Afghanistan and Iraq where the mission not only consists of destroying transnational terrorist infrastructure and pacifying insurrections, but where doing so has also often involved the broader goal of building what are viable states with effective governments. The state-building enterprises in Afghanistan and Iraq, which one can argue with the benefit of hindsight seem to have been largely unsuccessful, have been ostensibly undertaken to prevent the re-emergence of security vacuums and safe havens that can be leveraged in the future by al-Qaida, its affiliates and other like-minded organisations.[7] At

---

[7] To some degree, the inclusion of state building into what was – at least initially – intended to be a pure counter-terrorism campaign was the direct result of what have been constantly shifting goal-posts in the GWoT. At the same time, this shift may also have occurred to some degree in response to an expanding literature that discredited the kinetic approach adopted in Afghanistan and Iraq on the one hand, and argued that the 'battle for hearts and minds' was central to allied efforts seeking to counter al-Qaida's ideology of violent Islamist extremism on the other. See, for example: A. P. Schmid and R. Singh, 'Measuring Success and Failure in Terrorism and Counter-Terrorism: U.S. Government Metrics of the Global War on Terror', in A. P. Schmid and G. F. Hindle (eds.), *After the War on Terror: Regional and Multilateral Perspectives on Counter-Terrorism Strategy* (London, RUSI Books, 2009);

the same time, researchers and practitioners alike are recognising that asymmetry is now part and parcel of the existing strategic and tactical security environment that the West finds itself in. Indeed, writers like David Kilcullen[8] and Andrew Bacevich[9] see the 'fundamental mismatch between US military capabilities and those of the rest of the world'[10] as a core characteristic of the contemporary security environment. It is worth recalling that it was with the end of the Cold War that the US entered a period in which it enjoyed what was an unprecedented military preponderance within the international system. This meant that no adversary, or indeed combination of adversaries, could engage the US in a conventional war and hope to win. While advances in global military technology are increasingly challenging[11] and eroding US post-Cold War military–technological advantage, at least for the time being, it still continues to hold an unmatched advantage over both its friends and its rivals. At the same time, it also continues to exert an exceptional ability to project both air and ground forces as well as an extraordinary competency at combined and joint warfare. More significantly, the US has as yet unmatched levels of defence spending. Indeed, in 2013 alone the US defence budget amounted to a total of $640 billion and represented more than that of the next eight countries combined.[12]

But what we are seeing in the years since 9/11 is that many twenty-first-century adversaries of the United States and its allies have adapted in ways that make this US military and technological might largely irrelevant. In short, US air power, military and technological superiority are no longer enough to decisively 'win' contemporary conflicts. Instead, Iraq and Afghanistan have taught us that twenty-first-century conflicts demand a new strategic vision and an ability to adapt just as quickly as our foes. Such adaptation demands a new sort of capability on the part of the US and its allies. It requires enhanced military intelligence, 'Special Forces and small-unit capabilities even more than the traditional big divisions, large carrier task groups and long-range

---

A. E. Hunt et al, 'Beyond Bullets: Strategies for Countering Violent Extremism', *Solarium Strategy Series* (Washington, DC, Centre for a New American Security, 2009).

[8] D. Kilcullen, *The Accidental Guerrilla: Fighting Small Wars in the Midst of a Big One* (London, Hurst & Co., 2009).

[9] A. Bacevich, *Washington Rules: America's Path to Permanent War* (New York, Metropolitan Books, 2011).

[10] Kilcullen, *The Accidental Guerrilla*, p. 22.

[11] C. Morrison, 'Technological Superiority No Longer Sufficient for US Military Dominance', *AEIdeas*, http://www.aei-ideas.org/2014/08/technological-superiority-no-longer-sufficient-for-us-military-dominance/ [accessed 5 August 2014].

[12] 'The US Spends More on Defense than the Next Eight Countries Combined', *Peter G. Peterson Foundation*, http://pgpf.org/Chart-Archive/0053_defense-comparison [accessed 23 July 2014].

strategic bombers.'[13] Indeed, traditional confrontations between nation-states with standing armies are on the decline – though this is by no means suggests that conventional, force-on-force, state-on-state wars are no longer plausible. However, the US seems to be facing what is primarily an unconventional conflict scenario today – characterised by irregular,[14] asymmetric[15] warfare waged by what Gary Hart categorises as 'dispersed terrorist cells, stateless nations, insurgencies, tribes, clans, and gangs'.[16] These groups, exemplified by al-Qaida and its various allies – such as al Shabaab, Lashkar-i-Taiba and the Taliban – practise a hybrid[17] form of warfare and tend to involve a relatively small number of combatants who are engaged in small-scale (and for the most part opportunistic and tactically uncoordinated) attacks against Western interests, forces and proxies. This hybrid form of warfare uses terrorism, insurgency, propaganda and economic warfare to sidestep what has been the West's conventional capability advantage.[18]

Of course, the question that then needs to be posed is: why has such a shift occurred? For writers like Kilcullen, the strategic logic of terrorism, insurgency and unconventional war is founded precisely upon the mismatch in military capabilities between the US and the rest of the world. This means that no rational adversary, irrespective of ideology, will willingly challenge

[13] G. Hart, 'After Bin Laden: Security Strategy and the Global Commons', *Survival: Global Politics and Strategy*, 53/4 (2011), p. 20.

[14] A type of warfare where the combatants are irregular military as opposed to regular forces. The term can include enemies of 'any genus who choose to fight in an irregular mode; or it may refer to foes who are deemed to be irregular by definition because they are not the licensed sword arms of officially recognized polities'. See C. S. Gray, *Irregular Enemies and the Essence of Strategy: Can the American Way of War Adapt?* (Carlisle, PA, US Army War College, Strategic Studies Institute, 2006), p. 8.

[15] One of the most widely accepted definitions of asymmetry in the US context was provided in the 1999 Joint Strategy Review and stated that: 'asymmetric approaches are attempts to circumvent or undermine US strengths, while exploiting US weaknesses using methods that differ significantly from the United States' expected method of operations ... Asymmetric approaches often employ innovative, non-traditional tactics, weapons or technologies, and can be applied to all levels of warfare – strategic, operational and tactical – and across the spectrum of military operations.' See S. Metz and D. V. Johnson, *Asymmetry and U.S. Military Strategy: Definition, Background and Strategic Concepts*, (Carlise, PA, US Army War College, Strategic Studies Institution, 2001), p. 5.

[16] G. Hart, 'A National Security Act for the 21st Century', *Huffington Post* 11 December 2009 [accessed 4 July 2014]. See also G. Hart, *Under the Eagle's Wing: A National Security Strategy of the United States for 2009* (Colorado, Fulcrum Publishing, 2008).

[17] Hybrid threats are essentially combined threats: instead of 'separate challengers with fundamentally different approaches (conventional, irregular or terrorist)', hybrid threats reference 'competitors who employ *all* forms of war and tactics, perhaps simultaneously'. In other words, there is a 'fusion of war forms that blurs regular and irregular warfare ... traditional and irregular tactics, decentralised planning and execution and non-state actors ... using both simple and sophisticated technologies in innovative ways'. See: F. G. Hoffman, *Conflict in the 21st Century: The Rise of Hybrid Wars* (Arlington, VA, Potomac Institute for Policy Studies, 2007), p. 7.

[18] Kilcullen, *The Accidental Guerrilla*, p. 25.

the US in a conventional force-on-force confrontation, instead preferring to resort to asymmetric, unconventional, often hybrid means of engagement[19] to confront it and take tactical advantage of the fact that it is still largely mired in conventional military thinking. In response, it is necessary that the US and its allies move away from relying on traditional tactics, institutions and policies in order to address this new operating environment. In short, 'the West' needs to adapt just as quickly to the new realities of the twenty-first century by moving away from monolithic, all-encompassing policy responses such as the GWoT towards a much more pragmatic, proportionate, case-by-case response system. It needs to build an internationalist grand strategy – one that is founded upon shared concerns and goals and which can encompass a shared security response. Most crucially, given the current economic climate, it needs to accept that this will necessitate burden-sharing with all its caveats – perhaps to an (as yet) unprecedented degree.

Lesson II: The law of unintended consequences

Lesson number two is perhaps best described by Peter S. Probst when he talked about the 'law of unintended consequences'[20] – and it is worth spending some time discussing this with the aid of an illustrative case study. A key element of US response to the 9/11 attacks was the initiation of a policy that was vigorously promoted under the GWoT, namely that of capacity building and the formation of international partnerships against the perceived threat posed by al-Qaida, its affiliates and its particular brand of terrorist violence. The logic of capacity building was rooted in the idea that while a number of nations needed to fight extremism within their own borders, many lacked the capability to do so. As such, a key US policy in the GWoT involved assisting international partners to strengthen their capacity to 'fight terrorism, defend themselves, and collectively meet challenges to common interests'.[21] The US government believed that such assistance was vital for creating a global environment that would be inhospitable to terrorists and terrorist ideologies. However, as part of this policy the US not only worked with states that were willing partners but also cajoled, pressured and persuaded reluctant regimes

---

[19] Kilcullen, *Accidental Guerrilla*, pp. 22–23.

[20] P. S. Probst, 'Measuring Success in Countering Terrorism: Problems and Pitfalls', in G. Muresan, P. Kantor, F. Roberts, D. Zeng, and F. Wang (eds.), *Intelligence and Security Informatics: I.E.E.E International Conference on Intelligence and Security Informatics* (Berlin, Springer, 2005).

[21] Department of Defense, *National Defense Strategy of the United States of America* (The Department of Defense, 2005), p. iv.

to meet their international obligations to fight terrorism by compelling them to participate in the GWoT. These were essentially countries that may have had the capability to fight terrorism but were unwilling, for a whole gamut of reasons, to do so, ranging from the presence of 'external threats, internal schisms that enable[d] one faction to use the state to extend tacit or active disagreements over what constitute[d] "terrorist" … activity'.[22] It would not be misplaced to state that implementing this particular policy in relation to Pakistan contributed towards what may be effectively categorised as the rising strategic instability of both the Pakistani state and the South Asian region more broadly for reasons addressed in some detail below.

First, it is a well-known fact that Pakistani authorities have had longstanding ties with various militant groups based in or operating out of Pakistani territory as well as with those located within neighbouring states such as India and Afghanistan.[23] Indeed, Pakistan had been intimately involved with training and equipping the Taliban for almost a decade when it was asked to participate in the US-led counter-terrorism efforts targeting the very regime it had fostered.[24] Reports suggest that post-9/11 the US essentially armtwisted a reluctant President Musharraf into cooperating, pressuring him to either 'abandon support for the Taliban or to be prepared to be treated like the Taliban'.[25] This put the Pakistani regime in a difficult position, especially in light of the fact that, like the government, much of Pakistan's population also supported the radical Taliban regime, clearly indicating that any government action taken against the Taliban would inevitably alienate the Pakistani population, and also key players in the military and Pakistan's intelligence agency, the Inter-Services Intelligence Directorate (ISI).[26]

Similarly, the Pakistani government's support and use of terrorist groups based within its territory as proxies has been a fairly long-standing policy. It was in the period immediately after the loss of East Pakistan in 1971 that Pakistan first took a series of measures to counter not only the perceived

---

[22] The White House, *The National Strategy for Combating Terrorism* (Washington, DC, The White House, 2003), p. 21.

[23] S. Puri, *Pakistan's War on Terror: Strategies for Combatting Jihadist Armed Groups since 9/11* (Abingdon, Routledge, 2012).

[24] A. J. Tellis, *Pakistan and the War on Terror: Conflicted Goals, Compromised Performance* (Washington, DC, Carnegie Endowment for International Peace, 2008), p. 3; A. Rashid, *Taliban: Militant Islam, Oil and Fundamentalism in Central Asia* (London, I. B. Tauris, 2001).

[25] C. C. Fair, *The Counterterror Coalitions: Cooperation with Pakistan and India* (Santa Monica, RAND, 2004), p. 17.

[26] See, for example, the Gallup poll results as quoted in L. T. Hadar, 'Pakistan in America's War against Terrorism: Strategic Ally or Unreliable Client?', *Policy Analysis* (Washington, DC, The Cato Institute, 2002), p. 3.

threat from India but also Pashtun nationalism within its borders and, in the period after the 1979 Iranian Revolution, the threat posed by its Shi'a minority. Several measures were implemented, including the deliberate and steady Islamisation of society. This not only involved an incremental rise in the number of *madaris* (plural of *madrassa*, a seminary) but also the support of various militant Islamist groups that were used as proxies to safeguard Pakistan's strategic and security interests against nations and groups seen as threats.[27] One of the consequences of this steady Islamisation was a consolidating anti-Americanism in Pakistani society. This was rooted in a number of factors including the United States' support of Israel and failure to press for the establishment of an independent Palestinian state; what was perceived as the US abandonment of Pakistan after the Soviet withdrawal from Afghanistan in 1989; and also what can be best described as the slow but steady consolidation of hardline, radical Islamist forces within Pakistan. As such, forcing Pakistani cooperation in the GWoT placed it in a deeply vulnerable position as the radical and volatile religious populations in Pakistan viewed their government's participation, in what was effectively seen as a 'Crusade' against Islam and its holy warriors, as deeply heretical and rapidly turned against the state.[28]

Pakistan's internal stability was further compromised by the United States' drone strike campaign that targeted al-Qaida and Taliban commanders based in Pakistan's Federally Administered Tribal Areas (FATA) and the Khyber Pakhtoonkhwa. Operational since 2004, these drone strikes rose steadily under the Obama administration, so much so that the media eventually came to dub the campaign 'the US drone *war*'. While there is no doubt that these strikes decimated core al-Qaida and Taliban leadership, they also concomitantly strengthened the radical Islamist movement in Pakistan, boosting both radicalisation and recruitment processes within the country. This occurred in several ways. To begin with, in 2007 several Islamist militant groups based in the northwest of Pakistan coalesced under the banner

---

[27] See for example: S. Nawaz, *Crossed Swords: Pakistan, Its Army and the Wars Within* (Oxford, Oxford University Press, 2008); Z. Hussain, *Frontline Pakistan: The Path to Catastrophe and the Killing of Benazir Bhutto* (New Delhi, Penguin Books, 2007). It is worth noting that Christine Fair underscores that militants in Pakistan, with the exception of suicide bombers, are on average better educated and tend not to be the products of madaris. At the same time, evidence also suggests that madaris are an important source of suicide attackers in both Pakistan and Afghanistan and that students who emerge from madaris are more likely to support militancy than those from mainstream public schools. See C. C. Fair, *The Madrassah Challenge: Militancy and Religious Education in Pakistan* (Washington, DC, USIP, 2008), chapter 3.

[28] For details see, for example, H. Abbas, *Pakistan's Drift into Extremism: Allah, the Army, and America's War on Terror* (London, M. E. Sharp, 2005).

of the Tehrik-e-Taliban-e-Pakistan (TTP).[29] Some of these militant groups
had previously served as proxies but have, in recent years, started targeting the Pakistani state in reaction to its participation in the GWoT as well
as the increasing restrictions it had placed on militant activity in Kashmir.
At the same time, Pakistani military operations undertaken in FATA and the
Khyber Pakhtunkhwa to dismantle these networks along with the US drone
campaign put a lot of pressure on groups located in the tribal belt and effectively served to push them out of these areas and into Pakistan's mainland.
In other words, groups like the Afghan Taliban, al-Qaida and the TTP were
forced to flee the peripheral tribal provinces and entered what is in essence
Pakistan's political, cultural and economic centre of gravity.[30] Southern
Punjab also proved to be a much better sanctuary for these groups for several reasons. First, not only was the region a drone-free zone, it is also one
of Pakistan's most over-populated, poverty-ridden provinces. Moreover, the
area has a deeply entrenched madrassa culture. When taken together, these
factors not only helped provide ripe pickings of recruits for these groups
but also provided a more receptive and supportive environment for their
extremist Islamist ideologies. More significantly, this region also offered
access to the core of the Pakistani state in a way the frontier provinces never
did.[31] For all these reasons, these developments contributed significantly to
Pakistan's rising instability and insecurity.

Another fallout of these developments has been the increasing contact between various Punjabi groups and the groups moving into the heartland from
the tribal belt. As part of the GWoT, Pakistan had been forced to ban a number
of Punjabi groups that it had previously used as proxies.[32] A number of these
now-banned groups took sanctuary in southern Punjab and came into increasing contact with both al-Qaida and the Afghan Taliban.[33] Given that even
banned Punjabi groups can operate quite freely across the Punjab, stronger
ties with al-Qaida and the Afghan Taliban, who were in turn looking for new
alliances, should not come as a surprise. What has resulted is an obvious tactical and ideological cross-pollination between these groups. A good example

[29] See for example: S. M. A. Zaidi, *The New Taliban: Emergence and Ideological Sanctions* (New
York, Nova Science Publishers, 2009).

[30] A. Majidyar, 'Could the Taliban take over Pakistan's Punjab Province?', *Middle Eastern Outlook*
(Washington, DC, American Enterprise Institute for Public Policy Research, 2010).

[31] R. Singh, 'Thinking About the Law of Unintended Consequences', *Journal of Terrorism Research*,
1/1 (2010).

[32] B. Brandt, 'The Punjabi Taliban: Causes and Consequences of Turning against the State', *CTC
Sentinel*, 3/7 (2010).

[33] Although it is worth noting that a number of these contacts pre-date the GWoT and can trace their
roots back to the Soviet era.

of such cross-pollination is that of the Punjabi Lashkar-e-Taiba (LeT) – one of Pakistan's strongest, most favoured proxies and a group that has thus far, unlike other proxies, refused to conduct attacks against the Pakistani state. LeT's relationship with al-Qaida pre-dates the latter's movement into southern Punjab. Thus, LeT was instrumental in assisting in the exfiltration of al-Qaida cadres from Afghanistan immediately post-9/11 as well as in providing them with safe havens within and beyond Pakistan's borders. LeT has also not only shared but also run training camps for al-Qaida at several points over the past decade. The obvious outcome of this interaction was more than evident in the 2008 Mumbai attacks where LeT tactics clearly mimicked the hallmark al-Qaida style of simultaneous attacks on soft targets. The ideological hybridisation between the two groups is also clearly evident in the shifts in LeT objectives. Historically, LeT has primarily been an anti-Indian group focused on waging a jihad in Kashmir. However, in recent years LeT has steadily developed both global connections and ambitions. 'Various counter-terrorism and intelligence agencies believe that LeT today has ties with militant groups in the Arab world and sleeper cells in the US and Australia.'[34] In short, the policies adopted under the GWoT have had direct, if unintended, repercussions not only for Pakistan's internal security but also for South Asian regional security.

Lesson III: Macro-securitisation of the GWoT has fuelled al-Qaida's brand of ideology

Here I speak specifically of how the United States' propensity towards hyper-securitisation (i.e. 'its tendency to both exaggerate threats and resort to excessive countermeasures'[35]), has fuelled al-Qaida's position as well as its virulent ideology within the international system. However, this tendency towards hyper-securitisation needs to be contextualised by understanding not only the evolution of American self-identity but also its position within the international system at a very particular point in history. First, it is worth remembering that the US has been preoccupied with establishing international peace and stability through the promotion of liberal democracy for some time now. Indeed there is little doubt that US foreign policy has been shaped by its belief in the significance of not only adhering to liberal democratic values but also

---

[34] Singh, 'Thinking About the Law of Unintended Consequences', p. 72.
[35] B. Buzan, 'American Exceptionalism, Unipolarity and September 11: Understanding the Behaviour of the Sole Superpower', *International Studies Association* (Montreal, Canada, 2004), p. 18.

a perceived obligation towards spreading these values and norms internationally. In other words, the United States has traditionally viewed itself as 'an
agent of historical transformation and liberal change'[36] in the international
system. To this end, the use of military force by the United States for the cause
of democracy promotion is not a new phenomenon and, at least empirically,
one can argue that it has been a benchmark of American foreign policy since
at least the beginning of the twentieth century. However, till the advent of
the GWoT, US-armed interventions were largely what Freedman calls 'liberal
wars of choice', i.e. they were an exercise in choice and fought only when
resources were available. By the 1990s, these wars took the form of military
interventions undertaken ostensibly to 'protect the weak, shelter the poor, and
feed the hungry'.[37] In stark contrast, the GWoT was framed as a war fought for
survival and as such as a 'war of necessity … [where] no semblance of defeat
could be tolerated'.[38]

Implicit within the idea of both the promotion of liberal democracy and
an existential war of necessity is a clearly exceptionalist view of American
identity and foreign policy. In this exceptionalist view, liberal values are understood to transfer quite readily to foreign affairs and this essentially pushes
the US towards remaking international society and asserting its rights to be
different by 'taking individual action against threats'.[39] Inherent in this exceptionalism seems to be a very clear notion of what it means to be American
and the rights and responsibilities that come with being the United States.[40]
One also gets a clear sense that underpinning this thinking is a belief in the
universality and 'essential rightness of American values',[41] which is arguably
rooted in the liberal thinking of philosophers like Immanuel Kant and John
Stuart Mill who have historically exerted a deep influence upon American
politics and its political leaders. However, while this exceptionalist construc-
tion of self-identity may be historically rooted to some extent, it was further
bolstered by both the United States' victories in the ideological wars of the
twentieth century and, more crucially, by the position of unmatched advantage in which it found itself in the post-Cold War period. Given this background, the GWoT should then be understood as a strategic attempt on the

[36] J. Monten, 'The Roots of the Bush Doctrine: Power, Nationalism and Democracy Promotion in U.S. Strategy', *International Security*, 29/4 (2005), p. 113.
[37] L. Freedman, 'Iraq, Liberal Wars and Illiberal Containment', *Survival*, 48/4 (2006), p. 51.
[38] *Ibid.*
[39] Buzan, 'American Exceptionalism, Unipolarity and September 11', p. 6.
[40] R. Singh, 'Measuring "al-Qaeda": The Metrics of Terror', in A. Behnke and C. Hellmich (eds.), *Knowing al-Qaeda: The Epistemology of Terrorism* (London, Ashgate, 2012), p. 88.
[41] B. Buzan, *The United States and the Great Powers: World Politics in the Twenty-First Century* (Cambridge, Polity Press, 2004), p. 155.

part of the Bush administration to secure this position of primacy by extending US hegemony in the international system. In this regard the GWoT essentially represents the culmination of the long-standing 'neoconservative call for using force to check the rise of any potential challengers to US predominance that emerged in the period immediately after the Cold War ended'.[42] This was based in the logic that American preponderance in the post-Cold War period was impermanent, because system-level changes would ensure that the US would not remain the sole superpower forever. This was, in other words, America's 'unipolar moment' rather than a 'fixed power structure replacing the Cold War balance of power system'.[43]

What resulted was the realignment in US foreign policy under the GWoT, most clearly evidenced by the gradual shift from multi-lateralism to unilateralism which eventually culminated in first the Bush administration's refusal to allow a NATO-led response in Afghanistan after 9/11 and then again in its illegal attacks on Iraq in 2003.[44] At the same time, the challenge of transnational terrorism was framed as an existential threat to not only US capabilities and values but to its very identity within the international system. It was the exceptionalist view of US foreign policy, rooted in a very particular vision of the United States' mission abroad as well as a specific view of its rights and responsibilities in the international system, that enabled the successful hypersecuritisation of al-Qaida and transnational terrorism under the GWoT. In other words, as per this exceptionalist view, 9/11 demonstrated that as the sole superpower not only did the United States enjoy the 'advantage of exceptional powers and privileges in the international system but also that it attracted exceptional threats':[45] America was attacked because it was America. Thus, al-Qaida came to be framed as a threat to not only every liberal democratic norm, value and institution that the US historically upheld and promulgated but also to the unchallenged projection of US power and capabilities within the international system.

This is reflected quite clearly in the US government metrics of success and failure in the GWoT, which measure US performance in the confrontation with al-Qaida against the standard of the post-Cold War identity that the US created for itself, i.e. as the world's sole superpower, as an exceptional nation that not only enjoyed special rights and privileges within the

---

[42] Singh, 'Measuring "al-Qaeda": The Metrics of Terror', p. 87.
[43] C. Krauthammer, 'The Unipolar Moment', *Foreign Affairs*, 70/1 (1990–91).
[44] J. P. McSherry, J. Ehrenberg, J. R. Sanchez, C. M. Sayej (eds.), *The Iraq Papers* (Oxford, Oxford University Press, 2010).
[45] Singh, 'Measuring "al-Qaeda": The Metrics of Terror', p. 89.

international system but also shouldered great responsibilities and duties.[46] The extraordinary reach and influence of the superpower are also clearly evident in the metrics through which the United States gauged its own success against the al-Qaida network and international terrorism. These metrics included: a body-count of terrorist operatives captured and/or killed; restricting the geographical reach of al-Qaida and transnational terrorism; defeating al-Qaida in both the battle of arms and ideas; neutralising rogue regimes; controlling weapons of mass destruction; safeguarding the American homeland from future attacks; promoting democratisation around the world; and building an international coalition to fight transnational terrorism.[47] These metrics constructed a truly exceptional US in that only a true superpower could have the enormous ideological and material reach implicit in each of these. At the same time, these metrics were also a reflection of the United States' attempts at securing its position of preponderance in a unipolar world. Thus, in constructing 9/11 as exceptional the US not only underscored its unique and privileged status but also justified the GWoT as a legitimate and necessary response of an exceptional nation-state.

However, at the same time, in framing al-Qaida as the enemy these metrics simultaneously empowered al-Qaida and its ideology by constructing it as an exceptional, unprecedented threat on the one hand and an enemy worthy of the sole superpower on the other. Al-Qaida thus came to be framed as the counterpoint to the United States. If the US was the carrier of shared values and the upholder of liberty and justice then al-Qaida was the 'inherent agitator',[48] the anomaly threatening tolerant societies and the civilised world. It was the antithesis of all that the US stood for. Hence, it was backwards, barbaric, evil, inhumane and murderous. At the same time, as

[46] Metrics can be defined as standard measures to assess performance in any field. Problems exist with developing metrics in counter-terrorism as opposed to conventional war. In conventional state-on-state wars success can be determined on the basis of territory won, the quantity of enemy weaponry, ammunition and ranks decimated, infrastructure destroyed, etc. This is not so clear in the case of gauging success in counter-terrorism where 'the eradication of terrorist cells, decapitation of terrorist leadership, blocking of terrorist funds or the destruction of terrorist safe havens does not necessarily (and, in fact, rarely) result in the cessation of terrorist violence'. See N. Morag, 'Measuring Success in Coping with Terrorism: The Israeli Case', *Studies in Conflict and Terrorism*, 28/4 (2005).
[47] For a detailed treatment of US metrics of success and failure in the GWoT see: Singh, 'Measuring Success and Failure in Terrorism and Counter-Terrorism: U.S. Government Metrics of the Global War on Terror'; Singh, 'Measuring "al-Qaeda": The Metrics of Terror'; R. Singh and S. Marsden, *Assessing Success and Failure in Terrorism and Counterterrorism: Development of Metrics on the Global War on Terror and the Global Jihad* (The National Consortium for the Study of Terrorism and Responses to Terrorism (START), 2011).
[48] C. Mullin, 'Islamist Challenges to the "Liberal Peace" Discourse: The Case of Hamas and the Israel–Palestine "Peace Process"', *Millennium Journal of International Studies*, 39/2 (2010).

a worthy enemy, it had a formidable reach and capability within the international system, which is why it posed an existential threat to the United States and the modern world. Thus al-Qaida too was 'exceptional' in its systemic omnipotence, its material and ideological strength, its reach, capabilities and ambitions. It was a threat to the liberal values of freedom, democracy, civil liberties and human rights – indeed, to civilisation itself. A threat that was so great that it demanded an international coalition to counter and confront it. A threat so great that even the world's sole superpower found itself helpless to either act alone, or catch the elusive bin Laden and Zawahiri. Hence, 'in terms of agency, scope, geopolitical space, international agendas and the political and security policies of other states, the US metrics of the GWoT constructed a truly formidable al-Qaida, one that was the equal and opposite of the US-self'.[49] But in doing so, the metrics also constructed an al-Qaida that was capable of posing a direct challenge to the sole superpower – which was a gross overstatement. Thus, in exaggerating the threat posed by al-Qaida to both its security and status, the US and its metrics constructed it as a much more formidable entity than it may well have been in reality. In other words, the US, through the GWoT, breathed life into al-Qaida in a way that would not have happened if it had responded to 9/11 in a proportionate, pragmatic and less militaristic manner.

Conclusion

Since 9/11 we have seen some successes and some costly failures in monies and lives lost in the GWoT. In this chapter I have explored some of the reasons why policies against transnational terrorism have only produced infrequent and indecisive tactical victories as opposed to long-term strategic successes. I have argued that counter-terrorism policies that were adopted under the GWoT failed to score a decisive victory against al-Qaida and its allies for a whole host of reasons, three of which were identified and framed as crucial lessons to be learned from our experiences of counter-terrorism since 9/11. From the discussion above, it is clear that there has been a qualitative shift in not only the international system and the character of wars and enemies but also in the reach and ability of US power. It is imperative both to recognise the existence of this shift and also to understand it in all its complexity in order to formulate an adequate and accurate response to future challenges.

---

[49] Singh, 'Measuring "al-Qaeda": The Metrics of Terror', p. 94.

To some degree, formulating a more comprehensive, complex understanding is hindered by what some authors have argued is the US tendency
to employ 'a simple, all-encompassing, central organising principle as a
substitute for national strategy'.[50] During the second half of the twentieth
century this was represented by the containment of communism. In the post-
9/11 period this has come to be represented by the GWoT.[51] When combined
with an inability to recognise the complex new realities of a rapidly changing operating environment this can result in an overly militarised response,
which in turn not only engenders a host of unintended and undesirable consequences but also does not embody an adequately holistic reaction to what
is often a multi-faceted (and volatile) threat. This is precisely what we have
seen in the GWoT and indeed, as suggested in lesson III, one would not be
misplaced to argue that it was our failure to understand the true nature of
al-Qaida that not only contributed towards hindering counter-terrorism
policy but also greatly impacted upon how the group evolved. In other
words, the real nature of the threat tends to be more than just physical and
to this end requires a measured material and ideological response. However,
the distinct emphasis on the kinetic response has meant that the state has
failed to adequately address in a timely manner al-Qaida's most virulent
legacy: its ideology of global jihad.

Indeed, the manner in which al-Qaida affiliates across the Middle East and
Afghanistan/Pakistan have incorporated the al-Qaida ideology into their local
agendas, as reflected in a steadily increasing tactical and ideological hybridisation, suggests that this may well be the more significant future legacy of al-Qaida.
Thus, while local agendas are once again being prioritised, the foundational
ideology remains harnessed to that of al-Qaida, at least for this generation of
jihadists. This ideology has been further propelled by the West's overly military
response. Undoubtedly, the Arab Spring demonstrated that the abstract notion of
an 'Islamic Caliphate' does not really appeal to the majority of people across the
Middle East. However, local grievances with what are perceived to be repressive Western policies not only remain but also continue to grow. Unless
this is addressed though policies which are not purely 'kinetic' in nature,
local groups – both historically affiliated with the core and otherwise – will use
al-Qaida's ideology and rhetoric of global jihad to wage battles and promote terror ostensibly in the name of a more equitable and peaceful future. Thus, what
is required is a US grand strategy that looks beyond a purely kinetic response to
the transnational terrorist threat and responds on a case-by-case basis. Indeed,

[50] Hart, 'After Bin Laden', p. 19.
[51] Hart, 'After bin Laden', p. 19.

one can argue that the most crucial lesson of all in the years since 9/11 has been the undeniable advantage of a measured, calm, proportionate counter-terrorism response along with the fact that it is unwise to generalise across cases. All in all, while it is true that we have made mistakes we are also learning from these mistakes and adapting, slowly but steadily, to our new strategic realities. The million-dollar question given contemporary developments in the Middle East, and especially the rise of the Islamic State, is: have we left it too late?

Acknowledgements

Part of the research and writing for this paper was supported by the CAPES Foreign Visiting Professor Programme (2013–14) and undertaken at my host institution, Pontifícia Universidade Católica (PUC) de Minas Gerais (Brazil). I am grateful to the Department of International Relations at PUC Minas for their support and generosity over this period.

4

What Should be the Limits of Western Counter-Terrorism Policy?

DAVID OMAND

THERE IS NOW A WEALTH OF EXPERIENCE to draw on concerning Western counter-terrorism efforts since the attacks by al-Qaida on New York and Washington on 11 September 2001 (9/11), capable of illuminating the relationship between public security, civil liberties and human rights. In the light of the lessons from that experience, some learnt the hard way, it is time to consider what should be the limits of future counter-terrorism policy and of the intelligence effort to support it.

The fundamental dilemma for public policy is clear: how can a government best exercise its primary duty to protect the public in the face of a severe terrorist threat and yet maintain civic harmony and uphold democratic values and the rule of law at home and internationally? A comparison of British and US experience illustrates what could be described as the 'thermodynamics' of counter-terrorism. There is a relationship between the vigour of security measures, taken domestically and overseas, both to protect the public directly and to obtain intelligence to prevent future attacks, and the level of confidence among all sections of the community in the government's commitment to protect the liberties and rights of the citizen, including the right to life in the face of murderous terrorism and the right to privacy for personal and family life. As with the thermodynamic relationship between the volume, pressure and temperature of a gas, too sudden an application of force to compress it and the temperature may rise dangerously to explosive levels; too little pressure applied and the gas is uncontained and will expand out of control. The best approach may well be to cool things down as the pressure is gradually built up, and certainly not to do things that heat the gas up unnecessarily – the impact of the occupation of Iraq after 2003 comes to mind. There is, after all, no such thing as a risk-free world and experience shows that attempting ever-higher levels of security will become oppressive and counter-productive.

Proceedings of the British Academy **203**, 57–72. © The British Academy 2015.

The analogy is best not pushed further – the point to be registered is that there has been an inter-relationship between counter-terrorism efforts, their effect on the spread of the violent jihadist ideology and their effect on civic harmony, civil liberties and human rights. In that respect, there are some important new lessons to be learnt by governments from the last decade, and a much larger number of old lessons to re-learn. In the former category, by way of example, falls the impact that must now be expected from the spread of digital technology. On the one hand there has been the use of the internet and social media by terrorists and their associates to communicate and propagandise and on the other hand the exploitation of digital technology by the security and intelligence authorities to derive information on their suspects, as revealed in the documents stolen by Edward Snowden from the US and UK intelligence community and published in the media. In the latter category would, for example, come the following:

- The choice of counter-terrorism strategy – especially the selection of the strategic aim – is crucial to getting the thermodynamic judgment right.
- The need to understand and apply consistently the classic principles of risk management in order to mitigate the threats facing the public.
- The value to the counter-terrorism effort of having an intelligence community – spanning domestic and overseas services – that can generate pre-emptive intelligence to forestall attacks, cooperating closely and harmoniously with law enforcement.
- The value when terrorist attacks occur of having previously invested in building up national resilience to enable rapid recovery, especially in the critical national infrastructure supporting the fabric of everyday life.
- The importance of the narrative governments choose to tell their publics to explain what is going on based on their assessment of the threat and of the effects of the response, direct and indirect, and thus the enduring value of having an informed public that believes government is listening to its concerns and that therefore is prepared to support its security policies even when these inconvenience the citizen.

As an illustration of the importance of the strategic narrative consider the way that the surprise attack by al-Qaida on 9/11 reinforced a growing opinion in government circles in both the US and the UK that not only should states be prepared to use armed force to defend themselves against external attack by other states but they have a responsibility to their citizens to anticipate trouble brewing and to act before it is too late. In the face of such a catastrophic scale of terrorism, that responsibility would justify intervening in countries harbouring terrorism or that might support them in future by providing weapons and support. The terrorist weapons on 9/11 were box cutters, kinetic impact and burning jet-fuel but the question rightly imposed itself on the policy-makers: what if it had been a nuclear device, a dirty bomb or a biological weapon? If terrorists acquired such means, the argument ran, they had just shown by their fanaticism that they would use them, being fully prepared to give their own lives in the process if necessary. If that happened in any modern city then the core of our civilisation – the ability of very large numbers of people to be able to live together in cities without fear – would be called into question. It was no longer responsible policy to wait until the enemy was at the gates, or even inside the city. Action had to be considered before the threat crystallised, which of course would mean relying on pre-emptive intelligence.

The audacity of the 9/11 attacks, the symbolism of the targets and the instant availability of literally stunning visual coverage by the media provided unprecedented global media impact. The fear that it could be the first of many such attacks, and the realisation that al-Qaida with its base in Afghanistan had the capability to inspire and mobilise networks capable of further such attacks, came as a highly unwelcome surprise to Western governments. Applying the logic of pre-emption and 'never again', it was inevitable – and fully justified – that the UK government immediately supported the US intervention in Afghanistan in the autumn of 2001 to overthrow the Taliban and destroy the al-Qaida support structure they were protecting.

The way the threat was subsequently framed has to be seen as part of the wider narrative then current about the nature of the post-Cold War world. While in opposition before 1997, New Labour had condemned the international community for ignoring the warnings of massacres in Rwanda. New Labour had also criticised perceived weakness of resolve during the Bosnian war, and the way that a deep policy rift had been allowed to develop between the political classes of the US and the UK. The US Senate had refused to support the actions of the Royal Navy enforcing the UN arms embargo on the Bosnians, arguing that the Serbs were committing genocide whilst Europe refused to allow the Bosnians to be armed to defend themselves. The Senate had even passed a resolution cutting off intelligence cooperation with the UK on enforcing the arms embargo. In the end, the lesson had been drawn that it was only UN acceptance of the role of air and military power provided by the US and its NATO allies that enabled the international community to uphold its will.

The lesson does not seem to have been lost on Tony Blair as Labour Party leader. Later, as Prime Minister, he was the leading international figure arguing for the NATO intervention in Kosovo to protect the Albanian minority.

One month into the Kosovo war, on 22 April 1999, Blair made his speech in Chicago setting out his 'Doctrine of the International Community', later referred to by the media as the 'Blair doctrine.'[1] In it he argued that the post-Westphalian order of sovereign states entitled to order their internal affairs as they pleased within their own borders was over. The international community had not only the right, but the duty – if certain conditions were fulfilled – to intervene inside sovereign states when the government concerned was unable or unwilling to protect its own population or to enforce international law. The Kosovo operation was then followed in 2000 by Prime Minister Blair authorising the military intervention by the Royal Marines in Sierra Leone, a highly successful use of the ability to project force.

It is an irony of history that the general lesson of the importance of pre-emptive action, reinforced by the shock of 9/11, came to be applied to the very different circumstances of Iraq, given the fear of the threat that Saddam's Iraq might pose if sanctions were lifted with the no-fly zone stood down and he became free fully to pursue his WMD ambitions. Not that the UK authorities ever believed at any level – as did some in Washington – that there was collusion between Saddam's Iraq and leading figures in al-Qaida – the British Government's chain of logic was an indirect one, that the UK must support the US in taking anticipatory action to deal with future dangers. The US decision to invade Iraq with questionable UN authority and with inadequate preparation for the consequences now seems a major error of judgment and an over-reaction to the perceived threat at the time, let alone to what is now believed to have been the actual state of Saddam's WMD programmes. The intervention made the al-Qaida radicalisation threat worse, as the UK Joint Intelligence Committee before the Iraq war had warned the government it would.[2] The long and bloody occupation campaign in Iraq after the invasion hardened attitudes in sections of the British Muslim community against the US orientation of UK foreign policy and made the US brand more toxic internationally, as subsequently recognised by the decisions of the Obama administration to alter aspects of counter-terrorism strategy.

It really matters how threat and response are framed in strategic terms at the outset of any campaign. Facing terrorism, time and effort must be afforded at the outset to judge the underlying nature and potential gravity of the future threat. Only then can leaders be in a position to calibrate the response appropriately and proportionately across all the levers open to government at home

---

[1] Available at http://webarchive.nationalarchives.gov.uk/+/www.number10.gov.uk/Page1297.
[2] Chilcot Inquiry evidence at http://www.iraqinquiry.org.uk/media/48331/20100720am-manningham-buller.pdf, p. 6.

and abroad. Such an assessment will never be an easy undertaking, especially in the face of public outrage after an attack, and there cannot be a ready-made heuristic to apply. Attention will understandably be focused on achieving successes at the operational and tactical level. The experience of the last decade on both sides of the Atlantic shows, however, that the importance of establishing the appropriate strategy cannot be over-estimated. It really does matter how governments understand and thus come to conceptualise and characterise the threat and their response to it.

At such a moment governments need careful strategic intelligence assessments judging the situation based on the best evidence that can be gathered, that identify the best explanation of events that can be devised consistent with those facts and draw on our historical understanding and interpretation of the motivations of those posing the threat, leading in turn to careful predictions of how the threat might develop and how all those involved and affected might respond to the measures we and our allies might take. With the benefit of such strategic assessment, modelling may be possible to examine the 'what ifs' corresponding to the policy choices open. For some purposes, governments need to analyse what might be the worst case they could face, even if far from the most likely, so as to be able to consider how best to protect the public.

The overall level of risk represented by such low probability/high impact cases, as they are known, has to be mitigated by sensible security investment. Thus, stockpiling smallpox vaccine effectively removes the risk of terrorists trying to obtain and spread that disease; having heavily armed guards at nuclear sites similarly makes a successful attack with catastrophic consequences vanishingly unlikely. Such investment can only be afforded sparingly. Nor is the worst-case scenario usually what we forecast as the most likely outcome. This poses an obvious problem for public communication. Ministers have to communicate a sense of the general level of risk to which the public is likely to be exposed, and the rationale for the measures taken and expenditure and inconvenience incurred. Honest reassurance can, for example, convey the sense that the individual risk to a citizen of being caught up in a terrorist incident remains low, for example relative to other everyday risks such as accidents, but also not disguise the fact that not all attacks can be expected to be pre-empted by the authorities. Given terrorists have the initiative there may be from time to time unwelcome surprises. It is also necessary to explain how it is planned that the authorities will manage the unwanted consequences of security and intelligence measures and counter-terrorism legislation, for example effects on individual privacy, freedoms, liberties and human rights. Like the thermodynamic relationship between volume, pressure and temperature, actions taken to affect one variable have consequences for the others, with not always desirable consequences.

In developing its preferred strategy for reducing the threat to the public, government will have to have some feel for what the public can be brought to tolerate by way of risk of continuing terrorist activity as counter-terrorist effort builds up. That sense of risk appetite, as it is called, is key to the pace and intensity of the measures that government authorises to get a grip on the situation. At one extreme of national danger, it is possible to envisage a state of emergency being declared with draconian powers, justifying derogation from human rights obligations.[3] At the other extreme, for example after a single 'lone-wolf' attack, there can be the expectation of a swift arrest and prosecution of the perpetrator under existing powers, no doubt with a public inquiry to follow into the circumstances.

Parliament, public and the media will also have (vivid) ways of expressing their often conflicting and inconsistent risk appetites. In the aftermath of some atrocity these are unlikely to be the same as those of the security authorities. To return to the main lesson, only with a strategic and explicable view of the nature of the threat and the consequences of possible responses can the different considerations be brought into an acceptable equilibrium that the public will accept in the circumstances.

Looking back, a strong case can be made that the relevant UK risk judgments in the period after 9/11 have been shown to be broadly correct in the light of hindsight, although with some hard lessons learnt on the way. But the experience of recent years provides a warning against too stark a caricature of the mantra that 'terrorism is a matter for criminal justice alone' on the one hand, and the extremes of the Bush 'War on Terror' on the other hand. The criminal justice paradigm is indeed a necessary condition but by no means a sufficient condition for success. The ability to mount a successful prosecution of the terrorist is important but will not by itself sufficiently protect the public, especially when the terrorist is prepared to be a suicide bomber.

The magnitude of the shock of 9/11 came as a complete tactical surprise. For most observers outside the intelligence community the capability of al-Qaida to plan such a complex attack had also come as a strategic surprise. The public had not been prepared for the possibility of an atrocity on such a scale, least of all in the American homeland. What the mass murders of 9/11 in New York, Washington and Pennsylvania did, therefore, was to crystallise for

---

[3] Circumstances considered by the House of Lords in 2004, in the case of A and others v. the Home Secretary, [2004] UKHL 56, available at http://www.publications.parliament.uk/pa/ld200405/ldjudgmt/jd041216/a&oth-4.htm.

the first time an understanding at the political level that the al-Qaida movement was a major threat to domestic public security. The global terrorist campaign against the US and its allies that bin Laden had announced several years
before was finally hitting its target. Al-Qaida now appeared a very different
kind of terrorist organisation in comparison with other earlier terrorist groups in
terms of ambition, ingenuity, reach, suicidal fanaticism and intended lethality.

It should not perhaps have taken the attacks of 9/11 to produce a sense
amongst political elites of the real and present danger from al-Qaida given the
openly declared desire of bin Laden and his deputy Ayman al Zawahiri to attack the US and major European countries, for example in their fatwa of 1996.
Bin Laden was already a major intelligence target after the 1998 bombings of
US embassies in Dar es Salaam and Nairobi and the attack on the *USS Cole*
in Aden in 2000, but despite the publicity surrounding the US bombing of al-
Qaida camps in Afghanistan that followed those attacks violent jihadism had
not entered public and political consciousness as a significant domestic threat.
In 2001 the position was scarcely different in the UK, where security and
intelligence effort and funding remained at their reduced post-Cold War level.

Some differences between US and British interpretations of the situation created by 9/11 were to be expected. The Provisional IRA campaigns,
including the detonation of massive bombs in the City of London in 1992
and 1993 and again in 1996 in London Docklands and in Manchester, had
hardened British attitudes to the personal risk from urban terrorism. The UK
policing, security and intelligence community was used to assess risk. The
UK entered the campaign against jihadist terrorism with a security and surveillance infrastructure around urban centres far more advanced than then
existed in the US or most other European partner nations. The Northern Irish
experience may well thus have helped London arrive at a more balanced
assessment of the al-Qaida threat than Washington. The suicidal nature of
the 9/11 attack, however, forced the British authorities to recognise the vulnerability of international aviation and its use as a terror weapon, and the
openness of much critical infrastructure and of UK public life generally to
suicide terrorism carried out without warning, with no specific demands and
with the intent to cause mass casualties, characteristics not associated with
Irish terrorist campaigns.

The merits of adopting the law enforcement 'police primacy' approach
had been learnt the hard way through the experience of using the army
on the streets in counter-terrorism duties in Northern Ireland and the dire
consequences of emergency measures such as internment without trial
(from 1971 to 1975) and the use in 1971 of coercive interrogation methods (later condemned by the European Court of Human Rights as inhuman

and degrading although falling short of torture). Portraying al-Qaida terrorism as simply a criminal act ran the risk, however, of under-estimating the ideological component of the al-Qaida message and the power of its religious wrapping to radicalise elements of the domestic population to be part of a global movement. The ready assumption in British security circles that working within the law was the natural basis for any counter-terrorist strategy in a democracy may also have helped blind the authorities in the UK to the way that President Bush, in order to uncover and destroy al-Qaida, was prepared to authorise extraordinary extra-legal measures in highly secret (NOFORN) Presidential findings not released at the time to the UK.

A further speculation about perceptions of threat may be justified. Older members of the British population may have retained an unconscious feeling from the long Cold War of being unavoidably vulnerable to potential attack and a pride in the historical record of the Second World War blitz spirit. The British population had also experienced PIRA terrorist bombs, and seen how the pattern of everyday life returned to normal. Although 9/11 brought the largest loss of British lives (67) ever from a terrorist incident, the psychic shock of 9/11 in the United States was clearly deeper precisely because of a longstanding sense of continental invulnerability. President Bush's response echoed the message from President Truman in founding the Central Intelligence Agency, 'No more Pearl Harbors'. For the US public, Congress and the Administration in 2001 the attacks on 9/11 were regarded as those of a foreign enemy who had dared to conduct a sneak attack and with whom the US was therefore in an armed conflict to the finish.

US intelligence officers, along with special forces, became active hunters rather than passive gatherers of intelligence including using extraordinary extra-legal rendition, coercive interrogation including techniques that amounted to torture, and extra-judicial targeted killing of identified high-value al-Qaida leaders, most notably using guided weapons launched from remotely piloted drones. At the same time, massive sums were made available to build up the defence of the US itself against external attack through a new Department of Homeland Security. Looking back, we can see how the conceptualisation of the threat also carried the risk of overlooking signs of domestic radicalisation and under-estimating extremist reaction to US counter-terrorist behaviour overseas.

In Europe, by contrast, the threat from outside represented by al-Qaida was being mirrored on the inside of society as support for jihadist violence could already be found in small networks within European Muslim communities, and these feelings heightened with the increasing insurgent and terrorist violence following the occupation of Iraq. What was being diagnosed in the UK by 2003 could be described as a growing disease of the body politic, resulting in the presence in the UK of a small number of violent radicalised individuals in loose overlapping networks alienated from society and actively supporting the aims of al-Qaida. At first their activity may have been mostly propagandising, for example over Kashmir, collecting funds and organising volunteers in the UK to pursue jihad overseas, but later – especially as the news from Iraq worsened – it included planning to attack targets in the UK itself.

Just over a year after 9/11 the Bali nightclub bombing killed 202 people, including many young Australian and British students, and re-ignited public concerns over the effectiveness of counter-terrorist measures. The danger was growing of domestic jihadist extremists inspired by the al-Qaida ideology, with radicalising material easily accessible through the internet as well as through personal and familial ties overseas. The effort against PIRA and its British bombing campaigns had already led to important prevention of terrorism legislation being on the UK statute book. After 9/11, measures were rushed through in the Anti-Terrorism, Crime and Security (ATCS) Act 2001 and further counter-terrorist Acts then passed every year defined new offences, gave new powers to the authorities and provided new penalties for the Courts.

The creation in 2002 of the Cabinet Office Security and Intelligence Co-ordinator post was another recognition that in the face of the al-Qaida threat more senior central effort on the coordination of government counter-terrorist effort was needed. As Coordinator, I quickly came to feel that such was the nature of the al-Qaida threat, spanning as it did domestic and overseas spaces with the ever-present risk of a catastrophic attack on the UK itself, that a broad strategy was needed that would engage to the greatest extent possible all our national civil and military resources, and harness all our national inventiveness and talent from government, academic and private sectors. In October 2002, therefore, I launched an inter-departmental team, under the acronym CONTEST, short for COuNter-TErroriSm sTrategy. The term CONTEST quickly became the shorthand for the strategy itself as it emerged early in 2003 and was presented to and accepted by the Cabinet.

Having a simple enough strategic intent was particularly important given the many different organisations involved from national and local government, law enforcement, the private sector and civil society not under central command. A clear strategic goal was felt to facilitate devolved decision taking, allowing each organisation to contribute towards a shared objective. Clarity of strategic aim can also help guard against the natural tendency for the cumulative effect of many tactical decisions, each correct against their own logic yet together leading further away from the strategic goal. The right aim also helps moderate the natural argument emanating from the front line to be allowed to take the gloves off, almost always at the expense of creating adverse propaganda opportunities and setbacks in public support. It helps too to have a compass bearing on where you want to head when the winds of the red-top media are blowing fiercely demanding 'something must be done'.

CONTEST was couched as an interim strategy, only looking five years ahead. At that stage there were too many unknowns – not least how the intervention in Iraq would change the international situation – to make long-term planning possible. There was, however, confidence in the strategic logic of the approach taken in CONTEST – and that has been borne out by the fact that the strategy remains in force now some twelve years after its initiation and is on its third major iteration and third Prime Minister. The value of such continuity in basic policy in terms of maintaining effective counter-terrorist effort is itself an important lesson.

The intelligence assessments supporting the development of CONTEST did correctly identify the al-Qaida attacks on 9/11 and subsequent plots as following a strategy that Fawaz Gerges later vividly characterised as the al-Qaida leadership attacking 'the far enemy':[4] only by directly terrorising Western populations and demonstrating the incapacity of their governments to protect the public would the US and its allies cease to support what al-Qaida characterised as pro-Western, apostate and corrupt regimes in the Islamic world. Without such Western support, Islamist revolutions would then eventually install Islamist regimes that would follow strict sharia law, and thus contribute to the long-term goal of the restoration of the Caliphate across the Islamic world.

US policymakers seem to have drawn from this common intelligence analysis the primary importance of eliminating as quickly as possible the senior al-Qaida operational leaders who were assessed to be likely to be working on further major attack planning against the US. UK and European policymakers had an additional concern drawn from the historical lessons of revolutionary action[5] – the logic of the deed – of the danger of being provoked into disproportionate reaction, thus justifying the revolutionary narrative in the eyes of the communities from whom the terrorists sought support. In particular, the al-Qaida strategy relied upon building amongst disaffected young European Muslims a sense of primary loyalty to their membership of the umma, the global Islamic community, and their perceiving that community as under

---

[4] F. Gerges, *The Far Enemy* (Cambridge, Cambridge University Press, 2005).
[5] A. Camus, *L'Homme Revolté*, (Paris, Gallimard, 1951).

attack by the West. And terrorism could then be justified in their eyes as the fulfilment of the duty to take part in a defensive jihad.

The European historical experience reinforced the understanding that to be successful terrorists must disturb normality and destroy a sense of security on the part of citizens, business and the community to the point where governments feel pressure to concede to the terrorist agenda. The British strategic intent in CONTEST was thus chosen to be the maintenance of normality. Success would be achieved if the terrorists were denied what it was assessed they were most seeking, namely attacks that would destabilise confidence in the ability of government to protect the public, and would radicalise their support base.

It is, therefore, possible now to see more clearly than was possible at the time why the US and European governments were led to construct different strategic counter-terrorist narratives. That was despite the traditional patterns of cooperation on intelligence, defence science and technology and homeland security, applying to such measures as border control, fitting strengthened cockpit doors on aircraft to make hijacking difficult and introducing security arrangements for sea freight. Tensions came later, for example as the British government learnt of the detention of British residents in Guantanamo and US extraordinary rendition policies. A change of administration in Washington in 2009, together with the recognition that the US itself has to deal with 'home-grown' violent extremists active inside the US, has of course now brought transatlantic thinking closer on these issues.

Casting the CONTEST intent in terms of normality was, therefore, a fundamental policy choice. The aim was formally stated as to reduce the risk from international terrorism so that people can go about their normal life freely and with confidence. By 'freely' was meant without having to suspend the rule of law and interfere with individual liberties; by 'with confidence' would mean visitors coming to the UK, markets stable, people still travelling by air and using the underground.

A further important feature of the UK CONTEST approach was that it embodied risk-management principles, trying to reduce each factor in the risk equation that measures the level of threat from a terrorist attack as the product of the likelihood of an attack attempt × vulnerability to the type of attack × immediate impact should the attack succeed × duration of the disruption caused by the attack. For each of those factors government could deploy a number of policy instruments:

- The likelihood of an attack can be reduced by significantly expanding intelligence and police efforts and bringing terrorists to justice (the *Pursue* campaign of CONTEST).

- The length and depth of the terrorist campaign can be shortened by measures to counter the terrorist narrative and reduce the level of violent radicalisation in the community and tackling its roots overseas (the *Prevent* campaign).
- The vulnerability of the public can be reduced through measures such as aviation/transport security and safeguarding infrastructure essential for normal life (the *Protect* campaign).
- The impact of an attack can be mitigated by equipping, training and exercising the emergency services together to respond quickly *when* (rather than *if*) terrorists succeed in mounting an attack; and the duration and intensity of disruption can be reduced by building up national resilience so as to restore the essentials of normal life (the *Prepare* campaign). This investment in emergency services response and in national resilience has, of course, value in dealing with many other kinds of civil emergencies.

This British CONTEST strategy with its '4P' campaigns was subsequently exported to other nations, including forming the basis of the EU's own counter-terrorism strategy.

Managing the risk down to allow normal life to continue rather than adopting a 'War on Terror' metaphor is, however, an approach that involves reassuring the public that the major risks are being satisfactorily managed but without the false promise that life can be made risk-free. It may lead to media accusations that the government believes there is an 'acceptable' level of violence and inevitably carries the implication that sometimes, despite everyone's best efforts, there will be tragic attacks. For the general British public (although not to the security authorities) it seems to have come as a great shock that the attacks on London transport on 7 July 2005 (7/7) were perpetrated by radicalised young British Muslims attacking their fellow citizens and declaring that their victims were legitimate targets in their suicide videos. It was not until 2006, a year after 7/7, that the British government published a white paper describing its strategy (CONTEST) for countering international terrorism[6] but with only a few sentences of explanation as to what lay behind the al-Qaida movement. The French government published its own white paper on counter-terrorism around the same time[7] and dealt at length with the origins of al-Qaida and its ideology.

---

[6] HM Government, *Countering International Terrorism* (London, HMSO Cm 6888, July 2006).
[7] Secrétariat Général de la Défense Nationale, *Livre blanc sur la sécurité intérieure face au terrorisme* (Paris, La Documentation Française, 2006).

Good intelligence is needed to uncover networks, forestall attacks, identify potential vulnerabilities and as evidence in court. If the authorities are to risk pre-emptive action then sound intelligence is essential on which decisions can be based over when to intervene and when to leave alone. In the UK, external and domestic intelligence services improved their ability to work with the police as a single counter-terrorist community, and with allies and partners overseas developing the use of digital technology to track individuals and their identities, movements, finances and communications around the world. Two notable innovations were the creation of JTAC, the Joint Terrorism Analysis Centre spanning all the dimensions of policing and intelligence, both civilian and military, and the CPNI, the Centre for the Protection of National Infrastructure within the Security Service – bringing technical security and policing expertise together to improve protective security advice to government and industry.

Another advantage of having adequate pre-emptive intelligence is that by making it easier to manage the level of threat, political pressures are relieved that otherwise would build up on government to take more draconian measures so as reassure the majority.

At the 7/7 inquest Christopher Coltart QC, representing seven of the victims' families, claimed the state may have breached its obligations under the European Convention of Human Rights (ECHR) to protect the lives of its citizens because if more action had been taken to put more suspects under close surveillance prior to July 2005, 'it may have been possible' that the attacks could have been prevented. That was an extreme argument, but reflected the position that the citizen has a right to expect that the security authorities will be allowed to use all lawful and reasonable means to manage the risks from such dangers. It also supports the contention that public security requires the authorities to balance rights, such as the victims' right to life – the right not to be blown up – and the right to privacy and family life. The balancing act required is within the framework of human rights, not imagining that security and rights are in opposition. Indeed, where there is no security there will be no rights.

Since 7/7 it has been estimated that up to a dozen terrorist plots against the UK have been uncovered or have otherwise failed in their intent. That is a remarkable tribute to the efforts of the security and intelligence authorities. Pre-emptive intelligence has been critical in delivering a higher chance of terrorist networks being identified in time and individuals brought to justice. Without it, the pressure would have been to resort to cruder measures – the bludgeon of state power – to try to protect the public. Such measures applied to minority communities are likely to disrupt civic harmony and increase a sense of alienation, feeding in to the narrative of the extremist.

The revelations from the intelligence documents stolen in 2013 by Edward Snowden revealed much about how since 9/11 the US and UK signals intelligence community have exploited the rapid advances in electro-optics, cheap data storage, digital global communications networks, the internet, mobile personal devices and the massive use of social media. Bulk access to digital information has enabled the NSA in the US and GCHQ in the UK to supply information about the communications, location, movements, contacts, spending and beliefs of terrorist-related suspects and organisations of legitimate interest to the authorities.

A vocal minority have equated the Snowden revelations with state monitoring of the population and the advent of a surveillance state, fear that resonates especially in nations that have been subject to foreign occupation or to totalitarianism. Such critics often make the category error of not distinguishing bulk access to the internet – which the US and UK certainly do have, for example through underwater cables – and so-called mass surveillance which they do not conduct.

Mass surveillance is about pervasive observation or monitoring of the entire population or a substantial sector of it. Observation implies observers, human beings in the security authorities who are examining the thoughts and actions of the population. No such mass surveillance takes place on the UK population, and it would be comprehensively unlawful if it did. On the other hand, there is sophisticated selection by computer from the massive volumes of traffic on the internet of the very small percentage that is of legitimate intelligence interest. Even if the exaggerated fears of the Panoptic State have been shown to be misplaced, certainly insofar as the work of British intelligence is concerned,[8] the challenge for the future remains that of maintaining public confidence that these powerful tools in the hands of the intelligence authorities will not be misused.

A further lesson to be learnt from the last decade is about getting better at handling issues of responsibility and avoiding a blame game for operational decisions made in good faith: we need to learn that sometimes, inevitably, operational decisions do not pay off. Stuff happens in everyday life as it does in sport. We want our football team to win every game. They set out to win every game. But mistakes get made and sometimes the opposition is just too clever. It would be quite unreasonable to have the expectation that the team, and their manager, will never lose a game.

What everyone is searching for is how to redefine for the modern digital age the implicit contract between people and government under which in

---

[8] *Annual Report of the Interception Commissioner* (London, House of Commons HC 1184, 2014).

return for a reasonable assurance of protection, including protection of human rights, the people empower government with coercive means, including armed forces equipped with technologies such as the drone and security and intelligence agencies equipped with bulk access to the internet.

Such an understanding might take the form of a series of lessons from the last decade representing a balance of the competing principles and interests involved.

All concerned – government, its agencies and the public – have to accept that maintaining security today remains the primary duty of government and they will have the necessary call on resources. But the public should be invited to accept that there is no absolute security and chasing after it does more harm than good. Providing security involves applying consistently the classic principles of risk management in order to mitigate the threats facing the public.

The thermodynamics of security and intelligence activity has to be better understood if civic harmony is to be maintained at an acceptable level of public security. It makes a difference where on the threat spectrum a threat is situated by government. At one extreme, it could be just one more serious modern risk to be managed by the authorities, along with other threats to the citizen such as from organised crime or from natural hazards such as pandemics or extreme weather; and, at the other extreme, an existential risk, challenging the very existence of the democratic state, the safety of our cities and our long-term prosperity and quality of life. Great care is needed to select and apply appropriate responses that will be proportionate to the assessment of each of these very diverse threats.

The choice of counter-terrorism strategy – especially the selection of the strategic aim – must be reflected in the narrative governments choose to tell their publics. Clear explanation is needed early on based on assessment of the threat and of the likely effects of the response: direct and indirect. There is enduring value in having an informed public that believes government is listening to its concerns and that therefore is prepared to support its security policies even when these inconvenience the citizen. There is considerable value when risks to the public arise of having previously invested in building up resilience at national and local levels to enable rapid recovery, especially in the critical national infrastructure supporting the fabric of everyday life.

As part of the strategic narrative, the public should be reassured that terrorists will be treated as criminals and dealt with under the law but reminded that pre-emptive secret intelligence is an essential means to reduce the risk from terrorism, so that normal life can continue. There will always be intelligence gaps and ambiguities, but overall the work of the intelligence and security services shift the odds in the public's favour, sometimes very significantly.

Effective counter-terrorism effort requires the support of an intelligence community – spanning domestic and external services and with overseas liaisons – that can generate pre-emptive intelligence cooperating closely and harmoniously with law enforcement to forestall attacks and uphold the rule of law. If the secrets of terrorists are to be uncovered, therefore, there will be inevitable intrusions into privacy. These intrusive methods are powerful and they get results.

The public must accept that there is no general 'right to know' about intelligence sources and methods, but the public has a right to oversight of the work of intelligence agencies by cleared parliamentary representatives on the public's behalf, and should expect judicial oversight of the exercise of statutory intelligence gathering powers, with independent investigation of allegations of abuse.

So public trust that the security and intelligence machine will only be used for public protection against major dangers will continue to be essential. The policing, security and intelligence community have to accept, in turn, that ethics matter: there are 'red lines' that must not be crossed. So some opportunities will have to be passed over and the principles of proportionality, necessity and due authority will have to be followed. In my book[9] I set down six such principles. Richard Rusbridger, the Editor of the *Guardian* newspaper, in his blog[10] has suggested that these principles could also be applied to govern the use of intrusive investigative methods by newspapers and other media in the wake of the phone-hacking scandal by the *News of the World*.

The overall challenge for the future is to maintain public confidence that it is possible for government, having absorbed such lessons, to discharge its responsibilities for public safety and security whilst behaving ethically in accordance with modern views of human rights, including personal privacy, in a world where deference to authority and automatic acceptance of the confidentiality of government business no longer holds sway.

[9] D. Omand, *Securing the State* (London, Hurst, 2010).
[10] http://www.guardian.co.uk/commentisfree/2011/jul/07/phone-hacking-alan-rusbridger.

5

No Golden Age

The Deep Origins and Current Utility of Western Counter-Terrorism Policy

CONOR GEARTY

Introduction

IN THIS CHAPTER I AM CONCERNED with how democratic states have responded to the supposed challenge posed to them, both individually and collectively, by terrorism.[1] My interest lies in exploring how and why the language of counter-terrorism has become so ingrained in such societies despite its apparent hostility to the values that democratic societies say they uphold, a mismatch that is evident in the sorts of things that states feel able to do in the name of counter-terrorism – arbitrary arrest, restrictions on speech, banning associations, even on occasion the torturing and killing of opponents at home and abroad. All of these (and more) sit uneasily with the principles of representativeness, accountability, the rule of law and human rights that are supposed to be the ethical basis of democratic society. Explanations which point to the need to balance 'liberty' and 'security' do not get us very far;[2] they could be said merely to beg further questions about how much liberty pre-existed the security threat, what the nature of that threat is in fact, and why it should now be so readily assumed that improvement of the latter must necessarily be at the expense of the former. Declaring that the state must be entitled to defend the freedom of its people at (nearly) all cost is likewise a lazy argument, one designed to appeal not to reason but to a low common denominator of national solidarity; one of the oddest because so self-evidently contradictory features of such an approach is

[1] On which see, among other works, R. English, *Terrorism: How to Respond* (Oxford, Oxford University Press, 2009); L. Richardson, *What Terrorists Want. Understanding the Terrorist Threat* (London, John Murray, 2006).
[2] J. Waldron, *Torture, Terror and Trade-Offs. Philosophy for the White House* (Oxford, Oxford University Press, 2010) is excellent, especially (on this point) chapter 2.

how relaxed it is about giving up the basic democratic freedoms whose vital importance is so frequently stressed and whose protection therefore requires, it is said, their (temporary? selective?) disapplication.[3]

The contention developed here will be that these arguments (and others) have been mustered to defend a deeper position. Counter-terrorism law and policy of the sort identified above have been successful in democratic countries because they have gone with the grain of certain important, pre-existing features within such societies, elements that have long been inimical to what the victory of democratic forms of government has appeared to entail. On this reading, counter-terrorism law and policy have been more deep-rooted than might first appear to be the case, not compatible with the prevailing democratic ethos but rather connecting strongly with powerful pre-democratic impulses that have survived (albeit in reduced form) into the democratic era. These forces are now (not solely but not least off the back of the 'terrorist threat') enjoying a sharp revival. To put the point more aggressively, the counter-terrorist drive has succeeded to the extent that it has because it has found a weakness in the health of democratic society, inserted itself into the space left by this opening, and once safely in place has grown exponentially, to the point where it now (it will be argued) challenges the very political system into which it has insinuated itself. To say this another way using a familiar metaphor: the democratic body politic has had within it from its inception a virus that has impeded the growth to full health of its society of members, and now – expanding off the back of the introduction of 'counter-terrorism' – this virus has reached the point where it is threatening more and more of the vital organs of the democratic corporeality. If it is successful, the body itself will change, may already be in the process of changing, from a creature called (however imperfectly) democratic to one that is more accurately described as 'neo-democratic', a state which for present purposes we can define as one that may be wearing egalitarian clothes, embracing human rights even, but which has in fact precious little democratic substance or universal respect for human dignity within.[4] This chapter argues that where this has happened or is happening, it is because fear of the terrorism threat has fed a destructive urge within democracy which may always have been there (the argument demands that it has been), but to which the useful illusions of counter-terrorism have now given a new lease of life.

[3] See M. Ignatieff, *The Lesser Evil. Political Ethics in an Age of Terror* (Edinburgh, Edinburgh University Press, 2004); B. Ackerman, *Before the Next Attack. Preserving Civil Liberties in an Age of Terrorism* (New Haven/London, Yale University Press, 2006).
[4] For an elaboration of neo-democracy and its relationship with counter-terrorism, the rule of law and human rights, see C. A. Gearty, *Liberty and Security* (Cambridge, Polity Press, 2013).

As we move into the substance of the argument, a word on definitions may now be necessary. There is no need for a great deal of detailed precision to drive the thesis forward. We are dealing with the conduct of states, not individual actors, and, as the title suggests, mainly (but as we shall see, not solely) those located in the Global North, or West – it has been here that the idea of terrorism first took hold and began to do its destructive work.[5] What is meant by 'democratic' can also for present purposes be stated quite simply, crudely even: it is a descriptive label met by a country which has the rudiments of representative government, a functioning rule of law (overseen by an independent judiciary) and some dimension of respect for human dignity, manifested perhaps as a protection of human rights, perhaps as an ongoing guarantee of civil liberties, or possibly in some other way entirely.[6] Perfection is not demanded: some bona fide commitment to this sort of organisation of government, underpinned by reasonably free elections, is all that is required. To be 'democratic', therefore, it is on the analysis here not enough to have such freedoms on paper – some of the worst excesses of despotism are committed on citizens who 'enjoy' the very finest protection that mere words can guarantee. Such 'pseudo-democracies'[7] do not even try to deliver the substance of what their paper constitutions suggest, in contrast to the approach to democracy adopted by those states with which we are concerned, namely those that have some sense of democratic culture as well as having a democratic constitution. It will also be obvious that such democracies exist on a spectrum with levels of popular engagement in government, accountability and rights protection varying from state to state – across the world certainly and also within the Global North itself.

Imperfect origins

To paraphrase Rousseau, democracies are born free but are everywhere in chains. No democratic society emerges fully formed from its past, freed entirely from the circumstances to which this new governmental shape is

---

[5] See G. Duncan, O. Lynch, G. Ramsay and A. M. S. Watson (eds), *State Terrorism and Human Rights. International Responses since the End of the Cold War* (London/New York, Routledge, 2013). Also of interest as an indicator of how this view solidified after the attacks of 11 September 2001 is P. Berman, *Terror and Liberalism* (New York/London, W. W. Norton and Company, 2003).

[6] D. Held, *Models of Democracy*, 3rd edn (Cambridge, Polity Press, 2006).

[7] Belarus might be thought an extreme example – see its constitution at http://www.belarus.net/costitut/constitution_e.htm [accessed 19 September 2014]. Note Article One: 'The Republic of Belarus is a unitary, democratic, social state based on the rule of law.'

a reaction. Even those made afresh after defeat in war (such as Germany, Italy and Japan) have the baggage of a terrible past to confront and somehow to manage.[8] There are democratic states that grow out of a successful anti-imperialist revolution, but even here elements of the *ancien regime* survive into the new era: Ireland might be thought to be one of these though naturally this situation is mainly encountered among states in the Global South, the location of most of the European states' imperialist activities. Developments in new democracies after 1989 have seen the re-emergence of nationalist tropes that had been silenced by totalitarian control for generations – silenced but not obliterated.[9] In other less turbulent places, freedom has been hewn out of a pre-democratic past without any fundamental breach with the old order. The United Kingdom would be one example of such a state, the United States (whose 18th-century revolution was not a democratic one) another. The shift to fully representative models of government can never automatically displace the power relations that precede such a move, however this move is brought about. There is something of a 'Catch 22' about the democratisation process: a society which declares itself immune to its history (even in the name of democracy) is bound quickly to repeat it as the past rushes to fill the vacuum so ambitiously but meaninglessly declared; or the new order explicitly respects the past in which case the influence of its prior power-holders subsists, despite revolutionary appearances.

So what is the old order that lingers on in opposition to the new, the virus in the democratic child that would do its utmost to hinder its growth, and of which (on the argument here) the counter-terrorism tendency has been able to make such use? However they come about, democratic societies tend to emerge out of circumstances in which severe levels of inequality have been the norm; indeed, in some cases it has been the societal anger generated by such conditions of unfairness and injustice that has been the main driver of democratic change. These deep inequalities and injustices are reflective of the power relations that preceded the democratic shift, and neither the dynamics productive of such inequality nor their privileged defenders disappear

---

[8] See M. Mandel, 'A Brief History of the New Constitutionalism, or "How We Changed Everything so that Everything Would Remain the Same"', *Israeli Law Review*, 32 (1998), p. 250.

[9] On Ireland see J.J. Lee, *Ireland 1912-85: Politics and Society* (Cambridge, Cambridge University Press, 1989). For the colonial dimension more generally see P. Chatterjee, *Lineages of Political Society* (New York, Columbia University Press, 2011). On post-1989 democracies see G. Ekiert and D. Ziblatt, 'Democracy in Central and Eastern Europe One Hundred Years On', *East European Politics and Societies and Cultures*, 27/1 (2013), pp. 90–107. And see the disturbing article by Jan-Werner Müller, 'Eastern Europe Goes South. Disappearing Democracy in the EU's Newest Members', *Foreign Affairs*, 93/2 (2014) accessible at http://www.foreignaffairs.com/articles/140736/jan-werner-mueller/eastern-europe-goes-south [accessed 19 September 2014].

overnight: rather, this skewed perspective on truth becomes part of what democracy is henceforth understood to mean. Of course, the depth of this resistance to justice varies from place to place, but it is invariably to be found in some shape or other. The virus of inequality is there from the start.

To add detail to the argument we need to turn to the particular. There are of course many democratic states with their own separate histories, pressures and tensions. Three such states have been responsible for driving the language of counter-terrorism deep into the democratic vernacular. All three are in different ways the poster-children of twentieth-century democracy, the places where freedom and liberty has been understood to have thrived while all about has been disorder and chaos. The example each has set has been followed by others: they are collectively the makers of the 'counter-terrorism' weather. Yet none of the three has been able to escape the past that each has inherited, the strains of injustice and unfairness that, persisting into the new democratic order, have taken on various defensive shapes of which the most recent – and potentially most virulent – is that of counter-terrorism. These are the United Kingdom, Israel and the United States. Let us consider each in turn before returning to our central argument and its implications for how we practise democracy today.

Taming democracy

Britain's great success has been to adapt an ancient constitution to meet the demand of its people for equality and democracy. True, there has been violent disorder in the past but the shift to properly representative government has been mainly trouble-free. It has also occurred in a way which has never radically challenged the pre-existing status quo.[10] The wealthy have of course had to manage the effects of democracy but it has been regulation not confiscation that has been in the air. The continued ownership of land on a vast scale, rights of inheritance, private schooling, the purchase of privileged medical services – all have survived into, indeed thrived in, the democratic era.[11] The gap between the very rich and the rest, once narrowing, has begun in recent years once again to widen.[12]

---

[10] For the details of the relationship between democracy and the rule of law in early 20th-century Britain see K. D. Ewing and C. A. Gearty, *The Struggle for Civil Liberties. Political Freedom and the Rule of Law in Britain, 1914–1945* (Oxford, Oxford University Press, 2000).

[11] B. Fine, *Democracy and the Rule of Law: Liberal Ideals and Marxist Critiques* (London, Pluto Press, 1984).

[12] The Equality Trust, *A Divided Britain: Inequality within and between UK Regions* (August 2014): http://www.equalitytrust.org.uk/news/divided-britain-inequality-within-and-between-uk-regions

It was war that both produced democracy and at the same time provided the tools to protect the wealthy from its effects. The sacrifices made by all classes and by men and women alike in the Great War (1914–18) made the final push for equal representation impossible to resist. At the same time, the exigencies of that war produced a model for the control of radicalism that was to persist into the democratic era and thereafter to make impossible (or at least extremely difficult) the jolting of the democratic sensibility thus awoken into a truly social revolutionary state-of-being. The Defence of the Realm Act 1914 was the source for a wide range of regulatory controls on conduct (the defence of the realm regulations) which were legislated into permanent ordinary laws in the years following the end of the conflict. These provisions were supported by a reading of the ancient common law by the senior judiciary which was sympathetic to executive power in its effort to manage popular unrest. [13] It was a fast-emerging democratic Britain that defeated the General Strike of 1925, and it was first a Labour and then a national government of left and right (by now fully representative) which prevented the despair caused by economic depression in the 1930s from spinning out of control into a more fundamental attack on privileged institutions.[14] True, the Second World War gave further impetus to equality and social justice, but the constraints on radicalism so carefully constructed in the inter-war years remained firmly in place, and operated to stifle left-based criticism of the (democratic) status quo through the entire Cold War period.[15] Democratic Britain was born and brought up in an atmosphere of war: hot, cold and imminent.

Why did the egalitarian zeal of mass suffrage buckle before the exercise of these war-inspired state powers? In the nineteenth century it was taken for granted that democracy with its equal voting rights spelt disaster for the entrenched interests of what was, after all, a tiny elite.[16] Critical to the democratically based defence of privilege in post-1918 Britain was the plausibility of the argument that far from delivering truer and better governance, the radical popular movements that needed to be clamped down on put democracy itself at risk. The Communist transformation of Russia in 1917 and

[accessed 19 September 2014]. See, more generally, R. Wilkinson and K. Pickett, *The Spirit Level. Why Equality is Better for Everyone* (London, Allen Lane, 2009).

[13] The details of these war-time and post 1918 legislative and judicial interventions are in Ewing and Gearty, *The Struggle for Civil Liberties*, chapters 2–4.

[14] The story is particularly illuminating when told from the perspective of the Communist Party: see N. Branson, *History of the Communist Party of Great Britain, 1927–1941* (London, Lawrence and Wishart, 1985).

[15] J. Mahoney, *Civil Liberties in Britain during the Cold War* (Cambridge, Cambridge University Press, 1989).

[16] H. Cunningham, *The Challenge of Democracy: Britain 1832–1918* (London, Longman, 2001).

the support shown by the new Soviet authorities for world-wide Communist revolution meant that those who argued for greater equality within Britain could be relatively easily characterised as 'fifth columnists' intent not on the promotion of greater democracy at home but rather on driving forward the destructive interests of a hostile power.[17] That these radicals were often supporters of the Soviet Union, members of the domestic Communist party and even recipients of Russian money made the link easier to make and thereafter to sustain. Those pushing for greater social equality who were not associated with Moscow risked condemnation as fellow-travellers or even (quoting Lenin) as 'useful idiots' acting unwittingly for the foreign enemy.[18]

The language of counter-terrorism was not used to underpin the growth and explain the need for draconian police powers and their extensive deployment against radical political sentiment,[19] but these state actions against a hostile other were in the same tradition. The key to the success of this counter-revolutionary movement ('counter-terrorism') was plausibility: there had been a Soviet revolution; there were Soviet agents and sympathisers intent on the transformation of Britain; they were building a case by pointing to deprivation and inequality as a way of undermining a culture that was only apparently democratic. Local efforts to preserve an indigenous tradition of radical protest and to grow from it a wider movement of popular democratic renewal simply got squeezed in the middle.

If pre-existing structures of wealth and inequality were one hangover from the past that survived into the democratic era under cover of the plausible fear of subversion, then Empire was another. As early as the late-middle of the nineteenth century, the British Prime Minister Benjamin Disraeli pointed the way by showing how working-class men (not then women) could be sufficiently enthused by the imperial idea to vote for those who promoted it, however privileged these leaders might be or however indifferent to the material needs of those doing the voting.[20] Empire and afterwards the colonies and then later the Commonwealth (and later still 'humanitarian intervention') have long been the Achilles heel of British democracy, drivers of conduct abroad entirely inimical to the

---

[17] Many of the details are in Ewing and Gearty, *The Struggle for Civil Liberties*, chapter 3.

[18] For example, see 'Report (Political and Economic) of the Committee to Collect Information on Russia' (Cmd 1240 (1921)).

[19] But interestingly the 'Report (Political and Economic) of the Committee to Collect Information on Russia' did include a full translation of chapter 8 of Trotsky's *Terrorism and Communism*, the whole of which was said to be 'worthy of study': cited in Ewing and Gearty, *The Struggle for Civil Liberties*, p. 144.

[20] For an excellent study of this fascinating leader see R. Blake, *Disraeli* (London, Faber and Faber, 2012; first published 1966).

emerging self-image of fairness and equality at home.[21] This truth could be avoided by choosing to focus not on the underlying injustice in the way the colonies were administered or foreign wars waged but rather by foregrounding the violent expressions of such alienation and calling it 'terrorism'. This early illusion of counter-terrorism prevented damaging cross-over from the way Britain thought it should be governed to the way it governed other places. This is evident in much of the establishment reaction to India in the 1930s, for example, and also in Kenya in the 1950s and Malaya (as it then was) during the late 1950s and early 1960s.[22]

A version of it was also, and relatively early, to be found at home, in the 'quasi-colonial' Northern Ireland where special laws to control nationalist alienation were put in place from the start, and further legislation aimed at Irish republican violence in Britain was enacted in the weeks before the Second World War, in August 1939. This was called the Prevention of Violence (Temporary Provisions) Act 1939[23] – no mention of 'counter-terrorism' in the title, as had also been the case in the emergency powers legislation enacted specifically by the devolved Northern Ireland parliament from 1922.[24] By the time that the UK as a whole once again confronted via legislation the threat posed to the nation's integrity by Republican violence – a threat that had survived the Second World War, further clampdowns in the 1950s and had now re-emerged off the back of civil disorder at the end of the 1960s – the legitimising language of choice had become that of terrorism. The Prevention of Terrorism (Temporary Provisions) Act 1974 followed a campaign of violence in Britain which had culminated in a devastating attack by the Irish Republican Army (IRA) on Birmingham, and this law was frequently re-enacted in expanded and ever more comprehensive form as it bedded down fully into law. Eventually, the New Labour administration of Tony Blair dropped the myth of this

---

[21] On squaring the UK's evolving commitment to human rights with its colonial activities see A. W. B. Simpson, *Human Rights and the End of Empire* (Oxford, Oxford University Press, 2001).

[22] See P. Dixon, '"Hearts and Minds"'? British Counter-Insurgency from Malaya to Iraq', *Journal of Strategic Studies,* 32/3 (2009); J. Paget, *Counter-Insurgency Campaigning* (London, Faber and Faber, 1967); R. Thompson, *Defeating Communist Insurgency* (London, Chatto and Windus, 1967). There is a superb recent study of the whole subject: D. Porch, *Counterinsurgency. Exposing the Myths of the New Way of War* (Cambridge, Cambridge University Press, 2013).

[23] See D. Bonner, *Executive Measures, Terrorism and National Security: Have the Rules of the Game Changed?* (Aldershot, Ashgate, 2007); O. G. Lomas, 'The Executive and the Anti-Terrorist Legislation of 1939', *Public Law* (1980), p. 16.

[24] L. K. Donohue, *Counter-Terrorist Law and Emergency Powers in the United Kingdom, 1922–2000* (Dublin and Portland Oregon, Irish Academic Press, 2001); C. Campbell, *Emergency Law in Ireland 1918–1925* (Oxford, Clarendon Press, 1994). More general and comparative but highly detailed and therefore illuminating is L. K. Donohue, *The Cost of CounterTerrorism. Power, Politics, and Liberty* (Cambridge and New York, Cambridge University Press, 2008).

being a temporary measure and enacted a consolidated Terrorism Act in 2000. By then, and as a result of changes that had taken place as early as the 1980s, the legislation had been extended to embrace not just Northern Ireland-related political violence but all such violence wherever it occurred in the world, and the 2000 Act completed the picture by extending counter-terrorism powers to such threats emanating from within Great Britain as well as Northern Ireland.[25]

This was a huge change. Counter-terrorism laws which had previously been deliberately restricted to a specific problem of politically based violence in a particular part of the United Kingdom had become a tool for the resistance of subversion everywhere. The language of terrorism underpinning this statutory edifice of control had become so wide that it now embraced a spectrum of non-violent as well as violent activities and motivations that went beyond the traditionally political.[26] By 1989 the Soviet-inspired danger with which we began this section had of course lost its previous plausibility, but the state machinery which had been designed to counter it was simply shifted sideways to focus on this new emerging domestic and global 'terrorist' threat. Whereas during the Cold War the response to the threat of politically motivated violence of a sort we think of as 'terrorist' had been largely the responsibility of the police, during the 1990s (i.e. the years immediately following the point at which it became impossible to argue any more that there was a Communist threat) the lead role in counter-terrorism was handed to the old anti-Communist organs of state, the intelligence services, in particular MI5.[27] Of course, the police had long had an intelligence arm – Special Branch had itself been largely an early response to IRA violence.[28] But whereas the police were institutionally committed to the apprehension of suspected criminals and their prosecution through the courts, the security apparatus that had been constructed during the Cold War had no such concern with due process and open

[25] C. Walker, *Blackstone's Guide to the Anti-Terrorism Legislation*, 3rd edn (Oxford, Oxford University Press, 2014) is comprehensive on the law.
[26] Terrorism Act 2001 s 1. *R v Gul* [2013] UKSC 64. See A. Greene, 'The Quest for a Satisfactory Definition of Terrorism: *R v. Gul*', *Modern Law Review*, 77/5 (2014).
[27] See Security Service Act 1989 s 1. See the statement on counter-terrorism by the then Home Secretary Kenneth Clarke at HC Deb 8 May 1992 vol. 207 cc 297–306: http://hansard.millbanksystems.com/commons/1992/may/08/counter-terrorism [accessed 19 September 2014].
[28] B. Porter, *The Origins of the Vigilant State* (Martlesham, Boydell and Brewer, 1987); R. Allason, *The Branch. A History of the Metropolitan Police Special Branch, 1883–1983* (London, Secker and Warburg, 1983). A nice summary is B. Porter, 'Terrorism and the Victorians', *History Today*, 36/12 (1986): http://www.historytoday.com/bernard-porter/terrorism-and-victorians [accessed 19 September 2014].

justice: the defence of the state against enemies was its main focus, the out-come (the security of the state) mattering more than how this was achieved.[29]

On the eve of 11 September 2001, therefore, we can see that the UK had fully embraced the idea of a generic problem of 'terrorism' which may have had various shapes ('Irish'; foreign; domestic) but all of which, it was said, constituted both individually and collectively a threat to the integrity of the state. The law and the security practice it underpinned (increasingly law-based after the end of the Cold War[30]) found itself moving easily into a territory that, having been vacated by anti-Communism, was now a fer-tile breeding ground for anti-terrorism. The rhetoric of defending democ-racy was the same. Even before but especially after 11 September 2001, the threat was usefully easier to demonstrate than it had been when Mos-cow had been the enemy: the occasional killing of an agent could hardly compete with the deadly impact of a terrorist spectacular, however sporadic such atrocities might be. The previous challenge of Communist subversion might be thought to have been objectively more serious, but the high level of violence involved in 'terrorism' tends (not unnaturally) to obscure the low threat to the integrity of state institutions so far as an appalled general public is concerned. And whereas the revolutionary left had many friends (and not a few spies) in powerful places, the same could not be said for those engaged in terrorist struggles. In tandem with this internal face, 'counter-terrorism' also quickly developed an external aspect, becoming the expla-nation for military actions abroad which were redolent of times past, albeit now badged in a 'counter-terrorist' or 'humanitarian' vernacular. At the end of the first decade of the twenty-first century, with counter-terrorism clamp-downs at home and wars against terrorists being fought around the globe, it was not obvious that much had changed since the mid-nineteenth century. In the post-9/11 era Britain's early forays into counter-terrorism law stopped being embarrassing and short-term and grew instead into laws to be proud of and emulated elsewhere, a fact to which contemporary comparative studies of counter-terrorism laws bear eloquent testimony.[31]

---

[29] L. Lustgarten and I. Leigh, *In from the Cold. National Security and Parliamentary Democracy* (Oxford, Oxford University Press, 1994).
[30] Not just the Security Service Act mentioned above but the Intelligence Services Act 1994 and the Regulation of Investigatory Powers Act 2000.
[31] V. V. Ramraj and A. K. Thiruvengadam (eds), *Emergency Powers in Asia. Exploring the Limits of Legality* (Cambridge, Cambridge University Press, 2010); K. Roach, *The 9/11 Effect. Comparative Counter-Terrorism* (Cambridge, Cambridge University Press, 2011); V. V. Ramraj, M. Hor, K. Roach and G. Williams, *Global Anti-Terrorism Law and Policy*, 2nd edn (Cambridge, Cambridge University Press, 2012).

How did the language of terrorism come to so permeate the legislative and political responses of a state as confidently democratic as Britain appeared to be? Its first appearance in law in 1974 and the subsequent embedding (and embracing of all local and global violent subversion) that has been briefly described above reflects a shift in the pattern of international relations which took place at the end of the 1960s and early 1970s. Understanding how this happened is central to the underlying question posed in this chapter about how democratic states have come to allow the growth within them of the strong anti-democratic sentiments that we have seen recently, and which have flourished as the Cold War's traditional enemies have receded. This takes us to our second case study.

Militarised democracy

The difficulty facing the state of Israel has always been how to reconcile its birth in violence, and the conflict in which it has ever since been submerged, with the ideal of liberal democracy to which it aspires and to which it is strongly committed.[32] The very shape of the sovereign entity depends on an expansion beyond the designated UN borders of 1948 that occurred at its inception. This was later followed by further growth, albeit this time into territories occupied by rather than annexed to the state. There have been wars (1948; 1967; 1973), invasions (for example, into Lebanon in 1978 and again in 1982), and seemingly countless forays into the parts of Palestine seized after 1967. Civil unrest of a sort more associated with colonial rebellion than democratic disorder has regularly needed to be quelled both within and contiguously to the state. Like Northern Ireland before it, emergency laws have been part of the state's framework of legislation from the very beginning.[33] And yet Israel has been able throughout to present itself as a beacon of freedom in an illiberal region, what was earlier regarded as a 'poster-child' of democracy.[34] How has this been achieved?

---

[32] J. L. Gelvin, *The Israel–Palestine Conflict. One Hundred Years of War*, 3rd edn (Cambridge, Cambridge University Press, 2014). Compelling (albeit from the Israeli perspective strongly disputed) histories include I. Pappe, *The Ethnic Cleansing of Palestine* (Oxford, One World, 2006); N. Chomsky, *The Fateful Triangle. The United States, Israel and the Palestinians* (London and Sydney, Pluto Press, 1983). See also D. Hirst, *The Gun and the Olive Branch: The Roots of Violence in the Middle East*, 2nd edn (London, Faber and Faber, 1984).

[33] Drawing as Ireland also did on pre-existing British laws: Government and Law Arrangements Ordinance 1948, s. 11.

[34] Of the large number of books on terrorism which assume such an evaluation, see as typical examples B. Netanyahu, *Fighting Terrorism. How Democracies can Defeat Domestic and International*

Clearly Israel has always had two audiences: domestic and international. So far as the first is concerned, the story has been an easy one to tell, since only the supporters of the state within Israel are those at whom it has been directed: this is the well-known narrative of a brave small nation committed to freedom surrounded by authoritarian states dedicated to its destruction, with a suspect community within (the Palestinians) some of whom would be more than happy to play willing executioner.

The international audience has been harder to crack. Even after 1948 there was disquiet about the appropriation of territory in defiance of the settlement envisaged by the relevant UN resolution. After 1967, the analogy with colonialism appeared unavoidable: here were vast tracts of land occupied by indigenous communities upon whom was imposed an Israeli military order. In due course there arrived waves of Jewish settlers whose quality of life has been as reminiscent of colonial settlors everywhere as it has been removed from the grim circumstances of the Palestinians around them, now either living in vastly reduced circumstances in the locality of the settlements or expelled to refugee camps further afield.[35] We should recall that in the 1950s and 1960s, and despite the best efforts of (for example) the British authorities as noted above, there was growing acceptance of the right of a people to self-determination, and by the late 1960s many leaders of new nations had achieved their people's right through the use of political violence – perhaps not viewed as unequivocally legitimate when it had occurred but nevertheless more often than not seen in retrospect (with the benefit of hindsight, it is true) as, at the very least, excusable.[36] The Palestinian movement never quite pulled off this transformation into a guerrilla force that the times demanded: the Israeli authorities were harsh and also effective, and the state's continuously proclaimed democratic commitments made it attractive to Europeans and Americans alike (even among those not committed to a Jewish homeland in principle and whatever the cost).

At exactly this time three separate developments transformed attitudes to politically motivated subversive/insurgent political violence in the West

---

Terrorists (London, Allison and Busby, 1996) and B. Netanyahu (ed), *Terrorism: How the West can Win* (London, Weidenfeld and Nicolson, 1986). Cf E. W. Said and C. Hitchens, *Blaming the Victims: Spurious Scholarship and the Palestinian Question*, 2nd edn (London, Verso, 2001).

[35] There is basic but useful information at the web site of the United Nations Relief and Works Agency for Palestine Refugees in the Near East: http://www.unrwa.org/palestine-refugees [accessed 19 September 2014].

[36] The International Covenant on Civil and Political Rights and the International Covenant on Economic, Social and Cultural Rights, agreed in 1966, share a first article declaring the right of peoples to self-determination: http://www.ohchr.org/en/professionalinterest/pages/ccpr.aspx and http://www.ohchr.org/EN/ProfessionalInterest/Pages/cescr.aspx respectively [accessed 19 September 2014].

and made Israel's positioning much more straightforward.[37] First, there emerged from South America the notion of the 'urban guerrilla', a fighter (for freedom; justice; liberation) who took on the state in the cities, and whose definition of the enemy (and whom therefore it was permissible to attack) expanded as time went on, beginning with the army and the police and moving swiftly on to bankers, large property-holders and eventually all those with what was decided to be disproportionate wealth. Such thinking moved into Western Europe in the late 1960s, influencing a small number of radical left-wing groups in, for example, Germany, Italy, Belgium and the United Kingdom, and also (in due course) the United States.[38] The violence of these organisations (the Red Army Faction; the Red Brigades; the CCC; the Angry Brigade; the Weather Underground) was relatively trivial[39] but its impact on liberal democratic society was disproportionately severe: political violence was supposed to happen in other places, a thing read about in newspapers but not experienced (or even potentially experienced) for oneself.

The same was true of colonial violence, yet a variant of this also began to figure in Western society at this time, reflected in the growing violence of ETA in Basque Spain, the IRA in Northern Ireland, the FALN in Corsica and the FLQ in Canada – even the United States was not exempt, with some of the more determined Puerto Ricans doing their muscular bit for a freedom it was not obvious many of their people craved.[40] Here was the second of the three developments referred to above, which together with the first put a fear of political violence onto the domestic agenda of Western states for the first time. And then third, there was of course Palestinian violence, not explicitly the work of Yassir Arafat's mainstream Palestinian Liberation Army (PLO) but not obviously at far remove from that organisation either – the hijacking of aircraft; the gun and bomb attacks on passengers at airports; the hijacking of the *Achille Lauro*;[41] and (most infamously of all) the brutal assault on the Israeli team at the Munich Olympics in 1972.

[37] The ground is well covered in P. Wilkinson, *Terrorism and the Liberal State*, 2nd edn (Basingstoke, Macmillan, 1986). See also A. Guelke, *The New Age of Terrorism and the International Political System* (London, IB Tauris, 1995) and C. A. Gearty, *Terror* (London, Faber and Faber, 1991), chapters 3, 7 and 8.
[38] A. Vercher, *Terrorism in Europe. An International Comparative Legal Analysis* (Oxford, Clarendon Press, 1992); A. Jamieson, *The Heart Attacked. Terrorism and Conflict in the Italian State* (London, Marion Boyars, 1989).
[39] Dealing with one specific example but in some ways representative is H. J. Horchem, 'The Decline of the Red Army Faction', *Terrorism and Political Violence*, 3/2 (1991).
[40] P. Wilkinson and A. M. Stewart, *Contemporary Research on Terrorism* (Aberdeen, Aberdeen University Press, 1987) is a voluminous snapshot of the global focus of terrorism studies in the mid-1980s.
[41] A. Cassese, *Terrorism, Politics and Law: The* Achille Lauro *Affair* (Cambridge, Polity Press, 1989).

In the 1970s, and assisted by this wave of often shocking activity by groups not implausibly associated with the wider Palestinian resistance, the Israeli authorities were able to recast their opponents as terrorists rather than guerrillas, as (vicious; psychopathic) murderers not (principled) freedom fighters.[42] It was out of this mix that the idea of international terrorism emerged, a contagion of irrational violence aimed at the innocent that could break out in different places and change shape at will but which was at bottom all part of the same global problem and therefore (crucially) not linked to place or particular circumstances.[43] Here was the marked break with the previous, locationally sensitive, discourse of colonialism and guerrilla resistance. The connection it made between groups across the world was largely spurious[44] but the negative effect it had on insurgents caught by the label was immense: being a terrorist was not something to be proud of; it was a description at all costs to avoid.

This new terrorism discourse proved invaluable to Israel in explaining itself not only to its own people (already increasingly on board, particularly after the suicide bombings used in a later stage in the conflict[45]) but to the wider world as well. It resolved the liberty-versus-security dilemma to the satisfaction of many, not least those with power in Europe and the US, already sympathetic to Israel as we have seen, and now able to explain to themselves that that state's aggression was justifiable 'counter-terrorism' rather than old-fashioned colonial occupation, part of what all states had to do today rather than what colonial powers had been doing in the past in their failed efforts to preserve their empires.

Moving now beyond Israel, this new language was also useful in the (then still continuing) Cold War, with linkages being made between the Soviet Union on the one hand and, on the other, various of the terrorist

[42] See Netanyahu *Fighting Terrorism. How Democracies can Defeat Domestic and International Terrorists* and Netanyahu (ed), *Terrorism: How the West can Win.* Other volumes focused on particularly fanatical Palestinian or Palestinian-supporting 'terrorists': for example, Y. Melman, *The Master Terrorist: The True Story Behind Abu Nidal* (London, Sidgwick and Jackson, 1987).

[43] B. Netanyahu (ed), *International Terrorism. Challenge and Response* (Jerusalem, Transaction Publishers, 1981 and 1989); W. Gutteridge (ed), *The New Terrorism* (London, Mansell Publishing Limited, 1986); N. C. Livingstone, *The War Against Terrorism* (Lexington, Lexington, 1982).

[44] E. Herman and G. O'Sullivan, *The 'Terrorism' Industry. The Experts and Institutions that Shape our View of Terror* (New York, Pantheon Books, 1989); E. Said, 'Identity, Negation and Violence', *New Left Review*, 171 (1988), 46–60. More recent but in a similar critical tradition is R. Jackson, 'Constructing Enemies: "Islamic Terrorism" in Political and Academic Discourse', *Government and Opposition*, 42(3) (2007) 394–426. And see *Critical Studies on Terrorism* (Abingdon, Taylor and Francis) for articles that cut against the orthodox grain discussed in the text.

[45] R. Pape, *Dying to Win: The Strategic Logic of Suicide Terrorism* (New York, Random House, 2006).

groups to which it was alleged the Kremlin gave succour and support.[46] This was mainly a foreign policy bonus, however.[47] While it is true that some states caught up in counter-terrorism were able to make reasonably credible arguments that the 'enemy within' was Communist-driven – South Africa comes immediately to mind[48] – this was not plausibly the case as far as colonial style conflict in Ireland or Spain was concerned. Nor was it believable that, for all their Moscow links and sympathies, the radicals behind the likes of the Red Army Faction and the Red Brigades were fifth columnists of the dedicated quality of the local Communist parties of the inter-war period, or that they were as supported by Moscow as these comrades had been.[49]

This takes us to an important difference in the nature of the challenges to power in the democratic era as between, on the one hand, domestically based resistance to inequality and injustice in the inter-war and Cold War periods (discussed above in the British context) and, on the other, the various kinds of terrorist assaults that have afflicted the West from the late 1960s. These latter groups have had no seriously realisable revolutionary agenda and nor has it been possible with any conviction to describe them as supported by a foreign power intent on transforming domestic power structures in any way, and certainly not to the disadvantage of those whose wealth and privilege has survived relatively unscathed into the democratic era. It was noted earlier that a terrorist atrocity tends to crowd out any discussion of the genuine nature of the threat posed by its occurrence: being noisier than the old Communist subversion does not make it more serious, but (as we have already stated in the British context) that is a difficult position to adopt in the face of its sometimes gruesomely violent impact. The large contribution of Israel to our subject has been the generalisation of violence-based assaults on particular states by their weak opponents into a global challenge ('terrorism' and 'international terrorism' and 'state-sponsored' terrorism) to the liberal democratic order itself. The United States was a keen participant in this new discourse, particularly under

---

[46] Most notoriously C. Sterling, *The Terror Network: The Secret War of International Terrorism* (London, Weidenfeld and Nicolson, 1981).

[47] Exemplified by the US Defense Department, *Terrorist Group Profiles* (Washington, US Government Printing Office, 1988).

[48] And the African National Congress (ANC) in South Africa does make its appearance in US Defense Department, *Terrorist Group Profiles*.

[49] There were clearly links but perhaps not as focused and organised as many believe, for example, the dramatic assumptions in N. Lockwood, 'How the Soviet Union Transformed Terrorism', *The Atlantic*, 23 December 2011: http://www.theatlantic.com/international/archive/2011/12/how-the-soviet-union-transformed-terrorism/250433/ [accessed 19 September 2014].

the Reagan and Bush administrations in the 1980s.[50] But it was that country's reaction to the attacks on it on 11 September 2001 that gave our subject the impetus that it now has.

Imperialist democracy

Like the UK, democracy gradually insinuated itself into the American political system in a way that did not immediately challenge pre-existing power structures. Like the UK too, support for controlling radical opposition to on-going inequality and unfairness was secured and fuelled by fear: fear of a Soviet-inspired domestic political agenda that might have talked about greater fairness and better democracy but was intent in truth on the transformation of American society along Soviet lines. The Red Scare after the First World War was driven by this fear, as was what has come to be known as McCarthyism after the 1939–45 conflict.[51] It was not absurd for those whose disproportionate prosperity left them open to the greatest risk of revolution to argue that support for radical change and greater equality would in fact lead to just such an inevitably chaotic (and for many terrifying) outcome: Russia in 1917 and Soviet aggression in 1945–48 were recent memories or current facts and Moscow's power was still many decades away from the collapse of 1989. As in Britain, radical social democratic critiques of the status quo got squeezed between these larger foes: even the US's much applauded guarantee of free speech (in its constitution's famed first amendment) could not deliver such dissidents much room to operate.[52] Unlike Britain, however, no trade-union-based political party ever secured a strong enough foothold in the US body politic to protect organised labour from being swept into irrelevance under cover of this fear of the Communist threat – the closest the country came to this was the Roosevelt New Deal Democratic party of the 1930s but even this was always an uneasy alliance between northern and southern states on the one hand and Tammany Hall and privilege on the other.[53]

Democracy in America has not needed the 'War on Terror' in order to stop looking dangerous to the privileged. Narratives of freedom, liberty and

---

[50] See Sterling, *The Terror Network* and US Defense Department, *Terrorist Group Profiles*.

[51] S. Walker, *In Defence of American Liberties*, 2nd edn (Carbondale, IL, Southern Illinois University Press, 1999).

[52] Walker, *In Defence of American Liberties*. Perhaps the most notorious of the many cases upholding restrictions on radical speech is *Dennis v US* 341 US 494 (1951), essentially legitimising the Senator McCarthy-led assault on left-wing political comment.

[53] J. E. Smith's compelling biography *FDR* (New York, Random House, 2008) has the details.

opportunity for all dominate a political agenda which is in reality now almost entirely throttled by the power of money, in a way that has been sanctified by successive decisions of the country's Supreme Court.[54] Far from being threatened by the disappearance of its enemy in 1989, America's corporate democracy has taken to the new opportunities for aggrandisement offered by the end of the Cold War without fear or (it would seem) even a residual sense of guilt or anxiety about those who are (increasingly) being left behind. US commitments to counter-terrorism, therefore, have not needed to be deployed to prevent an upsurge in mainstream political activity: its main impact domestically in the US has been as a mechanism for aggressive action against suspect immigrants[55] and as a coercive means of suffocating discussion of Israel's conduct in the Middle East, punishing those who wander even a little from 'Israel-at-all-costs' orthodoxy.[56]

We need to look elsewhere to find the more general utility of this language, and, as with Britain during the 1930s to 1950s, we find it in imperialism. US control of territory outside its jurisdiction has only rarely been colonial in the traditional sense of occupation supported by administration by the external power. It has generally operated by one remove, via local leaders who are in theory free but in reality controlled by US interests. It has been a system that has worked well on the whole, allowing the US to believe itself the exceptional defender of democracy while its own interests have been carefully disguised (not least from its demos). As with Britain when its power began to fade away after the Second World War, challenges to US authority have tended to be characterised by it as terrorist threats, and its own military action abroad explained as 'counter-terrorism'. Particularly hostile governments have found themselves being designated leaders of 'terrorist states'.[57] The main theatre has been the Levant. The defeat of American interests that occurred in the Iranian revolution of 1979 led to concerns about 'Islamic fundamentalism' which were then fuelled by Hezbollah's damaging actions in Lebanon, in

---

[54] See *Citizens United v Federal Election Commission* 558 US (2010) at http://www.supremecourt.gov/opinions/09pdf/08-205.pdf [accessed 19 September 2014].

[55] M. Welch, *Scapegoats of September 11th: Hate Crimes and State Crimes in the War on Terror* (New Brunswick/New Jersey/London, Rutgers, 2006).

[56] For a recent depressing example see 'Professor Fired for Israel Criticism urges University of Illinois to Reinstate Him' *Guardian* 9 September 2014: http://www.theguardian.com/education/2014/sep/09/professor-israel-criticism-twitter-university-illinois [accessed 19 September 2014]. A good general treatment is I. Cram, *Terror and the War on Dissent: Freedom of Expression in the Age of al-Qaeda* (Berlin, Springer, 2009).

[57] For more details on the argument that follows, see C. A. Gearty, 'Human Rights in an Age of Counter-Terrorism', in C. Miller (ed), *'War on Terror'* (Manchester, Manchester University Press, 2006), chapter 3. There is an interesting response by Sandra Fredman in pp. 99–104.

particular the car bombs that drove American and French troops from Beirut in 1983.[58] As anxieties about the Cold War weakened in the late 1980s, and ended altogether in 1989, so a concern about the 'new terrorism' of radical Islam found itself drifting up the agenda of US foreign policy-makers. There were occasional forays by such subversive militants into the US itself, but the issue remained largely a matter of external relations – frequently linked to Israeli interests (as described above) but also extending to descriptions of other conflicts in which the US has been either directly or indirectly involved. The attacks of 9/11 brought this hitherto distant language of terrorism and counter-terrorism directly to the 'homeland', and led to a clampdown not only on the far enemy abroad but also on those perceived to be its supporters at home. The rhetoric of freedom and democracy was deployed to justify the 'necessary evil' required (it was said) to ensure the Republic's survival.[59] As in earlier decades, though, the targets here were those critical of or suspected of being estranged from US foreign commitments. There was no need to redeploy to curb domestic dissent since (as already noted) this had already been largely obliterated (at least from institutional politics).

The enemy within

Until the attacks on Washington and New York by al-Qaida in 2001, the 'terrorism' threat posed to liberal democratic states did not enjoy anything like the level of credibility that had accompanied the fear of Communism during the inter-war and then the early Cold War periods. True, as we have seen, the term itself had begun to be deployed in a generic way during the early 1970s, as a global problem rather than as a series of specific problems, but (Israel apart) its worst practitioners tended to be far away, caught up in disputes about the reach of Western/US power and therefore not particularly interested in subverting the structures of power at home. The one exception to this, the violence of separatist movements like ETA and the IRA, was (despite occasional suggestions otherwise) primarily driven by the need to own bits of land, not to transform the political structures on them. The 9/11 attacks, and the reaction to them in the United Nations and across the democratic world, propelled to centre stage new frameworks of laws for the control of violent domestic dissent, focused it is true on al-Qaida

---

[58] M. Levitt, *Hezbollah: The Global Footprint of Lebanon's Party of God* (Washington, DC, Georgetown University Press, 2013), chapter 2.
[59] Ignatieff, *The Lesser Evil.*

and al-Qaida-related militancy but capable of being deployed against other groups and individuals deemed subversive as well. The US example is well known: the assertion by the President of Commander-in-Chief powers to wage a new 'War on Terror'; the deployment of legal precedents from previous eras of war to justify indefinite detention without trial; the use of torture and other forms of degrading treatment against suspects; the covert surveillance of Americans as well as foreigners under the same supposed powers; and more recently the emergence of an asserted legal right to kill citizens and non-citizens alike, usually (but from the logic of the position not necessarily) when they are outside the jurisdiction.[60] Off the back of the same perceived threat, the UK introduced measures such as the indefinite detention of suspected international terrorists in 2001 and when this was challenged by its highest judicial authority a system of coercive administrative control outside the criminal law, and also the enactment of many new terrorism offences, the enhancing of police and security powers to deal with the terrorism threat, and much else besides.[61] Where the US and Britain have gone, others have tended to follow. The first decade of the twenty-first century saw the embedding of such legislation and policy across not only the Global North but much of the Global South as well.[62]

We may note three characteristics of such laws as we move to our concluding remarks. First they are now on the whole permanent. The old idea of terrorism producing a special challenge requiring a draconian but time-limited response has been replaced by a new sense of counter-terrorism laws being available to the state to assist it in its 'war' on terror, an endless conflict not least because the enemy (not being a state) cannot surrender and even if it could new ones would be quickly found to replace it.[63] Second, the definitions of 'terrorism' are generally very broad, going beyond violence

---

[60] The literature is of course vast: see J. J. Paust, *Beyond the Law: The Bush Administration's Unlawful Responses in the 'War' on Terror* (Cambridge, Cambridge University Press, 2007); D. Cole and J. Lobel, *Less Safe, Less Free: Why America is Losing the War on Terror* (New York and London, The New Press, 2007); S. Holmes, *The Matador's Cape. America's Reckless Response to Terror* (Cambridge, Cambridge University Press, 2007); M. Welch, *Crimes of Power and States of Impunity. The US Response to Terror* (New Brunswick, New Jersey and London, Rutgers University Press, 2009); J. Bravin, *The Terror Courts* (New Haven, Yale University Press, 2013). For an international perspective see the International Commission of Jurists, *Assessing Damage, Urging Action. Report of the Eminent Jurists Panel on Terrorism, Counter-terrorism and Human Rights* (Geneva, International Commission of Jurists, 2009).

[61] Walker, *Blackstone's Guide to the Anti-Terrorism Legislation* has the details.

[62] Ramraj and Thiruvengadam (eds), *Emergency Powers in Asia* and Ramraj *et al.*, *Global Anti-Terrorism Law and Policy* have many of the details on world-wide terrorism legislation.

[63] T. Becker, *Terrorism and the State: Rethinking the Rules of State Responsibility* (Oxford, Hart, 2006).

potentially to embrace conduct which is at worst on the periphery of such violence, at best merely the robust exercise of our civil liberties. The UK case of *R v Gul*[64] is instructive here, with Britain's Supreme Court expressing deep misgivings about how wide the UK definition of terrorism is, and how much discretionary power this gives to the prosecuting authorities. Third, as the laws on terrorism have bedded down they have tended to attract arrays of procedural safeguards which may be thought beneficially to have served as compensations for the lack of the sort of safeguards against state abuse that are thought essential to the criminal process, but which have also served to embed further into legal discourse procedures which only a very few years ago would have been thought unconscionable from the liberal rule of law perspective: the exceptional does quickly become the norm.[65]

How does this all potentially affect the health of the democratic polity itself, the claim with which we commenced this discussion? True, the 'terrorist threat' is rarely directed at conduct aimed at the transformation of liberal democracy into a different system, as was the aim of Communists and socialists of earlier eras; even the most robust hawks hesitate to argue that a Western Caliphate is around the corner. The laws and procedures created off the back of the terrorist threat are, however, not only (as we have already noted) of a permanent but also of a general nature: their reach is theoretically into the whole of society, their capacity for the inhibition of political discussion potentially deep. The old laws from the anti-Communist eras of the past also remain largely in place in all Western states; their most useful work in controlling radical speech may be in the past but their utility in curbing unacceptable political activism remains high.

Following the capitalist crises sparked off by the world-wide financial collapse of 2008, we have seen the imposition of 'austerity' policies across Europe with a consequent plunge in the living standards of many, and in the prospects of the young in particular. Meanwhile the wealth of the few soars. Never has democracy been more gentle or unthreatening.[66] Resistance has been intense and widespread, but it no longer has the ideological force of the Communist alternative. It tends to be expressed through demonstrations, sit-ins, occupations, efforts at direct democracy designed to circumvent the blocked challenges of conventional political discourse. Such assertions of citizen-power fall foul not only of the old laws designed to deal with past

---

[64] See Terrorism Act 2001 s 1. *R v Gul* [2013] UKSC 64 and Greene, 'The Quest for a Satisfactory Definition of Terrorism.

[65] Gearty, *Liberty and Security*.

[66] T. Picketty, *Capital in the Twenty-First Century* (Cambridge, Massachusetts, The Belknap Press of Harvard University Press, 2014).

left-wing radicals but also now increasingly of the new terrorism laws.[67] The virus is growing to such an extent that the only form of dissent permitted may soon be that taking place in orthodox political assemblies which have already doomed themselves to irrelevance by their submission to money and power. If and when we get to that point, it will be time to acknowledge that democracy, always imperfect, virus-infected from the start, has finally died. Its successor, neo-democracy, will show all the signs and symbols of democracy – elections; human rights protection; equality laws – but the rich will be getting richer and richer.

---

[67] C. A. Gearty, 'Terrorism and Human Rights' *Government and Opposition*, 42/3 (2007); Campaign against Criminalising Communities (CAMPACC), *A Permanent State of Terror* (London, CAMPACC in association with Index on Censorship, 2003).

6

Secrets and Lies

Misinformation and Counter-Terrorism

ADRIAN GUELKE

A SPATE OF RECENT BOOKS dealing with different aspects of Western counter-terrorist policies and practice paint a shocking picture not just of disregard for basic principles of the rule of law but of cruelty and inhumanity.[1] Their descriptions of the torture of suspects, murder by drone and the lengths to which the police in both the United States and the United Kingdom have been prepared to go to manufacture terrorist plots, where no threat to the public existed without the active encouragement of agents provocateur, constitute an indictment of those involved in this wrongdoing, as well as of political leaders who authorised these actions and then lied about it. The gulf between political rhetoric and events on the ground could scarcely be wider. The actions of whistleblowers of one kind or another have ensured that this gulf has not gone unnoticed. Most damaged as a consequence has been the reputation of President Barack Obama, particularly as he had raised hopes in his election of a change of course from the excesses of his predecessor. At the same time, almost alone of Western political leaders, President Obama has acknowledged the danger that the actions of Western liberal democracies in the name of counter-terrorism pose to constitutional government and the rule of law. His acknowledgement of this problem stands in marked contrast to other political leaders who have relied on secrets and lies to gloss over the conflict between their words and deeds. How has this state of affairs come about? Above all, why has it happened in societies in which respect for human rights has been widely proclaimed as a fundamental principle of

---

[1] See, for example, Arun Kundnani, *The Muslims are Coming!: Islamophobia, Extremism and the Domestic War on Terror* (London and New York, Verso, 2014); Jeremy Scahill, *Dirty Wars: The World is a Battlefield* (London, Serpent's Tail, 2013); Medea Benjamin, *Drone Warfare: Killing by Remote Control* (London and New York, Verso, 2013); and Ian Cobain, *Cruel Britannia: A Secret History of Torture* (London, Portobello Books, 2013).

Proceedings of the British Academy **203**, 95–110. © The British Academy 2015.

good governance? The trite answer is that terrorism tends to bring out the worst in any society. A fuller explanation is attempted below.

It is common to see the events of 11 September 2001 as a turning point in global politics, as well as in the practice of terrorism and responses to it in the form of counter-terrorism. But while the scale of the attack was indeed unprecedented in the number of deaths it caused, the challenge that 9/11 presented in security terms was by no means entirely new. The possibility that terrorism would cause destruction on the scale of natural disasters has been debated in the literature on terrorism in the 1990s, mainly under the rubric of new terrorism. Further, long before this debate, all manner of possibilities had been considered, in which wrongdoers of various kinds – whether conceived of then or later as terrorists – caused numerous deaths in a single incident, including during the anarchist wave of terrorism that an airship might be used as a flying bomb. While at this distance, this speculation might seem rather fanciful, consideration needs to be taken of some of the attacks that did occur during the anarchist wave, most notably the bomb attack on Wall Street in 1920 in which 30 people were killed instantly and many more wounded, eight of whom died as a consequence of their injuries. And though 9/11 was larger in scale than previous events, there had been a number of prior mass-casualty attacks, including the simultaneous bombing of American embassies in Kenya and Tanzania in 1998.

However, there is no gainsaying the huge impact that 9/11 had on the public throughout the Western industrialised world. That was compounded by the fact that people of many different nationalities worked in the twin towers of New York's World Trade Center, which was a potent symbol of global capitalism in the post-Cold War world. The shock both to the public and to policy-makers was palpable. Prior to 9/11, terrorism had seemed to be of declining importance. This was partly because of peace processes in Israel/Palestine and Northern Ireland, conflicts that for decades had been associated with terrorism. Further, fresh horrors, ethnic cleansing in the Balkans and genocide in Rwanda, attracted greater attention than what appeared to be the waning problem of terrorism. Indeed, one way of interpreting the debate on new terrorism was as an attempt to revive fading interest of both the public and policy-makers in the subject.[2] 9/11 propelled terrorism to the top of the world's political agenda and meant that for the first decade of the twenty-first century, the Global War on Terror became the dominant theme of the times.

---

[2] The failure of the term 'new terrorism' to gain an entry in the *Oxford Dictionary of English* (Oxford, Oxford University Press, 2005) can be taken as one indication of the limited impact of this debate on public discourse.

Reference has already been made to the concept of a terrorist wave. Though he was by no means the first person to apply the term wave to different periods of terrorism, this idea has been most fully expounded by David Rapoport.[3] He identifies four waves of modern terrorism: the anarchist wave dating from the 1880s; an anti-colonial wave following the end of the Second World War; a New Left wave from the 1960s; and a religious wave going back to the Iranian revolution in 1979. By the same token, the story of counter-terrorism might readily be conceived as a series of reactions to these waves. Such a chronology broadly holds up, with 9/11 giving a major impetus to the adoption of fresh measures to tackle the threat posed by the mass-casualty attacks linked to the global jihad of al-Qaida.

The interpretation of 9/11 as part of a terrorist wave meant that it was viewed as just a part of a larger and ongoing assault on the West. In the light of subsequent attacks in Bali, Kenya, Madrid, London and Boston, this would seem a perfectly reasonable supposition. Indeed, one might go further and argue that being part of an ongoing campaign is practically speaking a defining characteristic of an act of terrorism. On this basis, one might contend that the assassination of President John F. Kennedy in 1963 by Lee Harvey Oswald (assuming no larger conspiracy) does not meet this criterion of an act of terrorism, whereas that of Rajiv Gandhi in 1990 by the Tamil Tigers does. The distinction rests on the recognition that, however loose the term terrorism has become in common usage, by no means all murders, including even politically motivated assassinations, should be considered acts of terrorism. Indeed, one of the first questions that is asked after any violent event in which large numbers of people have been killed or which has attracted wide attention because of its shocking nature is whether the act in question is one of terrorism or not. The pressure from the media for an answer to the question is a common reason why the actions of individuals acting on their own acquire the label terrorism, which then sticks despite subsequent investigation of the case. At the same time, some reassurance is generally taken if the authorities are able to establish at an early stage that the act in question had no connection with terrorism.

The reason for that is primarily terrorism's association with ongoing campaigns of political violence. Hence, the characterisation of an act as one of terrorism raises the spectre of further similar outrages. By the same token, the assumption commonly made is that a violent outrage without any link to

[3] David C. Rapoport, 'The Four Waves of Modern Terrorism' in Audrey Cronin and James Ludes (eds), *Attacking Terrorism: Elements of a Grand Strategy* (Washington, DC, Georgetown University Press, 2004), pp. 46–73.

terrorism is likely to be a one-off. However, it is possible to give examples that contradict this assumption. In particular, the blow at the centre, as the assassination of Tsar Alexander II by the terrorist group Narodnaya Volya was dubbed, was conceived as an act that on its own would have a trans-formative impact and be the 'final blow' to the system.[4] By contrast, gang warfare provides many instances of ongoing campaigns of violence that tend not to be characterised as terrorism. In particular, violence between the gangs themselves is unlikely to be described as terrorism, even if it includes bomb-ings. However, if the lives of innocent bystanders are frequently put at risk by gang warfare then it may attract the description of terrorism. While it is by no means easy to draw a water-tight distinction between terrorism and other forms of violence, the following are typically seen as characteristic of an act of terrorism:

- it is part of a larger campaign with political objectives;
- it is carried out by a group of people or, if by an individual then someone with links to a group;
- it is normatively transgressive.

While the leaders of Narodnaya Volya were plainly mistaken in believ-ing that the assassination of Tsar Alexander II would usher in a new society, at least their strategic thinking was evident. In the case of 9/11, it is by no means evident what Osama bin Laden expected the outcome of the as-sault on America to be. The most plausible explanation is that he hoped that America's reaction to the assault would revive the fortunes in Muslim coun-tries of the Islamic resurgence that was then on the wane. Of course, strate-gies do not remain static. They change in response to events. Indeed, they are commonly more flexible than the narrative used to legitimise the cam-paign. In the case of the Provisional IRA, for example, the organisation's initial strategy had been directed at forcing the early withdrawal of British forces from Northern Ireland through maximising the level of violence, with the aim of victory within the year. Only after that approach had failed was the strategy of the long war adopted. It was based on sustaining the cam-paign of violence over many years, with the objective of securing a British declaration of intent to withdraw through a process of attrition. As any form of violence, including terrorism, is a means to an end, understanding the strategy of any group engaged in violence is at least as important as grasping

---

[4] Charles Townshend, *Terrorism: A Very Short Introduction* (Oxford, Oxford University Press, 2002), p. 58.

the appeal of their objectives. For people to be persuaded to risk their lives by participating in a campaign of violence, they need to be persuaded not merely of the rightness of its objectives but also, and just as importantly, the effectiveness of the means proposed. A major weakness of Western counter-terrorism in relation to jihadi violence has been its focus on why people might be attracted to the political objectives of jihadi groups, as opposed to how they are persuaded that violent means will achieve these ends.

An advantage of characterising terrorism in terms of campaigns is that it facilitates comparison with violent political conflict more generally. Relevant in this context are the phases that are characteristic of the most intractable of such conflicts, including a stage of rapid escalation from small beginnings to a peak, followed by a flattening out of the violence over a long period of time, prior to the onset of negotiations and an eventual political settlement. These phases are commonly mirrored in the reaction of the authorities. State responses to violent challenges to political order can be characterised in terms of a simple typology of suppression, criminalisation and accommodation.[5] The basis of the typology is how the state treats politically motivated violent offenders and suspects in comparison with those not so motivated or what in Northern Ireland parlance were known as ordinary decent criminals. Where the state treats those politically motivated much more harshly than ordinary decent criminals, this can be labelled suppression. During this phase, those suspected of any involvement in the campaign of violence threatening the society may be detained without trial and subjected to coercive interroga-tion methods that go far beyond what is normally permitted even in the in-vestigation of the most heinous of crimes. Further, in the suppression phase, expressions of support for the actions of the terrorists or even their political objectives may be outlawed.

In the criminalisation phase, there is reliance on the normal processes of law enforcement to meet the challenge of those rebelling against the state and during this phase the state may seek to delegitimise the campaign by deny-ing the political motivation of those involved, with the rebels being labelled mafias or bandits. The move away from a strategy of suppression to one of criminalisation is commonly a sign that the authorities are confident that they are capable of containing violence without the need for special methods. The attraction of this strategy in the context of an internal challenge to the state is the implication that the state is sufficiently legitimate that the problem can be

---

[5] The author first constructed this typology for John Brewer, Adrian Guelke, Ian Hume, Edward Moxon-Browne and Rick Wilford, *The Police, Public Order and the State* (Basingstoke, Palgrave Macmillan, 1996).

dealt with in the context of normal policing. If political violence does not fade away during this phase, but a stalemate develops in which those engaging in political violence are unable to advance their objectives but the state is also unable to prevent the continuance of the campaign of violence, then both sides may seek a negotiated end to the violence. The extent to which the terrorists or the men of violence, to use another Northern Irish expression, are able to advance their objectives will depend on circumstances. But during this phase of accommodation, concessions will commonly be made that mean that politically motivated violent offenders receive some form of special treatment that would not be accorded to ordinary criminals. This is usually premised on the organisation these offenders belong to ending its campaign of violence. In the past, amnesties were common that covered not just wrongdoing by insurgents but also that by the security forces. However, these tend to be out of fashion as contrary to the precepts of 'no immunity' and 'no impunity'.

While the state responses of suppression, criminalisation and accommodation may correspond to the different phases of conflict from escalation, through flattening, to negotiation, there is no necessary link between them and state responses may at times be out of sync with the evolution of the conflict on the ground. Further, the state may adopt all three strategies simultaneously in addressing different challenges. An example is how the Tony Blair government in the UK addressed the simultaneous challenges presented by al-Qaida, animal liberation activists and the situation in Northern Ireland in the late 1990s and 2000s. It responded with suppressive measures to the challenge posed by global jihadis, with new legislation enacted to address the threat of international terrorism even before 9/11. By contrast, it adhered basically to the rule of law in addressing the violent actions of animal liberation activists, an approach that reflected the government's recognition that there was considerable public sympathy for the issues that activists highlighted, though rarely for their methods. At the same time, the peace process in Northern Ireland required the altogether different approach of accommodation. The focus was on ensuring the durability of the paramilitary ceasefires, as well as ensuring that the number of defectors from the peace process remained as small as possible. In popular parlance, these became known as dissidents, though the government preferred the term residual terrorism to describe the continuation of political violence, albeit on a much reduced scale, after the achievement of a political settlement in the form of the Belfast Agreement of April 1998.

Justifying these different approaches presented difficulties when comparisons were made among them, especially because in the case of the Northern Ireland peace process the adoption of an accommodationist approach entailed the repudiation of the previous approaches of suppression and of criminalisation. In particular, there was wide acceptance during the peace process that the government's introduction of internment without trial had been a major error that had fuelled the conflict. Further, it was widely anticipated that the result of the setting up of the Saville inquiry into the events of Bloody Sunday when 14 civilians had been killed by paratroopers during a civil rights demonstration in Londonderry in January 1972 would be the prelude to the government's acceptance of wrongdoing by the army, as indeed it was, though conveniently without anyone in particular being held to account. In the case of criminalisation, what was repudiated was the denial of the political motivation of those engaged in paramilitary activities, whether as Loyalists or Republicans.

When pressed on the contrast between the government's response to al-Qaida and to the IRA, Blair emphasised that there were huge differences between the two in the form of terrorism they employed. In particular, he argued that the IRA would never have sought to have killed 3,000 people as al-Qaida had on 9/11. He also contended that the aims of Irish Republicans were limited and amenable to negotiation, unlike the objectives he ascribed to al-Qaida.[6] Yet, ironically, the assumption made by government ministers that Britain faced a generation of attacks by global jihadis seems to have had little other basis than simply the fact that the Provisional IRA's terrorist campaign lasted roughly 25 years. For the United States, without the experience in the twentieth century of terrorism within its borders on the scale of Northern Ireland's Troubles, the most relevant precedents for 9/11 were the Japanese attack on Pearl Harbor in December 1941 in which over 2,400 people were killed and the 1995 bombing of the Alfred P. Murrah Federal Building in Oklahoma City in which 168 people died.

In part because of the sheer scale of the attacks on 9/11, the first of these precedents proved far more influential in how the United States responded to the challenge posed by al-Qaida, though in retrospect it is possible to argue that the approach taken in response to the Oklahoma City bombing would have proved much less costly. However, the notion of seeking punishment of the perpetrators through a legal process lacked credibility in the context of a suicide mission in which those directly involved were already dead. A lengthy process of holding to account anyone alive who could have been linked to the plot did not seem to meet the immediate need to deter any possible further mass-casualty attacks and thereby to reassure the public that their safety was not in jeopardy. At the same time, from the outset,

---

[6] Discussed in Adrian Guelke, *Terrorism and Global Disorder* (London, I. B. Tauris, 2006), pp. 212–214.

the Bush Administration was determined that its response to 9/11 would serve its pre-existing foreign policy agenda. From the beginning, neo-conservatives pressed for the inclusion of regime change in Iraq as part of America's Global War on Terror. And one of the driving forces behind the use of torture at the start of the war in Iraq in 2003 was the quest for evidence that could be used to make a plausible case for the existence of links between Saddam Hussein and Osama bin Laden.[7] As with the quest for evidence of the regime's weapons of mass destruction, nothing was turned up to justify the confident assertions of Vice-President Cheney, among others, that were used to secure public support for the war. For the neo-conservatives, the overthrow of Saddam Hussein was not an end in itself but rather part of a much larger project to use American power, especially the country's military capacity, to secure American global hegemony. However, the neo-conservatives were not alone in pursuing this agenda. Liberal interventionists, too, sought to advance what had been dubbed the Washington consensus in the aftermath of the end of the Cold War.

In contrast to the controversy generated by the war in Iraq, there was wide international support for the military action that was taken by the United States, with the support of other Western states, against the Taliban regime in Afghanistan. As the Taliban had provided a safe haven for Osama bin Laden and al-Qaida, the justification for overthrowing the Taliban in order to root out al-Qaida was straightforward. And the ease and speed with which the regime was overthrown appeared to vindicate the actions taken. However, it became apparent relatively quickly that American assumptions about the nature of al-Qaida were mistaken. In particular, there was no vast terrorist fortress to be found in the caves of Tora Bora. Nothing like the den of a villain in a James Bond film had ever existed. At the same time, rooting out al-Qaida was to prove surprisingly difficult, with the interplay of regional geo-strategic interests acting as an obstacle to the achievement of American aims. Thus, it took the Americans nearly a decade following 9/11 to find and kill Osama bin Laden.

In the aftermath of 9/11, a number of measures were adopted to protect civilian airliners from being hijacked so as to be used as flying bombs or simply blown up in flight. And while civilian aviation continued to be a target of terrorist attacks, most of the attempts to interfere with passenger airlines failed. The main exception was the destruction of two Russian civilian airliners in 2004. It is worth noting in this context that since the start of civilian aviation, several planes have been blown up in bomb attacks during flight

---

[7] Scahill, *Dirty Wars*, p.150.

in episodes unrelated to terrorism or the pursuit of any political objective. Notwithstanding the Global War on Terror, the pattern of international terrorism in the decade following 9/11 was much the same as it had been in the previous decade. Despite the lethality of some of the attacks, international terrorism of all kinds, however widely defined, accounts for a tiny proportion of the numbers who have been killed in civil wars and other forms of violence within states, including terrorism. Admittedly, it is not easy to draw a sharp line between international and domestic terrorism in countries such as Iraq and Afghanistan that have been subjected to foreign occupation or in cases where the boundaries between states have become unclear.

Nevertheless, in one way or another, the vast majority of acts of international terrorism – at least from a Western perspective – in the last two decades could be characterised as part of the religious wave of terrorism, to use Rapoport's taxonomy. The modus operandi most closely associated with this wave has been simultaneous suicide attacks designed to cause the maximum number of casualties. While this methodology now tends to be seen as a hallmark of al-Qaida, it dates back to the early 1980s, most notably to the attacks on American and French troops in Beirut in 1983. At the same time, while many of the attacks since 9/11, such as those in Bali, Madrid and London, have been attributed to al-Qaida or seen as inspired by Osama bin Laden's message, it is open to question as to whether they should be considered part of the same terrorist campaign. Indeed, beyond the vague notion espoused by Osama bin Laden of attacking the far enemy, it is hard to discern a common strategic calculation behind the attacks. Further, it has been evident in the statements that perpetrators of these attacks have made that they were motivated for the most part by the pursuit of revenge for actions taken by the West in response to 9/11. The theme of revenge on society as a whole or a section of it has featured in a number of the cases of mass shootings in the United States that have occurred during the twenty-first century. Generally, these have been the acts of individuals, though there have also been cases of close friends or couples acting together. Very few of these cases have been described as acts of terrorism, notwithstanding their lethality. The exceptions have been where the perpetrator has been Muslim and wherever even the most tenuous association with jihadi groups has been found. However, it is arguable that a number of these episodes, which have received massive publicity in the media as proof of the continuing potency of the threat to the West of global jihadis and of terrorism with a global reach, properly belong in the realm of violent actions by the mentally disturbed.

Interpretation of attacks on the West or on Western tourists that have been carried out by jihadi groups since 9/11 is made difficult by the lack of a clear, let alone common, purpose to these attacks, other than as a response to the Global War on Terror. However, it is important not to conflate this issue with nativist reaction to the West's post-Cold War promotion of globalisation and the Washington consensus. In countries where a substantial proportion of the population are Muslims, such as Nigeria, Somalia and Mali, this has tended to take the form of support for religiously fundamentalist movements in which ethnic and regional identities also form part of the mix. A basis for linking these very different forms of violence has been attacks on tourists that have been carried out both by these movements and by much smaller groups linked in one way or another to global jihadi networks. Another complicating factor has been the recruitment of Muslims living in the West into movements such as the Taliban in Afghanistan, Al Shabaab in Somalia and, more recently, the Islamic State of Iraq and the Levant (known as ISIS) that has spread its control across large parts of both Syria and Iraq. The concern expressed in a number of Western countries has been that when these recruits return to the West, they will present a security threat on an analogy with the threat posed to a number of Arab countries in the 1990s by fighters returning from the jihad against the Soviet Union in Afghanistan in the 1980s. But the analogy is scarcely exact and any violence recruits engage in on their return home may not have the sanction of ISIS.

A notable feature of the interpretation of jihadi violence against the West or Westerners among both Western governments and in the media has been an unwillingness to accept the role that the West's own actions have played in provoking the relatively small number of attacks that have taken place since 9/11. Instead, the authorities have deployed a model of radicalisation within Muslim communities to explain the attacks. The model assumes that individuals who turn to violence progress through a series of stages under the influence of propagandists in these communities or on the internet. In this account, alienation from Western foreign policy is seen as one of the warning signs that an individual may be susceptible to radicalisation. Given the surveillance to which Muslim minorities in the West have been subjected, this has had a chilling effect on debate on foreign policy in these communities. In the light of governments' dislike of criticism of their policies, this effect perhaps enhances the appeal of the radicalisation model. Certainly, Western governments seem to go to absurd lengths to promote this model in the media and among researchers on terrorism, despite its very obvious flaws, including that nothing whatever can be learnt about the tiny number of individuals who engage in terrorism from the fact that they share certain views, when these views are also held by hundreds of thousands of people who have never broken the law.

Fear of jihadi violence within Western societies has been out of all proportion to its occurrence since 9/11 as numerous scholars, including, most
powerfully, John Mueller in voluminous writings on the subject, have
pointed out.[8] Perhaps the most egregious aspect of the exaggeration of the
terrorist threat has been a number of cases in both the United States and the
United Kingdom in which plots have been manufactured by the authorities
through the entrapment in sting operations of suggestible individuals quite
incapable of having acted on their own initiative.[9] They have included situ-
ations in which police agents have sought to bribe individuals close to or
below the poverty line with vast sums of money for participating in hare-
brained schemes in which all the material for the proposed outrage has been
provided by the authorities. Far from exposing these abuses, the media has
largely been complicit in lending credibility to the claims of prosecutors that
the victims of this entrapment were really dangerous terrorists. They have
also been failed by a legal system in the two countries. In the case of the
United Kingdom, there are similarities with how Irish suspects were treated
at the height of Northern Ireland's Troubles, when the Provisional IRA's
mainland bombing campaign led to a series of miscarriages of justice. As
the Irish were treated then as a suspect community, so are Muslims today
under the pervasive influence of Islamophobia, particularly in the press, including both tabloids and broadsheets.

To his credit, President Barack Obama has sought to extricate the United
States from the wars launched by his predecessor as part of the Global War
on Terror. During his first term of office, he sought, though without much
success, to substitute the notion that the United States was engaged in 'overseas contingency operations' rather than a 'Global War on Terror'.[10] His
objective was to move America away from the idea that it faced a never-
ending threat from global jihadis that required the persistence of extraordinary measures. At the inauguration for his second term as President, he
declared: 'A decade of war is now ending. We, the people, still believe that
enduring security and lasting peace do not require perpetual war.'[11] In terms
of the approaches discussed above, President Obama has clearly been seeking to shift American counter-terrorism policy and practice from one of suppression to the rule-of-law model of criminalisation. However, formidable
difficulties remain in his path, not least the opposition of neo-conservatives

[8] See, for example, John Mueller and Mark G. Stewart, *Terror, Security, and Money* (New York,
Oxford University Press, 2011).
[9] See, for example, Kandnani, *The Muslims are Coming!*, pp. 188–193.
[10] Peter Baker, 'The Words have Changed, but have the Policies?', *New York Times*, 3 April 2009.
[11] Quoted in Scahill, *Dirty Wars*, p. 513.

and others who regard any constraints on American action as a threat to their project of ensuring the country's global hegemony throughout the course of the twenty-first century.

President Obama spoke at length on his approach to counter-terrorism in a speech at the National Defense University on 23 May 2013. It is worth analysing this in some detail. At the outset, he sought to present a nuanced picture of the threats that America faces from terrorism. He argued that the core of al-Qaida no longer posed a major threat to America and he pointed out that al-Qaida had not carried out a single attack on the American homeland since 9/11. Thus, it had not been responsible for the attack on the Boston marathon in 2013. He accepted that al-Qaida affiliates, such as al-Qaida in the Arabian Peninsula, had attempted to attack the American homeland, but that generally the threat that such groups posed were to Americans working in the countries where these affiliates were based. He added that the home-grown terrorism of 'radicalised individuals'[12] also presented a threat, but he included a range of cases under this heading, including hate crimes against minorities and not simply the actions of people who might have been influenced by the concept of a global jihad. While his account did not exclude the possibility of further mass-casualty attacks, he largely discounted the likelihood of another attack on the scale of 9/11 itself. He assessed these threats to America and Americans as being on a similar level to those that the country had faced before 9/11.

Obama then went on to discuss how these threats might be met by a comprehensive counter-terrorism strategy that did not rely solely on the use of force. In this context, he emphasised the importance of the battle of ideas to counter the ideology that underpinned much but by no means all of the terrorism that threatened America. He also underlined the importance of partnerships with other countries in tackling terrorism. However, he then went on to examine the difficult cases in which the United States could not achieve its preferred option of detaining, interrogating and prosecuting terrorists. In particular, he argued that there were parts of the world where ordinary processes of law enforcement were not possible and where even the option of using special operations forces to capture terrorists was not feasible. And even if feasible, the costs of a mission to capture a terrorist or terrorists through these means might not be justified by the risks to the members of the special operations forces or to the local population. Political damage to America's relations with the country concerned might also rule

---

[12] *Remarks by the President at the National Defense University* (The White House, Office of the Press Secretary, 23 May 2013) – http://www.whitehouse.gov/the-press-office/2013/05/23/remarks-president-national-defense-university (accessed August 2014).

out this option. In these circumstances, he argued that the use of drones to kill particular individuals could be justified. However, he conceded that the deployment of this new technology raised 'profound questions – about who is targeted and why, about civilian casualties and about the risk of creating new enemies, about the legality of such strikes under U.S. and international law, about accountability and morality'.[13]

He then sought to address these points. While he insisted that America's response to 9/11 had been lawful, he accepted that the fight against terrorism had entered a different phase that required changes to the country's counter-terrorism strategy. He also acknowledged that the use of drones to target individuals, which had increased sharply under his Presidency, had caused civilian casualties. He announced that he had signed guidelines the day before his speech to impose constraints on the use of drones. He set out their import as follows:

> Beyond the Afghan theatre, we only target al Qaeda and its associated forces. And even then the use of drones is heavily constrained. American does not take strikes when we have the ability to capture individual terrorists, our preference is always to detain, interrogate and prosecute. America cannot take strikes whenever we choose, our actions are bound by consultations with partners, and respect for state sovereignty.
>
> America does not take strikes to punish individuals, we act against terrorists who pose a continuing and imminent threat to the American people, and when there are no other governments capable of effectively addressing the threat. And before any strike is taken, there must be near-certainty that no civilians will be killed or injured – the highest standard we can set.[14]

He went on to argue in the spirit of an accommodationist approach to counter-terrorist strategy that the underlying grievances that fuelled extremist views needed to be tackled.

Other issues that Obama addressed in his speech were his ongoing efforts to close the detention centre at Guantanamo Bay in Cuba that Bush had established; the need ultimately to repeal the Authorisation to Use Military Force that underpinned the Global War on Terror; and, more briefly, spying and leaks of government secrets. In this context, he spoke of the need for a balance to be struck between the protecting of classified information and a free press and between security and citizens' rights to privacy.

---

[13] *Remarks of the President*, May 2013.
[14] *Remarks of the President*, May 2013.

There were a lot of loose ends in Obama's speech that reflected debate within the Administration over the content prior to its delivery. Inevitably, it fell far short of satisfying critics of American wrongdoing after 9/11. In particular, the manner in which the Administration interpreted 'continuing and imminent threat' went far beyond any reasonable understanding of those terms. Nonetheless, it was a much narrower criterion than the one that Obama's counter-terrorism adviser, John O. Brennan, had put forward of the individual posing a 'significant threat to U.S. interests'.[15]

A number of factors undermined Obama's hopes for a fresh start. Thanks to Wiki-Leaks, amongst others, practically the full extent of American wrongdoing – and its authorisation at the highest levels of government under his predecessor – had been laid bare, but the wars that Obama inherited meant that he had very little political room to repudiate this misconduct. At the same time, his own reputation was severely damaged by the revelations of spying by the National Security Agency, even though this was, in large part, the culmination of a long process that went back to the beginning of the Cold War of the growth of a secret state that operated with a minimum of political accountability. Much the same process had occurred in the other English-speaking states – the United Kingdom, Canada, Australia and New Zealand – that made up the so-called five eyes. Yet, until Snowden's revelations, the idea of the Anglosphere had seemed a right-wing fantasy rather than a long-established geo-strategic alliance to advance these countries' security and financial and commercial interests. Terrorism with a global reach provided a convenient justification for the further growth of these secret states, while technological change was in the process of massively increasing the capacity of the secret state to gather information on many millions of people.

Yet the political chaos around the world created by the interventionist policies the West has pursued since the end of the Cold War is testament to the fact that the possession of huge quantities of secretly obtained data of widely varying reliability has not conferred on the political leaders of the Anglosphere either control over events or the capacity to manage change. Secrets very commonly include misinformation. I have personal experience of this point. When I was a student in South Africa in the 1960s, I was involved in a project that had been initiated by an international charity to set up a third-level college of adult education and training in Botswana. However, the project's acronym of CADET led the apartheid government to imagine that there was a sinister intent behind this wholly educational endeavour. This came to light as a result of the controversy generated by

---

[15] Quoted in Peter Baker, 'In Terror Shift, Obama Took a Long Path', *New York Times*, 27 May 2013.

the government's banning under the Suppression of Communism Act of a student leader who had invited Senator Robert Kennedy to South Africa to deliver a speech on academic freedom. Commentators who think that Western intelligence agencies are incapable of making similar mistakes are deluding themselves. In this context, I should note that after I came to the United Kingdom in the 1970s, I became aware that material on my South African special branch file had been passed on to British intelligence and, it seems, without any correction of its entirely false assumptions.

Another factor that has thwarted Obama's efforts to chart a new course for the United States in foreign policy has been blowback from the actions of the Bush Administration. Nowhere has this been more apparent than in the Middle East. In the face of the advance of ISIS in Iraq in 2014, the Obama Administration deployed drones, even though the situation clearly did not meet the criteria he had set out for their use in 2013, not least because ISIS could hardly be labelled an affiliate of al-Qaida, even if ISIS is similarly based on Sunni fundamentalism and acts as ruthlessly as al-Qaida. The Administration justified its action as a limited humanitarian operation to protect American citizens and vulnerable ethnic minorities in Iraq. Throughout his Presidency, Obama has faced calls to extend the scope of American military intervention, despite the failure of the wars in Afghanistan and Iraq to create the basis for stable, constitutional government in either country. His critics have latched on to the fresh horrors in the arc of instability across the Middle East and Central Asia to argue for further military intervention, while portraying President Obama's caution in the light of past failures of the use of American military power to effect constructive political change as weakness.

Obama's thoughtful approach to counter-terrorism strategy has been the exception rather than the rule among the West's political leaders since 9/11. Few other leaders have been willing even to acknowledge the dangers that the adoption of a suppressive approach to the threat of mass-casualty terrorism poses to democracy. Part of the explanation is the expectation that the public will blame them if they prove unable to prevent a fresh outrage on anything like the scale of 9/11 and avoiding that possibility has become their highest priority. Another part of the explanation is that those principally affected by surveillance and other measures that governments have adopted to meet the threat have been members of ethnic minorities with cultural practices that arouse considerable prejudice among significant sections of Western societies. Compounding the problem – and increasing the disposition of governments to sacrifice all manner of liberties in the quest to re-establish control over events – has been the transnational nature of the jihadi threat. At the same time, despite the moral panic within

Western societies over this threat, Western foreign policies have been in-fluenced by a multitude of factors, including the pursuit of geo-strategic advantage over rivals. As a result, in a number of instances – even after 9/11 – Western states have been de facto allies of jihadi groups, as in the ill-considered effort to overthrow the autocratic Assad regime in Syria. In these circumstances and especially in the light of the negative outcomes of their policies, it is hardly surprising that many government leaders have preferred to cover up or to lie about the actions they have authorised rather than provide a honest account of their motivation to a public generally indifferent to the complexities of foreign affairs.

7

How and Why Do Terrorist Campaigns End?

AUDREY KURTH CRONIN

THE THREAT OF RADICAL JIHADI TERRORISM appears to be endless. No sooner did Western governments speak of reduced danger from al-Qaida than a new off-shoot, the Islamic State of Iraq and Syria (ISIS)[1] emerged and launched a brutal campaign that even al-Qaida leader Ayman al-Zawahiri found excessive. In the midst of this violence and rhetoric it is difficult to make sense of the threat.

Studying how and why terrorist campaigns end enables us to put al-Qaida, ISIS and all other such groups into a broader historical and strategic framework. Most scholars focus upon the origins of groups, assuming that doing so will yield insight into what drives them and how to defeat them. My research indicates that this approach is only partly revealing, if not backwards. The causes of terrorist groups – the motivations that initially drive them to target civilians as a way to achieve political aims – rarely persist over the course of a campaign and are not the crucial elements leading to their demise. To develop effective counter-terrorism, it is much more important to understand and dissect what happens during the final phase of campaigns, and why. Looking at how terrorist groups decline and end enables us to identify and trace classic patterns of endings across campaigns, and it is a more promising way to push them in that direction.

Understanding how terrorist campaigns end informs (or should inform) policy. It is the only way for states to be strategic in their counter-terrorism. Processes of ending for terrorist campaigns hold within them the best insights into which counter-terrorism policies succeed and which ones fail, and why.

---

[1] This group is also known as the Islamic State (IS), the Islamic State of Iraq and the Levant (ISIL), or by a loose acronym of the Arabic words Dawlat al-Islāmiyya fī al-Irāq wa s-Shām, pronounced 'Daesh'. Many (including the French government) prefer to use this acronym, as it echoes the Arabic words *Daes* (meaning to tread underfoot, crush) and *Dahes* (one who sows discord). Daesh is also how it is referred to in the Arab world. See Adam Taylor, 'France is Ditching the Islamic State Name and Replacing it with a Label the Group Hates', *The Washington Post*, 17 September 2014, at http://www.washingtonpost.com/blogs/worldviews/wp/2014/09/17/france-is-ditching-the-islamic-state-name-and-replacing-it-with-a-label-the-group-hates/.

Proceedings of the British Academy **203**, 111–124. © The British Academy 2015.

Whether the group is gaining or losing strength and momentum, understanding classic patterns of endings enables thoughtful leaders to avoid common mistakes and gauge how well government counter-terrorism efforts are faring. It also helps to inure policy-makers and their publics from the classic strategies of terrorism, which are designed to enrage, provoke, inspire or intimidate. Reminding ourselves that terrorist campaigns end enlarges our perspective beyond the action/reaction dynamic that is central to terrorism's emotional manipulation of the audience. It helps to distinguish counter-terrorism measures that are hastening a group's demise from those that are interfering with it. The goal is to offer a mental framework for how to think strategically about the evolution of the threat of terrorism and the counter-terrorism response to it, so as to provide a broader context and gain a more balanced perspective of risk.

To accomplish this goal, we will first analyse four classic strategies of terrorism and consider why Western democracies have particular difficulty responding to them. Second, we will briefly review six historical patterns of endings for terrorist organisations that have emerged from scholarly research on hundreds of groups. In light of these six patterns, the concluding section assesses which counter-terrorism policies have hastened al-Qaida's demise and which have not, also reflecting upon the rise of ISIS and its significance going forward.

The strategies of terrorism

Terrorism is not a fight between peer competitors, except perhaps on the level of instinct and emotion. States are virtually always militarily, financially and institutionally stronger than terrorist groups. By arguing that they have no alternative, terrorist group leaders use symbolic violence against innocents to even the odds by challenging the state's ability to protect its most vulnerable citizens. Shocking violence aims to undermine state credibility, gain attention and elicit a passionate response. Officials, especially democratic leaders, cannot help but react to popular sentiments and anxieties among their constituencies, resulting in tactical responses that are satisfying in the short-term but undermine a state's long-term strategic interests. So a dynamic of interactive terrorist attacks and state reactions unfolds. It is deadly difficult for governments to be strategic in response to terrorism, and terrorist attacks are deliberately designed to exploit that vulnerability.

Indeed, the core concepts and foundational ideas of twentieth-century Western strategic thinking undermine effective counter-terrorism in the twenty-first century. The archetype of the last century's strategic theory is the development of air power, especially the (apparent) successes of strategic bombardment during the Second World War. Terrorist attacks typically involve bombings, kill civilians and challenge the public will. Anyone who witnessed the attacks of 9/11 would easily see the parallels with strategic bombing, in both their physical effects and their psychological impact upon survivors. It is a seductive, oversimplified paradigm. The instinctive response is to retaliate massively, as if the state were answering the actions of another state. The deep fear expressed by policy-makers in the Bush Administration – that the 2001 attacks orchestrated by al-Qaida were prelude to more devastating nuclear attacks on the American homeland – confirms the direct line they drew intellectually from strategic bombing, to nuclear attack, to terrorist attack. The regrettable extension of that logic into the 2003 invasion of Iraq (a state with no connection with bin Laden's organisation at the time) is further proof. US National Security Advisor Condoleezza Rice famously stated that while there would always be uncertainty about Iraq's nuclear capabilities, 'We don't want the smoking gun to be a mushroom cloud.'[2] From the perspective of senior US officials whose formative experience was the bipolar Cold War confrontation, those shocking al-Qaida assaults represented the opening salvo in a war of annihilation that might soon escalate to nuclear attack.

The problem is that this kind of strategic thinking is unsuited to the strategies of terrorism, which must be understood not from the perspective of the targeted state and its military frameworks but from that of the terrorist group and its aims. Terrorist groups are not peer competitors with the legitimacy and structures of other states. They may call their forces 'armies', but most terrorist groups lack the state's organised military apparatus and instead seek to build power by draining off a state's strengths. They cannot fight states as equals. Which strategy a group uses depends upon which target it is trying to influence and draw strength from at a given time. Terrorist groups gain strength and weaken states by using violence to do one of three things: either undermine the state's contract with its own citizens; elicit actions that are at odds with the state's interests; or draw support from third-party audiences. When terrorist attacks threaten a state's purpose or change its behaviour, they can drive the state to cede power and even defeat itself.

Unfortunately, many policy-makers persist in seeing the strategies of terrorism strictly within the two-sided frameworks of coercion and compellence,

---

[2] Wolf Blitzer, 'Search for the "Smoking Gun"', 10 January 2003, *CNN.com*, at http://www.cnn.com/2003/US/01/10/wbr.smoking.gun/ [accessed 9 October 2014].

concepts of nuclear strategy first laid out in the 1960s.[3] By this way of thinking, terrorism looks like a kind of counter-value targeting engaged in by non-
state actors. Sometimes the framework is accurate: terrorist attacks may try to
force states to withdraw from foreign commitments or make those commitments so painful that domestic pressure forces a government to abandon them.
Policy-makers cite the US and French withdrawals from Lebanon in 1983, the
US withdrawal from Somalia in 1993 and the Spanish withdrawal of troops
from Iraq in 2004 as examples of what al-Qaida and its associates were trying
to accomplish. ISIS has used numerous approaches, but compellence is its
primary strategy. American political scientists use the same framework: the
deeply embedded use of game theory, developed by economists and later used
as a foundation for nuclear deterrence theory, has led to causal models driven
primarily by the interaction between two rational actors: state and group.

But terrorism is a messy business and this two-sided framework does not
fully capture all of its purposes. It has always been an incomplete picture of
Osama bin Laden's logic and strategy, for example, which is obvious after
reading his speeches and *fatwas* (something few Americans do). When terrorist attacks are used to influence an audience, an attack upon a state and
its citizens may be the means to bring about an *irrational* state reaction or to
inspire, intimidate or even marginalise a completely different group of people
that is of interest to the group. Unfortunately, in creating its counter-terrorism
strategy, the US and its allies tended to focus exclusively on compellence
while ignoring other classic strategies of terrorism.

Provocation, polarisation and mobilisation are strategies of leverage that
are common in the history of terrorism. Provocation was most dominant
in the late-nineteenth century, often associated with the action–repression–
uprising cycle envisioned by Carlo Pisacane, Luigi Galleani and other
advocates of 'propaganda of the deed'. Its goal was to try to force the state
to *do something* – not a specific policy, but a brutal reaction that undercut
its legitimacy and worked against its interests. The best example was the
Russian group *Narodnaya Volya*, whose goal was to attack representatives
of the tsarist regime, force a brutal crackdown and bring about a peasant uprising. Brazilian revolutionary Carlos Marighella, in his 1969 *Minimanual
of the Urban Guerrilla*, further developed the concept in the twentieth century. There are many twentieth-century cases of provocation, including the
Basque group Fatherland and Liberty's (Euskadi Ta Askatasuna, or ETA)

---

[3] Some people use the term 'coercion' (the use of force or threatened use of force), but coercion can
be mixed with diplomacy and other positive inducements. Compellence refers here strictly to threats
or negative actions designed to change behaviour. The concepts were first developed in Thomas
Schelling, *Arms and Influence* (New Haven, Yale University Press, 1967).

early strategy in Spain, the Sandinista National Liberation Front's strategy in Nicaragua and the National Liberation Front's (NLF) strategy during Algeria's war of independence from France. From the perspective of a terrorist group, a strategy of provocation is risky and imprecise: it often drives a state to react in unforeseen ways that hurt state interests while also crushing the group. Then, as is so often the case with terrorism, everyone loses.

A second strategy of leverage is polarisation, where terrorist groups use violent attacks to divide the population and delegitimise the state from within, ultimately preventing it from governing. This strategy targets different ethnic, racial, nationalist, religious or sectarian residents, fracturing the domestic politics of the state, again driving regimes sharply to the right. Authoritarian behaviour emerges, compromising political freedoms and ultimately forcing populations to choose between aligning with the state or with the group. Polarisation strategies also appeared regularly during the twentieth century; they are especially useful to groups trying to force political change in democracies. It is difficult to respond effectively to this strategy, because the imperative to distinguish between those carrying out attacks and those targeted by them makes the problem even worse. It tempts governments to profile, perpetuate stereotypes and drive communities further apart along the very lines of attack that terrorists open up. Examples of groups that have deliberately tried to polarise communities include the LTTE in Sri Lanka and the PIRA in Northern Ireland. The Armed Islamic Group (GIA) in Algeria employed this strategy in a most extreme way, slaughtering as many as 100,000 people during Algeria's civil war in the 1990s.[4]

The last strategy of leverage is mobilisation, where leaders use terrorist attacks to inspire, recruit and mobilise a following. If a terrorist group is trying to mobilise supporters, its actions are not necessarily directed toward changing the behaviour of the state at all. State actions are a means, not an end in themselves. The group is far more interested in enlarging its resources, both people and assets, than in destroying the state – an aim that is unrealistic with strong states anyway.

A strategy of mobilisation aims to attack high-profile targets so as to bring attention to the cause, build stature and draw resources, including recruits, allies, sympathisers and passive supporters. For example, the 1972 Munich Olympics massacre rallied attention, sympathy and support for the cause of Palestinian nationalism in exactly this way. Before 1972, the Palestine Liberation Organisation (PLO) was a relatively unknown organisation: the horrified

---

[4] Rami Khouri, 'Algeria's Terrifying but Unsurprising Agony', *Middle East Review of International Affairs*, March 1998.

fascination of millions of television viewers permanently erased that obscu-
rity. Al-Qaida leaders' own public and private declarations clearly state that
mobilisation is the pre-eminent goal of the group and its associates. In 2001,
Ayman al-Zawahiri described mobilisation as a key reason for attacking the
'far enemy', namely the US and its Western allies, rather than focusing on
more controversial domestic enemies, meaning local regimes such as Egypt
and Saudi Arabia. The top goal was never to defeat the United States. The
logic, according to Zawahiri, was to use a clear-cut case of targeting 'in-
fidels', so as to mobilise the Muslim umma (community), hit high-profile
targets, attract vast media attention, lionise al-Qaida and draw jihadi recruits.[5] Indeed, strategies of mobilisation are extremely well suited for the
twenty-first-century globalised world, with its democratisation of access to
information, sharp reduction in cost of messages and virtually instantaneous
communications (especially images), allowing movements of all kinds to
mobilise on a scale and at a speed that is unprecedented.

These four strategies – compellence, provocation, polarisation and mobilisation – are not mutually exclusive and may be used in combination. Some
groups even use different approaches at different times, as the dynamic of
a campaign unfolds and both sides react. But wise counter-terrorism strategies must discern between them, because state reactions within one strategic
framework are counter-productive within another. For example, if a state assumes that a terrorist group is trying to change its behaviour through a frontal
strategy such as compellence, it may respond in a way that feeds into indirect
strategies of leverage such as provocation, polarisation and mobilisation. De-
pending on the context, states can respond with overwhelming military force,
for example, only to encourage increased mobilisation of support for a group.
The result is that the group or cause strengthens and the state loses ground. It
is easy to strike a blow against a terrorist group and kill current members; it
is difficult to end it.

This is why it is crucial to understand how terrorist groups end. In the
midst of a campaign it can be difficult to dispassionately assess the effects of
counter-terrorism tactics. The goal is not to achieve a temporary advantage
but to drive a group toward its own demise. And in the endings of hundreds
of terrorist campaigns, indirect strategies of leverage predominate far more
than direct strategies of compellence. Democratic governments who see the
group as an equal actor, answering its attacks in an action/reaction dynamic,
satisfy the short-term politics of domestic constituencies but prolong counter-
terrorism campaigns. Driving a terrorist group toward its *end*, on the other

---

[5] Ayman al-Zawahiri, *Knights Under the Prophet's Banner*, pp. 75 and 78.

hand, demands parrying indirect strategies of leverage through nuanced and historically informed counter-terrorism policies that take a longer view.

Patterns of endings for terrorist groups

As the preceding discussion of strategies of terrorism demonstrates, seeing any terrorist campaign as a two-sided battle between a group and a government is incomplete and misleading. Terrorism involves three strategic actors, each exercising differing influences on the termination of campaigns. Some pathways of decline are more under the control of the state, some are more related to the group and others are more influenced by outside observers. The only way to fully understand how groups end is to see the dynamic relationship between all three actors: group, target and audience. Patterns of decline and demise reflect factors that are both internal and external to a group, and do not always bear a direct relationship to state actions taken against them.

With this in mind, the research undertaken for my book[6] examines the experience of hundreds of groups. It includes scrutiny of some 457 groups, drawn mainly from a database covering organisations operating after 1968, although some prominent earlier cases are also covered. The book considers all types of terrorism, including left-wing, right-wing, ethno-nationalist, separatist and religious or 'spiritualist' terrorism. Thus it is not confined strictly to jihadi terrorism, although the conclusions reached are relevant to the violent Islamist groups that we currently face. The work does not minimise or discount in any way the current threat of jihadi terrorism: groups are at various points in their trajectory of rising and falling, with a few clearly gaining strength. It also does not imply that terrorism, as a phenomenon, will end – only specific terrorist campaigns. The purpose of the project is to understand consistent historical patterns of endings for terrorist groups so as to recognise them consistently when facing the threats of today and tomorrow.

Out of this analysis emerged six general pathways that reappear consistently. They are not mutually exclusive: a group can display more than one dynamic for ending. But each terrorist group demonstrates at least one of these patterns.

The first pathway is decapitation, the capture or killing of the leader of the group. In my book, cases where the leader was arrested included France's

---

[6] For a full explanation of the strengths and weaknesses of the data behind this research, see Audrey Kurth Cronin, *How Terrorism Ends: Understanding the Decline and Demise of Terrorist Campaigns* (Princeton, NJ, Princeton University Press, 2009), especially the appendices.

Action Directe, El Salvador's Fuerzas Populares de Liberación, Japan's Shoko Asahara (leader of Aum Shinrikyo) and Peru's Abimael Guzmán, leader of Sendero Luminoso (Shining Path). Cases of assassination included the Philippines' Abu Sayyaf, Russian and Chechen separatist leaders and Israel's campaign of targeted killings against Palestinian groups. On the basis of that study, I concluded that publicly delegitimising a leader in the eyes of his followers or potential supporters, especially by parading him before cameras as in the case of Sendero's Guzmán, was strategically more effective than killing him, because it had important political effects on the cause and on his image. Through painstaking military and police work, an effective capture can avoid creating a martyr (as with Ché Guevara), yield a storehouse of intelligence (as with Peru's Guzmán), and publicly de-romanticise a popular cause (as with Indonesia's Nazir Abbas). Sometimes killing a leader was unavoidable, but groups that ended through assassination were hierarchically structured, characterised by a cult of personality, younger than most other groups and lacked a succession plan.[7]

With the current fixation on the use of armed unmanned aerial vehicles, or 'armed drones', to kill members of the al-Qaida network in places such as Yemen, Pakistan and Somalia, this approach has gained a widespread attention and is the source of hot controversy.[8] Although some terrorist attacks have been disrupted or prevented as a result of using of armed drones beyond the battlefield, al-Qaida has demonstrated the capacity to replace leaders – even Osama bin Laden, who had a plan of succession in place to follow his 2011 demise. The widespread anger against the US tactic, which progressed well beyond leadership decapitation to include a much broader range of targets including Taliban members and low-level operatives, shifted the attention away from al-Qaida's terrorism and caused outrage among US allies and enemies alike. While the United States has sought to minimise civilian casualties, increase transparency and reduce its reliance on drones, the far-reaching negative impact of the campaign lingers in US foreign policy. There is no reason to believe that targeted killings are ending the al-Qaida movement, especially when jihadi affiliates and offspring such as ISIS are taken into account.

---

[7] Important work has subsequently been done in this area. See especially Jenna Jordan, 'When Heads Roll: Assessing the Effectiveness of Leadership Decapitation', *Security Studies*, 18/4 (2009); Bryan C. Price, 'Targeting Top Terrorists: How Leadership Decapitation Contributes to Counterterrorism', *International Security*, 36/4 (2012); and Jenna Jordan, 'Attacking the Leader, Missing the Mark: Why Terrorist Groups Survive Decapitation Strikes', *International Security*, 38/4 (2014).

[8] For an argument about the pitfalls of such an approach, see Audrey Kronin 'Why Drones Fail: When Tactics Drive Strategy', *Foreign Affairs*, 92/4 (2013) and 'The Strategic Implications of Targeted Drone Strikes for U.S. Global Counterterrorism', in *The Ethical, Strategic, and Legal Implications of Drone Warfare*, edited by David Cortright, (Chicago, University of Chicago Press, 2015).

The second pathway is negotiation. While it is unusual for negotiations to lead to the demise of groups strictly on their own, they often contribute to their decline and ending as an integral part of a state's comprehensive approach to counter-terrorism.[9] Yet, the rate at which groups enter talks is lower than generally thought. In my research, only about 18% of the hundreds of groups had negotiated at all. Groups that entered talks tended to be older (20–25 years) than the rest (average age 8 years), so were more established. And once they started, the talks seemed to persist: only about 10% of those who negotiated gave up on the talks altogether and walked away. The predominant pattern was for talks to drag on, neither succeeding nor failing completely. And there are numerous cases of progress: a wide range of organisations such as the Provisional IRA in Northern Ireland, the Philippine Moro Islamic Liberation Front (MILF), the 19th of April Movement (M-19) in Colombia and the Guatemalan National Revolutionary Unity (URNG) have either reduced their violence or ended it altogether in the wake of negotiations. Sometimes governments lose patience and crush terrorist groups with military force after stopping and starting talks, as was the case with the Liberation Tigers of Tamil Eelam (LTTE) in Sri Lanka. Other times, the two sides go in and out of talks, as has been the case with ETA, which has episodically stopped and restarted its violence yet gradually lost support over time.

From a state's perspective, negotiations are best sought with older groups where governments have prepared their constituencies for a long-term process.[10] Indeed, the best way to think about negotiations is as a means to shift the violence or energy of an established group into a different channel.

Sometimes terrorist organisations fulfil their political objectives, so success is the third pathway to the end. Here it is vital to distinguish between tactical or 'process' goals, and strategic or 'outcome' goals. It is not at all uncommon for terrorist groups to achieve process goals such as increasing the strength of one faction compared to another (sometimes called 'outbidding'), showing strength or ruthlessness, lionising leaders, publicising the cause, exacting revenge, signalling, or simply surviving. Terrorists often succeed in perpetuating a campaign but that does not mean that they 'win'. Groups set their own terms: they succeed when the organisation's goals are achieved. Fortunately, strategic objectives are easy to spot: they are what terrorist group leaders describe as the long-term purpose of the campaign. Strategic goals

---

[9] This discussion also draws from my forthcoming article, 'Hostage Negotiations and Other Talks with Terrorists: Price vs. Principle', *Georgetown Journal of International Affairs*, Winter/Spring 2015.
[10] Promising and unpromising conditions for negotiations are described in chapter 2 of *How Terrorism Ends*, as well as in my *Negotiating with Groups that Use Terrorism: Lessons for Policy-makers*, Centre for Humanitarian Dialogue, Mediation Support Project, Oslo Forum, 2008.

may be political (relating to the state – its regime, organisation, boundaries, population), economic (redistributing resources or wealth), social (racial or ethnic identity, modernisation) or religious (relating to spiritualist identity, values, strictures, virtues), or some combination of these.

Looking at the overall historical record, terrorism does not achieve its strategic objectives very often. Of the 457 groups studied in depth in *How Terrorism Ends*, only about 5% had by their own standards achieved their objectives (even those that evolved over the lifetime of a group). There are two especially well-known case studies of groups that have succeeded: Umkhonto, the military wing of the African National Congress,[11] which succeeded when apartheid ended; and Irgun, which reached its political objective with the withdrawal of British forces and the establishment of the state of Israel in 1948. Even when terrorism does succeed, the transition to legitimate governance involves distancing the new regime from any history of terrorist attacks. Terrorism succeeds only when the state bungles its response or the group can attract sufficient support to grow and transition to other activities.

The fourth pathway to the end of terrorist campaigns is failure. The short, eight-year average life span of terrorist groups attests to the difficulty of using this kind of tactic for long. A large proportion of groups find it difficult to keep going for two main reasons: either they implode, burn out and collapse upon themselves; or they lose popular support and fizzle out that way. Implosion can occur because groups fail to pass the cause to the next generation, as with left-wing and anarchist groups of the 1970s such as the Weatherman and the Symbionese Liberation Army. Or they may succumb to in-fighting, disagreements about ideology, arguments over tactics, or other kinds of internal dissent. Brutal disputes can lead to fratricide: the Japanese group Aum Shinrikyo, the British 'White Power' group Combat-18 and the West German Second of June Movement all killed members who were suspected of disloyalty. On the other hand, popular support may be lost because the ideology becomes irrelevant (as with many Marxist groups post-1990), government counter-action makes it too risky to participate (as in Chechnya), or the government offers a better alternative, such as new spending, jobs and public benefits (as in Northern Ireland). And sometimes groups lose contact with their constituencies because they are isolated and under pressure.

---

[11] The degree to which the activities of Umkhonto we Sizwe (meaning 'Spear of the Nation', abbreviated as MK) led directly to the end of apartheid is debatable. Many argue that the counter-productive government response to the unrest played a more important role. In any case, the ANC formally renounced violence in August 1990 and declared that its campaign had ended. For an argument that MK played an insignificant role, see Adrian Guelke, *Terrorism and Global Disorder* (London, Tauris, 2006).

But a principal way to lose popular support is through targeting errors, where attacks cause revulsion among the very constituency the group is trying to attract. The resulting backlash can damage a group more dramatically than any state counter-terrorism measures. Two famous examples are GAI's killing of 62 tourists at the pyramids in Luxor, Egypt in 1997 and the Real IRA's car bombing of Omagh in 1998, both of which mobilised public anger against the groups. When a terrorist group commits a targeting error it undercuts the only source of its legitimacy, which is the claim to be acting altruistically on behalf of a larger constituency. If the constituency revolts, the group suffers because its members are revealed as nothing more than murderers.

Repression, the fifth pathway out of terrorism, is the approach states pursue most instinctively. This is hardly surprising. Modern nation-states base their legitimacy on the ability to protect their citizens; terrorism threatens this. Many counter-terrorism campaigns begin with overwhelming force either deployed internally, when the threat is mainly domestic, or externally, when the threat is based beyond the state's borders. Notable case studies of repression include Uruguay and the Tupamaros, Russia and Chechen rebels and Egypt and the Muslim brotherhood (1928–66).[12] Because of the enormous military advantage of most states, it is possible to end a terrorist campaign through repression, especially if the government is willing to destroy *everything*. But sometimes repression exports the cause to another place (as with Chechnya and Ingushetia, for example) or mutates it into a new form (as with Egypt and the origins of al-Qaida). Repression is particularly costly for democracies as it requires 'profiling' or discrimination of targets, tramples on civil liberties and human rights, places a strain on the fabric of the state and, by alienating its own citizens, weakens its ability to anticipate future terrorist campaigns. Especially in an age of globalised communications, brutal state action can worsen the terrorist threat over time by engendering a violent international backlash.

The last pathway is reorientation, meaning that terrorist campaigns transition out of primary reliance upon terrorist attacks toward either criminal behaviour or more traditional types of warfare. Criminal behaviour and terrorism overlap; indeed, the former often funds the latter. But converting fully to criminality means shifting away from acquiring assets as a means of achieving political objectives to amassing them as ends in themselves. Those fighting violent criminal networks sometimes argue that terrorism and criminality have become indistinguishable; but if the profit motive eclipses any altruistic political objective, it can affect a group's legitimacy in the eyes of

---

[12] All of these, and others, are analysed in greater depth in chapter 5 of *How Terrorism Ends*.

their constituencies and thus influence the degree to which they threaten state existence. Here the Revolutionary Armed Forces of Colombia (Fuerzas Armada Revolucionarias de Colombia, or FARC) and the Philippine group Abu Sayyaf come to mind. Some criminal groups need government infrastructure and would rather pay off corrupt officials than kill them.

The other way that groups transition is to escalate into full insurgency or even conventional war, especially if they are supported by states or can mimic state governance in a particular territory. Organisations that have successfully transitioned into insurgencies include the Sri Lankan Tamil Tigers (Liberation Tigers of Tamil Eelam, or LTTE), the Cambodian Khmer Rouge and the Communist party of Nepal-Maoists. Like crime and terrorism, insurgency and terrorism overlap – it would be foolish to posit a clear distinction between these evolving concepts. But there are differences of degree and emphasis, particularly in the strength of a movement and the nature of its targeting. Unlike terrorist groups, insurgencies operate as military units, are strong enough to engage military forces directly, are numerically larger and can seize and hold territory, even if temporarily. When groups become insurgencies it is always bad news for the state. The only good news is that this development puts a terrorist threat on more familiar ground for military forces.

Assessing al-Qaida and ISIS

As I first wrote in 2006, this analysis of how groups end indicates that al-Qaida's demise will unfold either through outright failure or transition to a different kind of threat.[13] The other four pathways are implausible and unpromising. Al-Qaida does not fit the profile of a group that ends through decapitation and, indeed, decapitation through drone attacks and even the killing of Osama bin Laden have not ended it. As for the second pathway, although there have been efforts to talk with some members of the Afghan Taliban, no negotiations are possible with core al-Qaida. Strategic success for al-Qaida is likewise impossible, as efforts to mobilise popular support behind bin Laden's group have fallen flat. Lastly, the limits of military repression have unfolded through two conventional conflicts in Iraq and Afghanistan, as well as a dramatic increase in both US Special Operations and targeted drone strikes. While these measures have degraded the al-Qaida leadership, especially in Pakistan and Afghanistan, and reduced its ability to carry out operations, military force has not ended the group and will not be able to do so. That leaves the pathways of failure and reorientation: while

---

[13] Audrey Kurth Cronin, 'How al-Qaeda Ends', *International Security*, 31/1 (2006).

failure is the outcome that we should have been striving hard to facilitate (or at least not impede), transition into an entirely new kind of insurgency is the result I fear is fully underway.

For years al-Qaida has had all the hallmarks of a group that could fail. Its popular support began to dissipate in 2007, as the group's killing of civilians, sectarian targeting, lack of religious authority and condemnation of other Muslims as 'apostates' repulsed Muslim populations throughout the world. Then the dramatic changes of the Arab Spring exposed the hollowness of al-Qaida's claim to be the vanguard of a Salafist revolution. The elation of popular uprisings in places like Egypt, Libya and Syria was followed by a devastating second act of governance failure, political struggle, violence and civil war. Some argued that the 'Arab Spring' had merely provided radical jihadis greater space in which to organise and take over; but nowhere in the aftermath of the uprisings did al-Qaida emerge as the dominant force. Al-Qaida had failed to be the catalyst for change – the role it had always promised to play in building a new future for all Muslims – and by 2011 al-Qaida core was a shadow of its former self.

Still, the United States failed to understand the political context for its regional counter-terrorism policies, removing political pressure from al-Qaida and placing it squarely upon itself, thus enabling al-Qaida spin-offs to draw recruits and pose a growing threat through the movement's metastasis. Ironically, those who argued that the United States should stay the course with its use of drones and special operations tended to be the same people who warned that the al-Qaida threat was spreading throughout the Middle East and Africa. Any strategic connection between one and the other was discounted or ignored. Al-Qaida affiliates especially in Yemen (al-Qaida in the Arabian Peninsula, AQAP), the Sahara (al-Qaida in the Islamic Maghreb, AQIM), Somalia (al-Shabab), Nigeria (Boko Haram) and Iraq (al-Qaida in Iraq) lost leaders but gained strength with a wave of popular anger fanned both by perceptions of US drone policy and the perceived lack of concern for the tens of thousands of Syrian civilians killed by chemical weapons and other atrocities. At the time of writing, half of the population of Syria has been displaced from its homes or residences, having fled to Lebanon, Turkey, Jordan and other neighbouring states.

In the middle of all this, the al-Qaida affiliate in Syria, Jamat al-Nusra openly feuded with ISIS and the two became bitter enemies. In February 2014, al-Qaida disavowed any ties with ISIS, which has now proven to be the stronger of the two organisations. ISIS has since attracted an unprecedented number of recruits, including from Europe, to a traditional ground campaign that has crossed the Syrian border and swept across Western Iraq. In July

2014, ISIS declared itself the 'Islamic State' and announced the establishment of a new Caliphate in the Iraqi/Syrian territory it occupied. No longer 'al-Qaida', ISIS transitioned from terrorist group to an insurgency and then a conventional army, with formidable weaponry, tactics and capability captured from a US-built Iraqi Army that ran away as the group advanced. The situation as it currently stands is that al-Qaida and its partner al-Nusra are on the defensive, with core al-Qaida seen as an anachronism, dramatically overshadowed by a brutally violent group that emerged from the remnants of an organisation that would never have existed had it not been for the ill-advised 2003 invasion of Iraq.

Despite their common rhetoric about returning to pre-modern Islam, ISIS is a very different group from al-Qaida. The sources of its demise will likewise be different. Even as it engaged in horrific terrorist attacks, al-Qaida consistently sought to mobilise the Muslim umma, reaching out to ordinary Muslims to convince them to follow. By contrast, ISIS has no such nuanced programme. It is not a terrorist group. It is stronger, more numerous, more wealthy and more dangerous than any terrorist organisation forced to rely on asymmetrical violence and strategies of leverage. Although it has a very sophisticated media presence, the goal of ISIS is old-fashioned territorial conquest and despotic governance. It is an unprecedented regional challenge that Iraq, regional neighbours, European allies and the United States must now struggle to meet. The only ray of hope in this picture is that, like other groups that have transitioned from terrorism to conventional warfare, ISIS is now a truly military threat that traditional militaries should be better suited to meet. In our failure to understand and shrewdly answer terrorist strategies, we may have found ourselves a brutal conventional enemy that we fully understand.

8

Why Terrorist Campaigns Do Not End

The Case of Contemporary
Dissident Irish Republicanism

RICHARD ENGLISH

WHO ARE IRELAND'S CONTEMPORARY DISSIDENT REPUBLICANS? Not all Irish republicans who dissent from Sinn Fein's contemporary peace-process orthodoxy have endorsed the use of violence, but the focus of this chapter will be upon those who have done so, and the term 'dissident republican' will be used to refer to these people. According to the UK Security Service (MI5), violent republican dissidents have represented the most sustainedly serious ongoing terrorist danger to the United Kingdom in recent years. At the time of writing, MI5 assessed the threat to the UK from international terrorism as 'substantial' ('a strong possibility'), while the threat from Northern Ireland-related (principally dissident republican) terrorism in Northern Ireland itself was judged to be 'severe' ('a terrorist attack is highly likely').[1] The fissiparous terrorist community which has generated this severe threat emerged out of militant Irish republican disaffection from a peace-process politics in Northern Ireland which they considered to be politically unacceptable. Some dissidents have been ex-PIRA members, providing experience, expertise, leadership, commitment, continuity, legitimacy and also some practical materials. In the words of the then Deputy Chief Constable of the Police Service of Northern Ireland (PSNI), Judith Gillespie, in 2011: 'There seems to be a slow seepage from old hands, old experienced hands from PIRA, either going back to dissident activity or at least lending some support from time to time, in terms

---

[1] UK Security Service web site, accessed on 31 July 2014. In descending order, MI5's UK threat levels are: Critical, Severe, Substantial, Moderate, Low. Even if other forms of terrorist threat are judged over time to grow, the broad point remains true: that dissident Irish republican violence in Northern Ireland has been assessed by the UK authorities over recent years as their most sustainedly serious terrorist challenge.

Proceedings of the British Academy **203**, 125–144. © The British Academy 2015.

of technical expertise, bomb-making expertise, advice.'[2] But this is a process with deep roots and (as so often in the long history of terrorism) there has been a jagged sequence of changes in allegiance, rather than any neatly single fault line in historical development. In 1986 a small group broke away from the Provisionals in reaction to the latter's decision to end their abstentionist policy towards the Republic of Ireland's Dublin parliament; the Continuity IRA (CIRA) and its associated political party Republican Sinn Fein (RSF) were the result. Another rupture came in 1997, when the Provisionals decided officially to endorse non-violent politics; here the Real IRA (RIRA) and its associated political organisation the 32-County Sovereignty Committee (later Movement, or 32CSM) emerged.

In addition to seasoned ex-Provos there have also been younger, newer recruits to dissident republican ranks (what might be called peace-process terrorists: people too young to have been involved in PIRA violence, and who might well have been born after one or both of the Provisionals' ceasefires of 1994 and 1997). Various groups have emerged in addition to the CIRA and RIRA, including rival groupings adopting the long-deployed republican name Óglaigh na hÉireann ('Volunteers of Ireland': the Irish-language title long claimed by those seeing themselves as the legitimate IRA) and, more significantly, in 2012 a body styling itself 'The IRA' and bringing together various dissident republican actors.

In comparison with the sustained, high-level violence of the PIRA in its post-1969 campaign, dissident republican violence has been limited. But the violent threat from those Irish republicans who consider physical force to be justified and necessary against British rule in any part of Ireland has now endured for years, after history's most enduring bearers of that flame – the Provisional IRA – eventually changed their mind about armed struggle. Dissident violence baffles many, and generates understandable condemnation. On Tuesday 29 July 2014 in Derry, a dissident gun attack on a PSNI land-rover did not manage to kill anybody, but did prompt Ulster Unionist member of the Policing Board Ross Hussey to condemn those behind the attack as 'fascists'.[3] Similar denunciations have occurred many times, with dissidents being branded merely criminal, or psychopaths, or gangsters without political support.

By contrast, my argument here is that it is only by situating Ireland's contemporary dissident republicans within the framework of a very recognisable nationalist politics that we can explain them and their persistence.

---

[2] Judith Gillespie, interviewed by the author, Belfast, 15 April 2011.
[3] *Irish News*, 31 July 2014.

This requires that we clearly define what we mean by nationalism, and why we consider it to have proved such a uniquely powerful force in shaping the modern world. There are difficulties enough with defining the words 'nation' (a body of people considering themselves a distinct group characterised by shared descent, history and culture), 'national' (something distinctively characteristic of a nation) and 'nationality' (the fact of belonging to a nation, or the identity or feeling related to it); defining 'nationalism' is an even more complex process. My thesis is that the true definition and explanation of nationalism lie in the interweaving of the politics of nationalist community, struggle and power.[4] Crucial here is the apparent fact that the nationalist idea of community resonates with many of humanity's deepest instincts and needs: towards security, survival, safety and protection; towards the fulfilment of economic and other practical needs; towards membership of meaningful, stably coherent, lastingly special and distinctive groups.

For this process of meaningful group-belonging to work, people require shared means of communication: mechanisms for durable agreement, coherence and trusting interaction. These can be of various kinds, often being both practical and also emotionally and psychologically valuable and attractive. They include *territory* (an attachment to our own special place, to a land which we work, on whose resources we rely and from whose distinctive features we derive emotional and practical sustenance); practically and emotionally fulfilling alignment with a body of particular *people*; relatedly, notions of communal *descent* (with the partially persuasive claim that, as members of the same nation, we are linked to each other by blood); *culture* (another means of communication and another explanation of why nationalist community so appeals, whether through a distinctively shared language or religion or music or sport or diet or some combination of these kinds of cultural phenomena); perceivedly shared *history* (one's group being seen as enduring, purposeful through time, and rich in past achievements and legacies and potential); an *ethical* dimension (with one's national group not merely typical in what it embodies, but rather characterised by superior moral values, claims, purposes and obligations); and finally the rather darker feature of nationalist community, that of *exclusiveness* – what your nation *is* implies and requires a category of what it is *not* (again, a potentially appealing colour in this picture, in telling a tale of good-versus-evil, in providing comfort and moral certainty and definitive clarity at the same time).

---

[4] For a fuller exposition of my argument about nationalism, see R. English, *Irish Freedom: The History of Nationalism in Ireland* (London, Macmillan, 2006).

National communities need not possess all of these features (shared attachments to territory, people, descent, culture, history, ethics and exclusivism). But they do require some of them, and the practical as well as emotional appeal and strength inherent within each of these features helps to explain the existence, durability and pervasiveness of such communal, national groups.

Nationalism also involves more than membership of such a self-conscious community, since it requires struggle: collective activity, mobilisation and even a programmatic striving for goals. Those goals might and do vary, including sovereign independence (of persistent relevance historically in our Irish republican case study here), secession from a larger political unit, the survival or rebirth of national culture, the realisation of economic benefit for the national group, or the recasting of the social order. Again, and tellingly, overlapping motivations can be detected here. Nationalist struggle can simultaneously fulfil an urge towards self-preservation, a very practical pursuit of material interests, a longing for individual and collective dignity, a response to actual or perceived threats and an urge to avenge past wrongs suffered by one's group. Such nationalist struggle repeatedly evinces a sense of putting right what is wrong in the present. And the dual allure of nationalist struggle should also be noted: there is the instrumental appeal (struggle moving you from undesirable point A to desirable and necessary point B), but there is also the attraction inherent within struggle itself (with its psychological rewards, and its conferring upon both individual and group of the very qualities so prized and cherished by the nationalist movement).

Finally, nationalism is not merely about community in struggle, but also about questions of power. As in our Irish case here, power is what is frequently sought by nationalists (still very often in the form of a state coextensive with the preferred nation); but also the deployment of power in pursuit of nationalist objectives defines and helps to explain nationalist activity. In many historical cases, nationalism has centrally been a politics of legitimising power: the nation is assumed to be the appropriate source of political authority, and the legitimacy of national power involves the attractive prospect of those in power over your community being like yourself, coming from your own national group, and strongly representing your own interests and values. Again and again, much of the appeal of nationalism lies in this idea of the national community possessing full sovereignty over itself as a free, independent unit (the *leitmotif* of so much Irish republican politics over many years). Everybody within the nation shares equally in the sovereign power which rules over the group, so any law derives ultimately from one's own equally shared authority. As individuals within the national community we have an equal share in the sovereignty through which decisions are made for us; as such (if one agrees with this nationalist argument), we are supposedly liberated.

This is why state power and self-determination lie so close to the heart of nationalist histories and politics around the world (not least in Ireland itself). And power also lies at the heart of what it is that nationalists actually do, and why nationalism so appeals. Power is deployed by nationalist individuals and organisations and communities in their pursuit of their objectives; power is used as the key leverage in nationalist campaigns for the righting of wrongs, and can be wielded in violent, propagandist, intimidatory, administrative, verbal, literary and many other forms of persuasion and coercion. This involves mobilisation rather than merely individual action; and the attraction of wielding such power helps to explain the durable appeal of nationalism as part of one's way of life.

So community, struggle and power offer the interwoven definition and explanation of nationalism and its extraordinary dominance in politics and history. It is not that we cannot find other means of identifying and belonging, or of pursuing change and acquiring power. But the point is this: the particular interweaving of community, struggle and power in the form of nationalism have seemed to many people to offer far grander opportunities than do these other means.

If community, struggle and power between them do define and explain nationalism and its appeal, can this help more deeply to account for the persistence of violent Irish dissident republicanism into the twenty-first century? My argument here is that it can significantly help us to do so, and I want to interrogate a range of primary as well as academic sources in order to explore this.

Attachment to communal territory has been doubly involved. At the local level, much dissident motivation has grown from the belonging to and defence of one's particular area against (unionist or loyalist) neighbours and intruders. More broadly, dissidents are committed to the idea that the problems in Irish society (whether in the north or the south) derive from partition, and they remain wedded to the ideal of an emancipated island territory: a united Ireland free of all British rule.[5] Territorial integrity is at the core of their politics: as one RSF figure put it in 2008, republicans will 'continue the struggle until the Brits are gone from our shores'.[6]

---

[5] M. Frampton, *Legion of the Rearguard: Dissident Irish Republicanism* (Dublin, Irish Academic Press, 2011), p. 280; J. Horgan, *Divided We Stand: The Strategy and Psychology of Ireland's Dissident Terrorists* (Oxford, Oxford University Press, 2013), p. 106.

[6] Michael McManus, quoted in Frampton, *Legion of the Rearguard*, p. 76.

Complementing communal territory has been the attachment to particular people (some of them people from small communities of shared descent groups), a fact reinforced by the extremely localised nature of dissident resistance, which has often taken the form of small-scale networks of attachment and activity.[7] As in previous Irish republican militancy, ideological commitment has been reinforced (and at times dominated) by personal loyalties and associations.[8] The Independent Monitoring Commission (IMC – set up by the UK and Irish governments to monitor paramilitary activity) commented clearly in 2006 that 'one feature of dissident republican groups is a tendency for things sometimes to be personality-driven or dependent on family or local allegiances, rather than on ideology.'[9]

The role of communal culture has been conspicuous (with an advocacy, for example, of the advancement of Gaelic culture).[10] So too has the important attitude towards history. Dissident republicans have remained strong adherents to the idea of an inherited, militant tradition, seeing themselves as flag-bearers for the Irish republican community through time, and as mandated by an historical tradition of armed struggle against English or British rule in Ireland. RSF's paper *Saoirse* exemplified this well in reporting the group's commemoration of the 200th anniversary of rebel Robert Emmet's 1803 execution. The orator at the Dublin event (Sean Ó Bradaigh) resonantly testified to the martyr's inspiring quality, and also explicitly identified RSF with what he saw as a tradition encompassing a line of famous Irish republican rebels, including 1790s republican Theobald Wolfe Tone and 1916 rebel leaders Patrick Pearse and James Connolly:

> There is something special about Robert Emmet, something exceptional and even lovable ... He has inspired scores of biographies and hundreds of songs ... It was on this very day, September 20, 1803, at this very spot in front of St Catherine's Church [in Thomas Street, Dublin] and at this very hour that young Emmet died for Ireland on England's gallows tree. Emmet deserves our respect, our admiration

[7] Frampton, *Legion of the Rearguard*, pp. 247–248, 262; Horgan, *Divided We Stand*, pp. 71, 96–98, 150.

[8] R. English, *Radicals and the Republic: Socialist Republicanism in the Irish Free State 1925–1937* (Oxford, Oxford University Press, 1994), pp. 222–223; for more recent dissident republicanism, see J. Morrison, *The Origins and Rise of Dissident Irish Republicanism: The Role and Impact of Organisational Splits* (London, Bloomsbury Academic, 2013), p. 139; J. Morrison, 'Why Do People Become Dissident Irish Republicans?' in P. M. Currie and M. Taylor (eds), *Dissident Irish Republicanism* (London, Continuum, 2011), p. 25; Horgan, *Divided We Stand*, p. 42.

[9] Eighth Report of the IMC (1 February 2006), p. 13.

[10] R. W. White, *Ruairi Ó Bradaigh: The Life and Politics of an Irish Revolutionary* (Bloomington, Indiana University Press, 2006), p. 321.

and our gratitude. Were it not for him, and countless other patriots, the Irish nation would long ago have faded away and disappeared in the mists of history ... We of Republican Sinn Fein, who have gathered here today, hold true to Tone's and Emmet's teaching and purpose – to break the connection with England and establish an independent Irish Republic ... Tone and Emmet, Pearse and Connolly, saw Ireland as one nation of thirty-two counties. They regarded English rule in Ireland as an illegality. Now, two hundred years later, Republican Sinn Fein adheres to the same judgment.[11]

The celebration of anniversaries – the commemoration of heroes and heroic episodes from the Irish past – reinforces dissidents' committed identity, and strengthens their sense that Irish history mandates a certain form of purist politics in the present.[12] Certainly, key dissident figures have drawn on a very long historical root to their struggle: 'Irish resistance to English aggression ... goes back over 800 years to the original Anglo-Norman invasion and colonisation of Ireland';[13] 'The Brits – they're the problem, and will be. They have been since 1169, and will be until such time as they leave.'[14]

There is a powerful sense of ethical duty and superiority involved here, with dissident invocations of the famous dead carrying with them a sense of historically conditioned moral obligation to reject compromises of the kind that (for example) Provisional Sinn Fein have made in recent years. To engage in corrupting, partitionist Irish parliaments, to share in the administration of a UK Northern Ireland establishment, to endorse the PSNI, to accept (however reluctantly) the principle of northern consent as necessary to Irish unity, even (in the famous case of Sinn Fein's Deputy First Minister, and former Chief of Staff of PIRA, Martin McGuinness) to meet amiably with Queen Elizabeth II[15] – all of this is seen by dissidents as transgressing a principled ethical code of republican tradition. So dissidents have been emphatic and repeated in their

---

[11] *Saoirse* October 2003. The academic literature on Emmet, Tone, Pearse and Connolly is now vast and varied. But most historians would be wary of transplanting political programmes as directly as did Mr Ó Bradaigh from 1798 (the year of Tone's death), 1803 or 1916 into the twenty-first century, preferring instead to stress the historical, synchronic specificity of what motivated these significant rebels. See M. Elliott, *Wolfe Tone: Prophet of Irish Independence* (New Haven, Yale University Press, 1989); T. Bartlett, *Theobald Wolfe Tone* (Dundalk, Dundalgan Press, 1997); M. Elliott, *Robert Emmet: The Making of a Legend* (London, Profile Books, 2003); P. M. Geoghegan, *Robert Emmet: A Life* (Dublin, Gill and Macmillan, 2002); C. Townshend, *Easter 1916: The Irish Rebellion* (London, Penguin, 2005); F. McGarry, *The Rising. Ireland: Easter 1916* (Oxford, Oxford University Press, 2010).

[12] Frampton, *Legion of the Rearguard*, pp. 190–191.

[13] R. Ó Bradaigh, *Dilseacht: The Story of Comdt General Tom Maguire and the Second (All-Ireland) Dail* (Dublin, Elo Press, 1997), p. 1.

[14] George Harrison, interviewed by the author, New York, 30 October 2000.

[15] *Belfast Telegraph*, 28 June 2012.

condemnation of Sinn Fein apostasy within the transformed north. Former PIRA member Marian Price (who became involved with the 32CSM) put it to me this way, regarding Sinn Fein and the 1998 Good Friday Agreement: 'They've tried to sell a defeat as a victory'; republican support for peace process politics, according to this view, represented an immoral betrayal of those who had fought the Provisional republican war: 'To suggest that a war was fought for what they have today, it diminishes anybody who partook in that war, anybody who died for it, and went out and sacrificed their lives and their liberty.'[16] Rejecting Sinn Fein's unethical compromise, and sustaining principled resistance, therefore represents a necessary maintenance of the struggle, a keeping of the flame alive.[17] Thus Sinn Fein is added to the list of villains in this political tale: the UK government, the unionist political class and its supporters and now also treacherous republicans all constitute the excluded outgroup against which authentic and justified dissidents can righteously wage their Manichean campaign.

For the dissident community is also a community very much in struggle. The latter is judged necessary as a means of securing national rights, with dissidents aiming ultimately for an independent and united Ireland, and convinced of the need for armed struggle to bring it about.[18] On this, they are the ones who have remained consistent. Ruairi Ó Bradaigh, long the dominant figure in RSF, joined the IRA in the 1950s and he retained a largely consistent form of militant republican purism until his death in 2013: 'I haven't changed, I am still saying the things that I was saying down the years.'[19] Leading figures from another group (the RIRA splinter-organisation Oglaigh na hÉireann (ONH)) made clear in 2010 that, 'An Óglaigh na hÉireann capable of having a sustained campaign will take time to develop. It will take time to develop the structures, personnel, finance and weaponry'; but they retained confidence in future violent achievement: 'We think a war can create the conditions where republicans can create dialogue that will fulfil republican objectives. A 32-county democratic socialist republic.'[20]

But dissident struggle also appeals because of the inherent rewards that it offers as such. It is the argument of this chapter that we cannot account

[16] Marian Price, interviewed by the author, Belfast, 28 February 2002.
[17] S. A. Whiting, '"The Discourse of Defence": "Dissident" Irish Republican Newspapers and the "Propaganda War"', *Terrorism and Political Violence*, 24/3 (2012); Frampton, *Legion of the Rearguard*, p. 181; Morrison, *Origins and Rise*, pp. 183–185; Horgan, *Divided We Stand*, p. 5.
[18] H. Patterson, 'Beyond the "Micro Group": The Dissident Republican Challenge' in Currie and Taylor (eds), *Dissident Irish Republicanism*, p. 81; Morrison, *Origins and Rise*, pp. 1, 159.
[19] Ruairi Ó Bradaigh, quoted in White, *Ruairi Ó Bradaigh*, p. 326.
[20] ONH leaders, interviewed by Brian Rowan, *Belfast Telegraph*, 3 November 2010.

satisfactorily for dissident republican persistence unless we situate it within nationalist politics; but nationalist politics can involve within it, for some, a variety of types of reward and a complex and overlapping set of motivations. For republican dissidents there have been some financial and criminal benefits at times;[21] there are the immediate rewards of comradeship, purpose, kudos, excitement and adventure;[22] there is the satisfying catharthis of pursuing personal rivalries, individual enmities and localised resentments, feuds and hostilities; and there is the attraction offered by an unyieldingly simple, absolutist form of uncompromised struggle.[23]

Dissident republican nationalism has also been very much about power. In terms of their ultimate goal, republican dissidents are motivated by the need to undo what they consider the UK's illegitimate rule over the six counties of Northern Ireland. Theirs is a classic self-determination argument about sovereignty, embodying a nationalistic commitment to a free, independent and united Ireland. In the 32CSM's firm view: 'We reject Britain's right to occupy any part of our country ... Partition perpetuates the British government's denial of the Irish people's right to self-determination.'[24] The appeal of fellow Irish nationalists ruling the whole of the island, rather than the north being shaped partly to suit unionist political preferences and agendas, seems clear enough in itself; and it partly explains the potency and durability of militant Irish republicanism, even now.

There seems no imminent prospect of their violence bringing about this sought-after united Ireland. But dissenting from the unacceptable and illegitimate *status quo* is seen as worthwhile in itself, as sustaining a long struggle towards the achievement eventually of legitimate arrangements of power across the whole of Ireland. Those who oppose Sinn Fein's compromises – like the 32CSM's Gary Donnelly – have sometimes shifted from initial enthusiasm for the peace process towards growing disaffection, on the basis that they consider central Irish nationalist rights to power not to have been properly addressed:

I embraced the IRA ceasefire in 1994. I thought, there's movement here, the conflict is over, the issues are going to be addressed. Twenty years on, that's not the reality. The root cause was not dealt with twenty years ago. And if you don't deal with the

---

[21] Morrison, *Origins and Rise*, pp. 193–195.

[22] Morrison, 'Why Do People Become Dissident Irish Republicans?', p. 33.

[23] R. W. White, *Ruairi Ó Bradaigh: The Life and Politics of an Irish Revolutionary* (Bloomington, Indiana University Press, 2006), p. 290.

[24] Quoted in Frampton, *Legion of the Rearguard*, p. 102.

Richard English

core issue, the causes of conflict are still there … it's about violation of national sovereignty.[25]

The short-term goal has more to do with undermining, thwarting, spoiling and rendering uncomfortable the existing peace process settlement, than it has about the immediate achievement of a united Ireland. But damaging their mainstream republican rivals in Sinn Fein and preventing a sustained normalisation of peace-process politics would represent a significant denial of what they see as wrongful power. Leading Sinn Feiners have sharp-sightedly noted this aspect of the dissident republican challenge:

> In broad societal terms, those who hold to those views – those oppositional, rejectionist views – are an incredibly small minority … So in wider societal terms, they are not making an impact. [But] their activities undermine the capacity for Irish republicanism to place itself as a champion of political change across the island. That's the difficulty that they pose for Irish republicanism: that they can actually fray the capacity and the coherence of Irish republicanism to become a truly popular, island-wide political alternative.[26]

As so often with previous republican violence, therefore, the intra-nationalist dynamics of tension and competition have been hugely important.

Power has been important and appealing also as a means of expression, with local fiefdoms and influence repeatedly evident, and with the violent maintenance of intra-communal power being one which has clearly appealed to dissident groups and individuals.[27]

The key points about all this are: first, that it is a familiar pattern the world over when nationalist movements emerge and survive; second, that there is nothing inherently insane or irrational about these attachments, albeit that they focus on an unobtainable goal (but then so too do many non-violent political movements). My argument is that it is indeed only by recognising the ways in which dissident zealotry fits the pattern of wider, serious nationalism the world over that we can understand the phenomenon properly. Respecting the seriousness of the issues involved in this nationalism in no way means that its demands should be ceded. But understanding republican dissidents within

[25] Gary Donnelly, quoted in the *Irish Times*, 30 August 2014.
[26] Sinn Fein's Declan Kearney, interviewed by the author, Belfast, 28 July 2011.
[27] J. Tonge, 'An Enduring Tradition or the Last Gasp of Physical Force Republicanism? "Dissident" Republican Violence in Northern Ireland' in Currie and Taylor (eds), *Dissident Irish Republicanism*, p. 105.

this normalising framework of explanation does, I believe, help explain why increasing numbers of people see this commitment as part of a sane and serious ideology, and as one which can be presented as being in tune with previous Irish politics. Like other political actors, dissident republicans display complex motivation,[28] and the widespread hostility people feel towards their violent politics should not blind us to this vital fact. To recognise the complicated, explicable nationalism which accounts for the phenomenon will facilitate a more effective response to it than will casual, misleading dismissals and denunciations.

Given that dissident republicans do resemble so many nationalist irredentists across the world and throughout history (including, of course, their PIRA predecessors in Ulster), could dissidents bring about the kind of conflict that endured in Northern Ireland during the 1970s and 1980s with much higher levels of violence? The evidence suggests not. There is not the combination now that there was then of Irish nationalist anger and millenarian expectation, of a perceived need for vigilante defence groups to protect Catholics from Protestant attack, of nationalist exclusion from Northern Irish power structures and the northern state, of unionist outrage coupled with unionist power, of heavy-handed state (especially military) clumsiness of response to instability, and of a widespread belief that constitutional politics would fail but that violence might yield victory. This last point is crucial, since even many disaffected members of the northern nationalist minority recognise that if the much stronger PIRA could not bomb their way to a united Ireland, there exists minimal hope of the much weaker forces of republican dissidents proving successful.

So what exists (and what is likely to persist) is a violent threat which is enduring, fissiparous,[29] episodically energetic and occasionally lethal, but far less extensive than the terrorist threats endured in the late twentieth century in Northern Ireland. The IMC reported that between 1 March 2003 and 28 February 2010 dissident republicans had killed 10 people,[30] compared with the far higher levels of fatal violence practised by the PIRA.[31] This should not lead us to assume a static situation. John Horgan's analysis of the period 31 August 1994 to 8 July 2011 suggests a notable rise during the phase from 2009 onwards,[32] but this has to be set in the long-term context. In April 2011 the PSNI's then Deputy Chief Constable (Judith Gillespie) sharply recognised

---

[28] White, *Ruairí Ó Brádaigh*, pp. xxii–xxiii.
[29] Frampton, *Legion of the Rearguard*, pp. 176–177, 180; Horgan, *Divided We Stand*, p. 35.
[30] Twenty-Third Report of the IMC (26 May 2010), p. 21.
[31] R. English, *Armed Struggle: The History of the IRA*, 3rd edn (London, Macmillan, 2012), p. 379.
[32] Horgan, *Divided We Stand*, pp. 49, 62–63, 71.

the growing seriousness of the dissident challenge, but also its limitations when compared to militant republicanism in the past: 'Is the threat growing? Yes. Even since it was assessed in February 2009 as severe, I believe it's got worse.' DCC Gillespie noted that, in early 2011, dissident activity was occurring with 'greater frequency, greater range, greater geographical spread, greater degree of targeting of police officers (on and off duty), greater degree of intelligence gathering, recruitment'. But she added an important note of perspective and proportion too: 'Is the threat level at the same level as it was at the height of the PIRA campaign in the '80s and '90s? No.'[33]

It is true that a sectarianisation of Ulster violence could change this, were Protestant loyalist paramilitaries to be provoked into retaliatory action against Catholics, and were we therefore to witness sustained, intense inter-communal violence. At present, despite occasional flare-ups, loyalist groups are comparatively quiescent and locally fragmented, and their remnants tend to be criminally or intra-communally oriented rather than leaning towards a sectarian conflict (despite the deep and ongoing sectarian division in Northern Ireland, and the effective erosion in recent years of a strong political middle ground there). But, were dissidents to try to provoke a loyalist backlash, then political violence might indeed increase. This is calmly reflected in the striking assessment of one ex-UDA leader (Jackie McDonald) in interview: 'If they really wanted to get into it, they would kill a loyalist, a senior loyalist. So they're only playing at it, really. The dissidents – the dizzies, as I call them – are more of a nuisance to Sinn Fein than they are to loyalism.'[34]

My argument about nationalist framework suggests that dissident republicanism is likely to represent a long-term phenomenon. As with IRA figures of previous generations,[35] so too contemporary dissidents do not consider a strong, popular mandate to be necessary in order to justify their violent struggle.[36] But the lack of popular support for that struggle means that it will almost certainly fail in its central, irredentist goal. It is worth noting here the emphatically repeated majorities that exist within Northern Ireland in favour of continued membership of the UK (and the comparatively limited levels even of Catholic nationalist support for the goal of a united Ireland).[37]

It is also true that the dissidents' capacity to gain ground is limited by the success of Sinn Fein in bringing the bulk of the northern republican community

[33] Judith Gillespie, interviewed by the author, Belfast, 15 April 2011.
[34] Jackie McDonald, interviewed by the author, Belfast, 31 January 2012.
[35] R. English, *Ernie O'Malley: IRA Intellectual* (Oxford, Oxford University Press, 1998), pp. 76–85.
[36] J. Tonge, '"No-one Likes Us; We Don't Care": "Dissident" Irish Republicans and Mandates', *Political Quarterly*, 83/2 (2012).
[37] English, *Armed Struggle*, p. 399.

with them in their peace-process politics, and indeed in expanding their support base to become the dominant nationalist party in Northern Ireland. There is no more effective constraint upon dissident vibrancy than an ex-revolutionary, republican movement, now in government, and vehemently opposed to dissidents' violent politics. Here, the key predictor of dissident weakness is not necessarily a normalised politics in the north, but rather Sinn Fein strength as seen by the republican community. Reflecting on dissident republicanism and on whether it might grow stronger, Sinn Fein politician Conor Murphy observed tellingly in interview that, 'It's marginal at the moment; that's not to say it couldn't become more serious. The strength of its seriousness very much depends on our ability to do things.'[38]

Relatedly, political expressions of popular support for dissidents have remained low. In the Northern Ireland Assembly Elections of 2007, the six RSF candidates averaged a minuscule 420 votes each, embodying only 0.4% of those who had voted; in the 2009 Republic of Ireland local government elections, RSF won only 0.01% of the total votes cast;[39] and one recent estimate had it that a mere 3% of the Northern Irish community offered support for politically violent republican methods.[40]

Taken together, all of this evidence suggests that dissident republicanism should not be taken to imply that we are going back to the Troubles; instead, it might be read as indicating that we have not yet entirely escaped them either.[41] If it is a terrorist illusion on the dissidents' part that their violence will bring them victory, it would also be a counter-terrorist illusion for the UK state to assume that republican dissidence is something that is likely to evaporate into non-existence.

But terrorism and counter-terrorism tend to exist in a mutually shaping relationship with one another. What can and should the state do in order to ensure that the ending of the PIRA era is not followed by a growth in serious post-PIRA terrorism? If dissident republican terrorism is indeed best read through the lens of wider patterns of explicable nationalist allegiance, then how should the state respond to it? I have argued elsewhere that the historical experience of terrorism and counter-terrorism suggests a seven-point framework for the

---

[38] Conor Murphy, interviewed by the author, Belfast, 16 December 2010.
[39] Frampton, *Legion of the Rearguard*, pp. 70, 79.
[40] R. Frenett and M.L.R. Smith, 'IRA 2.0: Continuing the Long War – Analyzing the Factors Behind Anti-GFA Violence', *Terrorism and Political Violence*, 24/3 (2012), p. 387.
[41] English, *Armed Struggle*, pp. 402–403; Frenett and Smith, 'IRA 2.0', pp. 391–392; A. Edwards, 'When Terrorism as Strategy Fails: Dissident Irish Republicans and the Threat to British Security', *Studies in Conflict and Terrorism*, 34/4 (2011), p. 319.

most effective response to non-state terrorist violence,[42] and I want now to situate our reflections on how best to react to violent, dissident nationalist politics within that argument, by considering dissidents to be explicable, violent nationalists.

The first point is surely that we have to learn to live with this phenomenon. In the heady wake of the 1998 Good Friday Agreement in Northern Ireland there were some who anticipated the complete ending of violence in the region and the establishment of entirely peaceful political processes. But, as we assess the possible futures for new generations of organisation calling themselves the IRA, we should humbly remember how long a sequence of organisational reinventions has taken in the past during the very long history of militant Irish republican nationalism. It would be naïve to suggest that the history of the IRA has come to an end; and Irish history does not compel us to expect an utterly harmonious relationship between Irish nationalism and a British state which claims and exerts sovereignty over part of Ireland.[43] To establish the goal of removing all dissident terrorism from the north of Ireland is likely to prove an unrealisable, self-defeating and rather pointless process. A better ambition would be to manage, contain and minimise such militancy and disaffection, so that it is as marginal and minor a problem as possible. In doing so, we should recognise both how great an achievement the reduction of republican violence in recent decades has actually been, and also how resilient and durable states and societies can prove in the face of terrorist challenges. Terrorist campaigns tend to end without groups having secured their central goals[44] – a pattern echoed in the experience of the PIRA, whose campaign was aimed at the destruction of the Northern Ireland state, but who ended it on the basis of sharing the administration of that very state;[45] and even such durably violent terrorist campaigns have seen the state adjust, cope and endure.

The second point is to bear in mind that, where possible, states should address the underlying root problems and causes behind the violent campaign. Serious terrorism (such as that evident in republican Irish history) tends to be a symptom of profound political difficulties and disaffection. Now the 1998 deal in Northern Ireland (modified at St Andrews in 2006 and Hillsborough in 2010) has so carefully responded to Irish nationalist grievances regarding the North as to dry up the vast majority of support for ongoing violence.

[42] R. English, *Terrorism: How to Respond* (Oxford, Oxford University Press, 2009), pp. 118–143.
[43] English, *Irish Freedom*.
[44] Cronin, *How Terrorism Ends*; M. Abrahms, 'Why Terrorism Does Not Work', *International Security*, 31/2 (2006).
[45] English, *Armed Struggle*.

As noted, the central dissident republican demand (for Irish unity) is almost certainly undeliverable at present, given widespread public opinion against it. So it is not the case that we should look at ongoing dissident violence and conclude that we should give them what they demand. But the ongoing process of entrenching the broadly popular settlement in Northern Ireland does have implications for the containment of republican violence in future. As in previous episodes of Irish republican history (with the Fianna Fail party in the 1930s and 1940s, for example),[46] the most credible people to undermine ongoing IRA violence after a settlement tend to be *former* IRA and republican zealots who have now opted for more constitutional politics and who can condemn and oppose dissenting IRAs with greater ease and credibility within their own community than can any British state on its own. This is not to say that, for example, a Sinn Feiner such as Martin McGuinness is in exactly the same position in which republicans Eamon de Valera and Frank Aiken found themselves in the 1930s. But it is to say that now, as then, people with republican pasts are a key resource in dealing with dissident violence, since they can delegitimise dissidents from the position of strong credentials and credibility within the nationalist community, and also because they are more deeply hostile to their republican rivals than anyone else and are, in practice, now on the state's side.

Here, the role of mainstream republicans is probably of greater advantage to Ulster unionists than most of the latter recognise or admit. What many unionists understandably resent – namely, Sinn Fein political strength and momentum – perhaps remains a necessary insulation against a worse experience of Irish republican militancy in Northern Ireland, since it offers a way of undercutting and limiting and delegitimising dissident campaigns of violence. Contrary to the arguments of some, therefore,[47] the Northern Ireland case suggests that addressing root causes can lead to a settlement far short of what terrorist groups were killing people to achieve, but popular enough with their constituency to allow for the terrorism broadly to stop. Such endgames seem to point away from the efficacy and sustenance of terrorist violence, rather than towards them.

Third, there remains a need to avoid an over-militarisation of response to dissident republican violence. It is now well recognised that in the early, crucible years of the Northern Ireland Troubles, certain clumsily implemented state initiatives helped to stimulate rather than end PIRA terrorism.[48] In the

---

[46] English, *Ernie O'Malley*, pp. 30–32; English, *Radicals and the Republic*.
[47] Alan Dershowitz comes to mind: *Why Terrorism Works: Understanding the Threat, Responding to the Challenge* (New Haven, Yale University Press, 2002).
[48] English, *Armed Struggle*, pp. 136–155.

current situation, dissident republican strength would also be enhanced were the state to over-react clumsily. This is something of which the UK authorities seem fully aware (hard-learned as it was during the 1970s and 1980s in the North). The police have been clear on the matter: 'We – the PSNI, as an organisation – have to be so careful not to over-react in any way' to dissident activity and provocation;[49] even some former Royal Ulster Constabulary (RUC) officers with lengthy experience of combating previous IRA campaigns in quasi-military manner have, at times, shown admiration for the restrained state response to contemporary dissident violence.[50] Relatedly, it has been recognised that restraint in the use of the military might well offer the best route forward in dealing with dissident terrorism. Dissidents themselves have been keen both to attack the British Army and also to draw them into a more prominent role in Northern Ireland.

From their own nationalist reading of the conflict, this makes sense. For dissident republicans, the struggle is at root between Ireland and Britain, and so the more that the battle lines can involve British forces other than Ulster-British ones, the better. Clearly, the British Army has played and still plays an important role in offering ultimate guarantees of order and security in Northern Ireland. But one sustainable lesson of the earlier Troubles is that police primacy makes best sense when dealing with various IRAs. Military action risks heavy-handed counter-productiveness and so military engagement should be kept to an absolute minimum, since there are risks of generating disaffection and of reinforcing dissident arguments that the issue in Northern Ireland is that of an occupying foreign power. The broader literature on terrorism tends to support such a conclusion, since the perception that there exists a militarily occupying, alien power in one's territory has repeatedly become one of the major sources of recruitment and strength for terrorist groups.[51]

Police primacy is emerging as a more widely accepted pattern for such crises across the world (including in Afghanistan),[52] and it certainly makes clear sense in our current case in Northern Ireland. Not only is such a pattern likely to minimise collateral damage and the counter-productive effect of kinetic methods, but police are more often deeply rooted in the local context and community than an army will generally be able to be. Intimacy of

---

[49] Judith Gillespie, interviewed by the author, Belfast, 15 April 2011.
[50] Former RUC Headquarters Mobile Support Unit Officer, interviewed by the author, Belfast, 7 June 2011.
[51] R. A. Pape, *Dying to Win: Why Suicide Terrorists Do It* (London, Gibson Square Books, 2006); R. A. Pape and J. K. Feldman, *Cutting the Fuse: The Explosion of Global Suicide Terrorism and How to Stop It* (Chicago, University of Chicago Press, 2010).
[52] S. G. Jones, *Counterinsurgency in Afghanistan* (Santa Monica, RAND, 2008).

understanding and nuance can be vital resources in fighting terrorism, and this is as true now as in Ulster's violent past.

The fourth point is to recognise that intelligence is the most vital element in successful counter-terrorism. There exists broad agreement in the terrorism literature, and among practitioners who have had experience on the ground, that accurate, extensive and well-interpreted intelligence is a vital resource in fighting terrorism;[53] this remains crucial in relation to contemporary dissident republicans. The range of questions addressed in such intelligence-gathering is wide. Who are the terrorists? What are they capable of doing, and when and where? How much support do they have? What are their strengths and weaknesses? What would increase, and what would undermine, their support base? How much material and expertise do they have? On a day-to-day basis, what are they planning and how best can these attacks be prevented?

The fifth point is related, as it affects and defines the practical nature of the intelligence work discussed above: respect orthodox legal frameworks and adhere to the democratically established rule of law. When a terrorist atrocity occurs there is an understandable instinct towards abandoning normal legal frameworks and restraints, in the desire to deal sharply with those behind such hideous violence. Internationally, this has been evident throughout the history of terrorism and counter-terrorism, from French responses to Algerian violence, through Israeli reaction to Palestinian terrorism, UK responses to the PIRA and, more recently, US post-9/11 policy.

But there are problems with this response. The main one is the practical matter of whether such (sometimes Draconian) legal policies actually work. Frequently, they seem to have at best ambiguous effects. Indeed, restraint and calm professionalism within the context of the normal legal framework will often be the best response, even in the wake of a large-scale atrocity when the temptation to extend legal powers dramatically will be strongest.[54] Positively, the key thing to recognise here is that imprisoning people for lengthy terms for terrorist offences is a vital achievement and that this can be done largely through orthodox legal means. With small groups (and dissident IRAs are much smaller than was the PIRA) lengthy, key arrests

---

[53] A. Roberts, 'The "War on Terror" in Historical Perspective', *Survival*, 47/2 (2005), p. 109; M. Howard, 'What's in a Name? How to Fight Terrorism', *Foreign Affairs*, 81/1 (2002), p. 9; M. Sageman, *Understanding Terror Networks* (Philadelphia, University of Pennsylvania Press, 2004), p. 180.

[54] This is the view of some of the most authoritative legal scholars (C. Gearty, *Liberty and Security* (Cambridge, Polity Press, 2013); L. K. Donohue, *The Cost of Counterterrorism: Power, Politics and Liberty* (Cambridge, Cambridge University Press, 2008)); but it also fits with what some key anti-terrorist practitioners have argued (M. D. Silber, *The al-Qaida Factor: Plots Against the West* (Philadelphia, University of Pennsylvania Press, 2012).

and imprisonment achieved through proper process can seriously undermine capacity.[55] Moreover, adherence to proper legal procedures reduces the risk of grievance-generation; the PIRA gained considerable propagandist advantage from some of the miscarriages of justice and transgressions of proper legal process that occurred during the lengthy Troubles period.[56]

Throughout Irish nationalist history it has been far easier to mobilise support for people wrongly imprisoned or badly treated by the British state than it has been to gather backing for the activities of violent republican groups whose activities have prompted such imprisonment. This lesson must be remembered. Should there be, for example, another mass-casualty dissident republican attack (something which is a serious possibility), then it will be vital that the right people are imprisoned and through proper and robust legal process, rather than that there be mistakes, transgressions of proper procedures, or anything open to manipulation and propaganda by republican dissidents. To date, most dissident republican campaigns focusing on prisoners have failed to resonate very widely;[57] from the UK state's point of view, it is important to keep it that way.

Sixth, there is a need to coordinate security-related, financial and technological preventative measures. The different wings of the UK state facing the dissident threat (the PSNI, the Northern Ireland Office, the British Army, the Security Service and others) are much more harmoniously cooperative than had initially been the case when the earlier phase of modern republican terrorism arose. Relationships with the relevant actors in other states (especially the Republic of Ireland) have also grown stronger. Nationally and internationally, one aspect of counter-terrorism which repeatedly hampers efforts to deal with terrorist violence is the tendency for different actors in the same counter-terrorist business to lack coordination of their various efforts in the process.[58] Equally important to note is the fact that many of the best successes the UK enjoyed against the PIRA occurred when inter-agency coordination was at its strongest.[59] All of the different aspects of counter-terrorist effort must be interwoven if the dissident threat is to be

[55] Frampton, *Legion of the Rearguard*, pp. 141–144.
[56] English, *Armed Struggle*, pp. 167–171.
[57] Frampton, *Legion of the Rearguard*, p. 72.
[58] D. Omand, *Securing the State* (London, Hurst, 2010), p. 175; G. F. Treverton, *Intelligence for an Age of Terror* (Cambridge, Cambridge University Press, 2009), pp. 5, 56.
[59] Former RUC Headquarters Mobile Support Unit Officer, interviewed by the author, Belfast, 7 June 2011; C. Andrew, *The Defence of the Realm: The Authorised History of MI5* (London, Penguin, 2009), pp. 784–785.

minimised; and a crucial part of this involves the building and sustaining of relevant personal relationships and trust.

Finally, there is a need to maintain strong credibility in counter-terrorist public argument. Credibility is a vital resource in counter-terrorism, and it is more easily lost than regained. It is of value in relation to the potentially disaffected groups who might or might not support dissident violence; and it is of value also in relation to the confidence and trust which the pro-state community in Northern Ireland has in the government and the authorities. For example, one crucial element in restraining loyalists from responding violently to dissident terrorism will be their confidence that the state is effectively and robustly identifying and dealing with the dissident challenge.

States can very often rely on an honest depiction of realities in countering terrorist argument, rather than on a series of tempting distortions; so it is a mistake to resort to caricature or falsifiable claims in trying to exaggerate the gap between the state and the terrorists. In relation to contemporary dissident violence, the UK government's basic case is such a strong one that it requires no exaggeration: dissidents offer no viable alternative to the existing arrangements in Northern Ireland, and their left-wing politics often tends towards the impossibilistic;[60] neither side in the North can expect to win through violence, given the balance of communal forces involved; terrorism causes appalling suffering for some and a worsening of life for very many; the economic wastage caused by dissident activity seriously damages education, health and other welfare provision; if bombing was going to solve the Northern Ireland problem by bringing about a united Ireland then it would have done so years ago; and so on. This being so, there is therefore no need to resort to the caricaturing of dissidents with claims that they are merely criminals and gangsters, that they are psychopaths, that they are evil and insane, that they have no politics or principles, that they have no support. Most people in Northern Ireland will never support dissidents anyway; those who might have some sympathy for them will have it reinforced if the government's depiction of dissidents lacks credibility.

I have argued that violent republican dissidents will continue to form part of Northern Irish reality, despite the extraordinary (and in many ways very benevolent) changes to that society in recent decades. The argument has been that they are entirely explicable within the framework of nationalism, and that reading them in this way allows for a coherent response which will limit their capacity to undermine peaceful politics. Dissident republicans represent the latest link of a seemingly indefatigable militant tradition; as such, they will

---

[60] Frampton, *Legion of the Rearguard*, p. 239; Horgan, *Divided We Stand*, p. 121.

probably prove enduring in one form or other. But it is important to conclude by recognising that, while Irish republican terrorism has not ended, nor does it carry the day with even most hard-edged republican enthusiasts. In the words of one (non-Sinn Fein, but also now emphatically non-violent) ex-PIRA Volunteer's view of republican dissidents, 'Physical force republicanism has been totally put beyond the Pale, and the existence of groups which misguidedly adhere to this philosophy only plays into the hands of the unionists and Sinn Fein, allowing them to claim the moral high ground.'[61] Irish republican terrorism may not have died out; but its dynamics have so changed that it might now become enduringly marginal.

---

[61] Ex-PIRA Volunteer, interviewed by the author, Belfast, 26 November 2012.

9

The Global Insurgency

Action and Reaction in
Contemporary World Politics

DAVID A. LAKE

THE UNITED STATES IS TODAY FIGHTING a global insurgency. The *Pax Americana* created by the international leadership of the United States has produced remarkable political order and unparalleled prosperity for states in Europe, Northeast Asia and increasingly Latin America. For decades, and especially since the end of the Cold War, the United States has been attempting to expand this liberal, democratic and market-oriented international order into other regions of the globe, particularly the Middle East. Although carrying enormous promise, this expanded *Pax Americana* is tremendously disruptive in traditional societies outside the already industrialised world. It is this disruption, and the American role catalysing it, that fuels the global insurgency.

Though noble in origins and likely a positive force for change over the long run, this effort to expand the *Pax Americana* has sparked a backlash against the United States, globalisation and Westernisation. The backlash is often led by religious fundamentalists who not only revere tradition and oppose change, but who have been the only form of permissible political opposition under decades of autocratic rule. With state elites in the Middle East largely coopted into the *Pax Americana*, opposition now takes the form of 'private', non-state actors who have little choice but to pursue their aims through violence. Unable to defeat their militarised states or the sole remaining superpower directly, the insurgents have taken up the weapon of the weak – terrorism – and attack relatively soft civilian targets both at home, in the 'West' and in the United States itself.

Taking advantage of the very political and economic openness of the *Pax Americana*, in turn, the insurgents, though largely regional in origin

Proceedings of the British Academy **203**, 145–164. © The British Academy 2015.

and focus, have gone global, hiding from the overwhelming power of their states and the United States in the interstices of the international system. The ungoverned spaces of the world, especially failed states, serve as havens for the global insurgency. From such havens, opponents of the *Pax Americana* can mobilise, grow and emerge to fight at the time and place of their choosing.

The US response to the global insurgency has taken a number of forms, including counter-terrorism and regime change. In unappreciated ways, however, state-building has become the dominant strategy. By creating effective governance in otherwise ungoverned spaces, the United States hopes to choke off the hiding places of the insurgents, forcing them into the open where it can fight them more effectively. The core problem in state-building, however, is that though the United States and its allies may seek legitimacy for the states they build, they also aim to appoint local leaders willing to cooperate in the Global War on Terror and other, larger elements of the *Pax Americana*. With policy preferences aligned with the United States but far from those of the average citizens in their countries, these 'loyal' leaders can govern only through high levels of repression. In promoting such autocrats, the United States alienates the population and foments further opposition to its role in the region. For this reason, state-building as counter-insurgency strategy is inevitably counter-productive. The United States must either go 'all-in' for a long-term strategy of political transformation in the Middle East or retrench and reverse its efforts to expand the *Pax Americana*.

This chapter is an interpretative essay that syntheses my prior writings on the topic of international hierarchy and its consequences. I paint with broad brush strokes to try to capture the broad horizons of the world we live in today, neglecting the details of any particular scene. This may displease some readers who prefer more finely rendered views but I hope it succeeds in revealing the 'big picture' for others. The first section explains the spread of the *Pax Americana* into Central America in the first half of the twentieth century and Europe and Northeast Asia in the second half of that same century. The next section briefly describes the expansion of the *Pax Americana* into the Middle East, especially after the end of the Cold War, the reaction to this expansion, with a focus on the current global insurgency, and the role of state-building as a form of counter-insurgency and the dilemma that lies at its heart. The final section argues that given the unattractive choice between expansion or retrenchment, the United States ought to lean towards the latter.

Expanding the *Pax Americana*

For over a century, the United States has pursued international order by constructing international hierarchies – authority relationships in which its rule over subordinate states is recognised as legitimate – first in Central America, then in Europe and Northeast Asia and later in the Middle East.[1] Economic hierarchies can vary from economic zones, in which the subordinate is restricted from giving special market access to third states, to dependencies, in which the subordinate cedes all authority over economic policy to the dominant state (for example, dollarisation). Security hierarchies vary from spheres of influence, areas of exclusive operation that prohibit third party alliances (such as the Monroe Doctrine), to protectorates, where the dominant state assumes control over the security policy of the subordinate. High levels of both economic and security hierarchy produce informal empires characterised by indirect rule and, at an extreme, formal empires governed directly from the metropole. Not all states are subordinate to another, of course, with relations between them and others approximating the anarchies traditionally assumed in international relations theory.[2] The United States today, by my estimates, exerts some degree of authority over approximately half the countries in the world, mostly in the comparatively limited forms of economic zones and spheres of influence.[3]

International hierarchies, like all authority relationships, have at their core an exchange of international order provided by the dominant state in return for constraints on the decision-making autonomy of the subordinate state. Security and open markets are the twin pillars of the *Pax Americana*, which both benefit and limit the foreign policy independence of subordinates. For its part, the United States protects its subordinates from foreign coercion and supports them in international crises, allowing them to spend less on defence, and adjudicates disputes between subordinates, permitting them to be more open to trade and, especially, more open to trade with each other. For their part, subordinates accept the constraints on their foreign policy autonomy and recognise certain limited actions by the United States in their affairs as legitimate or appropriate. This often includes giving the

---

[1] David A. Lake, *Entangling Relations: American Foreign Policy in Its Century* (Princeton, NJ, Princeton University Press, 1999); *Hierarchy in International Relations* (Ithaca, NY, Cornell University Press, 2009).

[2] Kenneth N. Waltz, *Theory of International Politics* (Reading, MA, Addison-Wesley, 1979).

[3] Lake, *Hierarchy in International Relations*, chapter 3.

United States basing rights that prevent subordinates from pursuing military options that might otherwise be available to them.[4] The costs to the United States of producing international order, and the loss of effective sovereignty by subordinates, are offset by the gains in peace and prosperity that all enjoy. The greater the potential gains from international cooperation and the more specific the assets that would otherwise be at risk, the more hierarchical will be the relationships between the United States and potential subordinates.[5]

The degree of hierarchy, however, is also a function of the differences in policy preferences between the dominant state and citizens of the subordinate state.[6] In all but the most extreme forms of hierarchy where the dominant state governs the subordinate directly, as in formal imperialism, the dominant state rules through a local leader sympathetic to its preferences who governs on its behalf. When the policies preferred by the United States and its subordinates are relatively similar, as during the Cold War when a common threat drove North America, Europe and Northeast Asia together, little hierarchy is necessary, as both dominant and subordinate states possess strong shared interests. In such cases, leaders sympathetic to the United States are also supported by their populations, allowing democracy at home to prevail. As the policy preferences of the United States and subordinates diverge, greater hierarchy is necessary to control the choices of the latter. The more loyal the local leader is to the United States, in turn, the more he will be perceived as a puppet, lackey, stooge or client of the United States, and the less legitimacy he will have in the eyes of the people over whom he rules. To sustain himself in power, such a loyal leader can govern only with relatively high levels of repression, and will do so with the support of the United States regardless of the 'lip service' given to democracy by Washington. In these cases, political opponents of the leader and his regime will also necessarily be 'anti-American', and will target both the client government at home and the United States abroad.[7]

[4] Alexander Cooley, *Base Politics: Democratic Change and the U.S. Military Overseas* (Ithaca, NY, Cornell University Press, 2008).

[5] See Lake, *Entangling Relations: American Foreign Policy in Its Century*, chapter 3.

[6] David A. Lake, 'Legitimating Power: The Domestic Politics of U.S. International Hierarchy', *International Security*, 38/2 (2013).

[7] On anti-Americanism, see Peter J. Katzenstein and Robert O. Keohane, *Anti-Americanisms in World Politics* (Ithaca, NY, Cornell University Press, 2006). On anti-Americanism in the Middle East, and how it shapes regimes and their opponents, see Amaney A. Jamal, *Of Empires and Citizens: Pro-American Democracy or No Democracy at All?* (Princeton, NJ, Princeton University Press, 2012).

The 'American Lake'

The United States began building an informal empire over states on the Caribbean littoral in the Spanish–American War of 1898.[8] Such a move had long been discussed and supported by American investors and imperialists. By the First World War, at the latest, the United States had consolidated its control over the region, managing to ensure that friendly leaders were in power in all states with the exception of Mexico, with whom relations remained strained.

Spurred by the desire to replace the European colonial powers entrenched in the region, the United States built a relatively hierarchical informal empire. This not only gave it monopoly control over the security and economic policies of subordinates in the region, limiting possible inroads by the Europeans, but also secured its southern flank – a move that allowed Washington to deploy its growing power projection capabilities toward Europe and Asia. The informal empire also protected the new Panama Canal at little additional cost.

The primary benefit to the United States was military expenditures not incurred in defending itself or the canal from other great powers who might have used the region for forward operations. The costs to the United States, on the other hand, were substantial, taking the form mostly of twenty major military interventions between 1898 and 1932.[9] Several of these interventions became protracted military occupations in what we would now call state-building operations.[10] What net gains there were, finally, were largely retained by the United States itself. There was little economic assistance or other aid to subordinates to compensate them for their lost sovereignty, at least not until President John F. Kennedy's Alliance for Progress beginning in the 1960s.

Policy preferences between the United States and the median citizens of various states in Central America were likely quite different. On the Caribbean

---

[8] On US expansion in the Caribbean, see Walter LaFeber, *The New Empire: An Interpretation of American Expansion, 1860–1898* (Ithaca, NY, Cornell University Press, 1963). On US–Latin American relations more generally, see Peter H. Smith, *Talons of the Eagle: Dynamics of U.S.–Latin American Relations* (New York, Oxford University Press, 1996); Jan. F. Triska, *Dominant Powers and Subordinate States: The United States in Latin America and the Soviet Union in Eastern Europe* (Durham, NC, Duke University Press, 1986); Brian Loveman, *No Higher Law: American Foreign Policy and the Western Hemisphere since 1776* (Chapel Hill, NC, University of North Carolina Press, 2010).

[9] Walter LaFeber, *Inevitable Revolutions: The United States in Central America* (New York, W. W. Norton, 1983); Stephen Kinzer, *Overthrow: America's Century of Regime Change from Hawaii to Iraq* (New York, Times Books, 2006).

[10] Minxin Pei, Samia Amin and Seth Garz, 'Building Nations: The American Experience', in *Nation-Building: Beyond Afghanistan and Iraq*, ed. Francis Fukuyama (Baltimore, MD, Johns Hopkins University Press, 2005); Paul D. Miller, *Armed State Building: Confronting State Failure, 1898–2013* (Ithaca, NY, Cornell University Press, 2013).

littoral, the United States inherited, so to speak, states with highly unequal societies already dominated by landowning, agro-exporting elites dominant under prior Spanish rule.[11] Rather than siding with the broad populations of these countries, the United States allied itself with existing elites who were, in turn, dependent on sales in the American market. In doing so, it reinforced the highly unequal and unstable political orders within these societies, which benefitted the elites, and shut off possibilities of political and economic reform that might have benefitted the public at large.

The informal American empire thus reinforced and bolstered authoritarian rule throughout Central America, including the dictatorial and often cruel reigns of Rafael Leonidas Trujillo in the Dominican Republic (1930–61), Anastasio Somoza Garcia and his sons in Nicaragua (1937–79, though with several intermissions), and Francois and Jean Claude Duvalier in Haiti (1957–86). As President Franklin Roosevelt once remarked about Trujillo, 'he may be an SOB, but at least he's our SOB'.[12] The net result was a political order that was skewed toward the United States and its local collaborators and highly undemocratic. Opposition to this order was relatively rare, given the collective action problems for the masses created by centuries of political and economic inequality. When it did arise – as in the Cuban Revolution of 1956, which took the country out of the informal empire; in the Dominican Republic in 1965, where a possible revolution was aborted by the landing of US Marines; and in Nicaragua in the 1980s, where the United States supported the Contras against the Sandinista regime – political opposition took a strongly anti-American cast. Washington responded forcefully to these challenges, including most visibly punishing Cuba for its defiance through a near-complete embargo.

More recently, US–Central American relations have been reset on a new track that permits greater democracy in the region. Under the press of globalisation, many states on the Caribbean littoral have reoriented themselves as labour-intensive export platforms, shifting the median voter away from opposition to the agro-exporting elite to support for policies of greater economic integration preferred by the United States. The Dominican Republic is, perhaps, the exemplar of this trend. In turn, the United States has credibly signalled a rolling back of its level of hierarchy. In the wake of the Vietnam

---

[11] On inequality in Latin America, see Kenneth L. Sokoloff and Stanley L. Engerman, 'History Lessons: Institutions, Factor Endowments, and Paths of Development in the New World', *Journal of Economic Perspectives*, 14/3 (2000).

[12] Quoted in Abraham F. Lowenthal, *The Dominican Intervention* (Baltimore, MD, Johns Hopkins University Press, 1995), 25. The Dominican Republic is an exemplar of the hierarchies built by the United States in the region.

War, President Jimmy Carter sought to reorient long-standing US hierarchies in Central America. He withdrew US support for the most oppressive dictators in the region, promoted human rights, and returned the Canal to Panama as a signal of his commitment to a new relationship. This strategy was reversed in part by President Ronald Reagan, especially in his support for the Nicaraguan Contras. Nonetheless, over the last several decades Carter's approach has generally prevailed and the United States has moved toward a less hierarchical relationship with its southern neighbours and greater support for democracy, a trend that was facilitated in the 1990s by the convergence on the so-called Washington Consensus on neoliberal economic policy. Although the United States undoubtedly retains the ability to intervene if necessary should an anti-American regime come to power – and perhaps the right, as witnessed by the regional support for its invasion of Grenada in 1983 – democracy appears more secure than at any point in the last century. This trajectory is, perhaps, the most optimistic model for the contemporary Middle East. After a period of first challenge and then change, a more legitimate and 'lighter' form of hierarchy can become compatible with greater democracy.

The 'Empire by invitation'[13]

The pattern in Europe and Northeast Asia after 1945 was dramatically different, though the eventual outcome was similar. To deter and, if necessary, fight the Soviet Union, the United States adopted a forward-based defence strategy after the Second World War. This strategy required substantial forces be deployed abroad on a long-term basis, a possibility enabled by the existence of willing subordinates in Europe and Northeast Asia. Given the conflict with the Soviet Union, the gains to the United States were enormous. States subordinate to the United States also gained substantially by not having to pay solely for their own defence against a possibly new imperialist power.[14]

Moreover, after the war at least, the policy preferences of the United States and average citizens in most of Western Europe and Japan were relatively similar. All feared the possibility of future regional conflict, which had resulted in two world wars. Despite significant socialist and communist movements in France, Italy, Greece and Japan, the fictive median voter likely feared the Soviet Union, albeit not to the same degree as most Americans. And despite

[13] The phrase is from Geir Lundestad, *The American 'Empire'* (New York, Oxford University Press, 1990).
[14] On the costs and benefits of hierarchy with Europe after 1945, see Lake, *Entangling Relations: American Foreign Policy in Its Century*, chapter 5.

some dissent on the left, nearly all supported the political order favoured by the United States with its reliance on embedded liberalism in the economic sphere and democracy in the political sphere.[15] The United States also shared its gains from hierarchy with its new subordinates, first through the Marshall Plan, and later unilateral policy concessions, including tariff reductions in early rounds of the GATT, that made participation in the *Pax Americana* more attractive.

The large gains from cooperation between the United States and its new 'allies', the redistribution of some gains to its subordinates, and their broadly similar policy preferences all made hierarchy both possible and, importantly, consistent with democracy. With much greater social equality than in Central America and in some cases past histories of democracy, imposing authoritarian rule in Europe or Northeast Asia after 1945 would have been difficult, and would likely have precluded the United States from creating spheres of influence if it had been necessary. The US did, of course, meddle in the internal affairs of its subordinates to prevent any electoral successes by communist parties after the war,[16] and it redefined what was mostly an internal struggle in Greece in international terms, leading to the Truman Doctrine and the dramatic expansion of the US role in Europe.[17] Likewise, it defined the struggle over the Korean peninsula as part of a global conflict with communism. Given the internal tensions within many post-war states, the US did not assume that its new allies would accept their subordinate positions without some potentially significant internal opposition. But in fact the gains from cooperation under hierarchy were large – broadly shared and political preferences were sufficiently similar that limited US rule over the foreign policies of its far-flung subordinates was established democratically and with at least some measure of domestic support.

The transformative effect of the *Pax Americana* over time cannot be overstated. Europe had fought two world wars, both over political control of

---

[15] On Europe and the US-led international order, see David P. Calleo and Benjamin Rowland, *American and the World Political Economy: Atlantic Dreams and National Realities* (Bloomington, IN, Indiana University Press, 1973); G. John Ikenberry, *After Victory: Institutions, Strategic Restraint, and the Rebuilding of Order after Major Wars* (Princeton, NJ, Princeton University Press, 2001), chapter 6; *Liberal Leviathan: The Origins, Crisis, and Transformation of the American World Order* (Princeton, NJ, Princeton University Press, 2011).

[16] See Irwin M. Wall, *The United States and the Making of Postwar France, 1945–1954* (New York, Cambridge University Press, 1991); James Edward Miller, *The United States and Italy, 1940–1950: The Politics and Diplomacy of Stabilization* (Chapel Hill, NC, University of North Carolina Press, 1986).

[17] Melvyn P. Leffler, *A Preponderance of Power: National Security, the Truman Administration, and the Cold War* (Stanford, CA, Stanford University Press, 1992), 142–146.

the continent and, in 1939, as a clash of ideologies between liberalism, fascism and communism. Japan had attempted to build its own empire in Asia. After 1945, rather than reifying differences with its new allies, the United States supported moderate Christian Democrats in Germany and Liberal Democrats in Japan willing to cast their lot with the US-led order.[18] Having induced new subordinates to join this order, the domestic political economies of the major powers solidified around a consensus on economic integration and military support for the United States. The success of state-building in Germany and Japan after the Second World War, a source of mystery to many contemporary analysts, had less to do with the particular strategies employed by the United States and much more to do with the large gains from international cooperation that, through a degree of enlightened leadership in both Washington and the new elites in these previously authoritarian states, were broadly shared.[19] The result was a remarkably stable and democratic international hierarchy led by the United States. Even the socialist and communist parties in Europe and Northeast Asia softened their opposition to US hierarchy over time, with the Italian Communist Party announcing in 1975 that it favoured continued membership in NATO.[20] Today, some European states and Japan remain strong supporters of US leadership, but most have moved from relations of hierarchy in the early post-war period to cooperation based on relatively similar policy preferences. Hierarchy has not diminished as a result of new demands for sovereignty or national control, but because the United States and its advanced industrialised subordinates have moved sufficiently together that authority is less necessary to reap the gains of pooling efforts and resources in world affairs.

A new world order

Since at least 1933, when Standard Oil first began investing in Saudi Arabia, the United States has sought a more prominent role in the Middle East and to recruit subordinates through which it could influence events in the region. This effort expanded somewhat after the Second World War, and became more intense in the late 1960s as Britain withdrew East of Suez. It was at this time

[18] On US support for moderates in Germany, see Leffler, *A Preponderance of Power*, esp. 318–319.
[19] On the mysterious success of state-building in Germany and Japan, see James Dobbins *et al.*, *America's Role in Nation-Building: From Germany to Iraq* (Santa Monica, CA, RAND, 2003), chapters 2 and 3.
[20] Robert D. Putnam, 'Interdependence and the Italian Communists', *International Organization*, 32/2 (1978).

that the United States made a decisive commitment to Israel during the 1967 War. The US effort expanded further in the 1970s after OPEC embargoed oil shipments to North America and Europe, dramatically increased oil prices and shifted enormous wealth to the oil-producing states. Long-standing ties to Saudi Arabia, which had frayed during the early 1960s, were strengthened, and deeper ties were formed with the Shah of Iran under the Nixon Doctrine, through which the United States attempted to court and prop up subordinate regimes in the region.[21] US involvement grew dramatically however, during the Persian Gulf War, when it deployed massive forces to the region for the first time, and in the invasions of Afghanistan in 2001 and Iraq in 2003. This effort to expand the *Pax Americana* into the Middle East is the centrepiece of the New World Order envisioned by President George H.W. Bush after the Cold War.

Today, the United States has limited hierarchies over many states in the Middle East, especially in the Persian Gulf. Due to its backing of Israel, no Arab regime can be seen as too close to the United States, and few are willing to sign formal alliances or host US bases or open-ended troop deployments, traditional vehicles through which the United States has exercised its authority elsewhere. Nonetheless, through more covert ties, overt but less permanent forms of cooperation like joint military training exercises, and the implicit dependence of many regimes in the region on the protection of the United States, Washington exerts considerable authority over the security and economic policies of Egypt, Saudi Arabia, Kuwait, the Gulf Emirates and others, now including Iraq and Afghanistan.[22]

The gains for the United States from these hierarchies are hard to estimate but likely limited. The United States is deeply involved at present in providing regional stability, which produces, first and foremost, a secure supply of oil at moderate prices for itself and other countries around the world (but see below). This appears to be the primary benefit to the United States. Other than oil security, it is difficult to see what strategic interests the United States has in the region that are not otherwise connected to the effort to create international hierarchies themselves. The cost of stabilising the region, on the other hand, has been enormous. The peace dividend, much anticipated after the

---

[21] On US–Saudi ties, see Madawi Al-Rasheed, *A History of Saudi Arabia* (New York, Cambridge University Press, 2010), esp. pp. 113–116 and 35–57. On Iran, see Robert Litwak, *Detente and the Nixon Doctrine: American Foreign Policy and the Pursuit of Stability, 1969–1976* (New York, Cambridge University Press, 1984), esp. 139–143.

[22] On the operationalisation of security and economic hierarchy and changing patterns of hierarchy in the Middle East over time, see Lake, *Hierarchy in International Relations*, chapter 3, updated in 'Legitimating Power: The Domestic Politics of U.S. International Hierarchy'.

Soviet Union imploded, has been largely swallowed by attempts to assert US authority in the region, including three wars (1993, 2001, 2003) and the larger Global War on Terror. Some significant fraction of the benefits earned by the United States through its regional hierarchies are also returned to subordinates in foreign aid, most importantly to Israel and Egypt (in 2010, a total of $4.6 billion). The benefits and costs to the United States of its Middle Eastern hierarchies are difficult to quantify, but on net the gains by the United States appear small.

States elites in the region, however, benefit significantly from the political order produced by the United States. For decades, the United States has been the ultimate guarantor of their security. Israel, which is largely capable of defending itself and has defeated its enemies at every turn in the past, is nonetheless dependent on the United States for weaponry and as a protector of 'last resort', to borrow a phrase from financial circles. As proven in 1991, despite billions of dollars of sophisticated weapons purchased from the United States, Saudi Arabia cannot defend itself against the regional forces potentially arrayed against it.[23] This holds even more so for Kuwait, which was overrun by Iraq in one night, and the Emirates, which are equally vulnerable because of their tiny size. If its subordinates had to pay for their own security, either the political landscape of the Middle East would be very different – with the many small states consolidated into a few larger ones – or their defence burdens would be greater than now, potentially bankrupting all but the richest.

The policy preferences of the United States and average citizens in the Middle East are likely quite distant. Even without US support for Israel, a flashpoint for most Arabs, history, culture and religion conspire to keep the West and this largely Muslim world apart. One need not subscribe to the clash of civilisations to recognise that these are distinct societies with different cultural traditions on the role of free markets, the role of women in politics and society, the balance between secular and religious authority and more.[24] Resource extraction typically does not breed entrepreneurship nor support economic liberalism, a key pillar of the US-led international order.[25] This implies that, to control policy despite these differences, the United States must aim to establish more hierarchical relations than was in the case in, for

[23] On military capabilities and strategy during the war, see Lawrence Freedman and Efraim Karsh, *The Gulf Conflict, 1990–1991: Diplomacy and War in the New World Order* (Princeton, NJ, Princeton University Press, 1993).
[24] Samuel P. Huntington, *The Clash of Civilizations and the Remaking of World Order* (New York, Simon and Schuster, 1996). For an alternative view of civilisational cleavages, see Peter J. Katzenstein, ed. *Civilizations in World Politics: Plural and Pluralist Perspectives* (New York, Routledge, 2010).
[25] Michael L. Ross, 'The Political Economy of the Resource Curve', *World Politics*, 51/2 (1999).

instance, Europe after 1945. As they consolidate, US ties with Middle Eastern states will likely resemble US–Central America relations in the early twentieth century.

Distant policy preferences further imply that US subordinates will be governed indirectly by highly authoritarian regimes that are, nonetheless, sustained in power because they are sympathetic to the United States and its interests in the region. The benefits of hierarchy appear insufficient to allow the United States to buy support from the local populations and thereby render these states legitimate in the eyes of their people, as it did with the Marshall Plan in a considerably more friendly Europe after the Second World War. Nonetheless, their ties to the United States can sustain authoritarian leaders in power for decades. Egypt under President Hosni Mubarak and now President Abdel Fattah el-Sisi is exemplary. In turn, regime opponents will be strongly anti-American, which appears to be the trend across the region.[26] From the Muslim Brotherhood in Egypt to al-Qaida, which turned its focus toward the 'far enemy' after US forces were stationed on Saudi soil in 1990, radical groups shut out of power have recognised that the road to revolution at home runs through Washington, DC.[27]

The reaction: global insurgency

Terrorism is the political strategy of necessity for opponents of the *Pax Americana* and the local autocracies it supports. With the United States having co-opted leaders in key states, opponents of those leaders and, in turn, the United States must be 'private' or non-state actors. Shut out of open competition for political influence within their states, moreover, opponents can only aim to overthrow the American-backed regimes through violence. Finally, unable to fight equally against their home governments or engage the military capabilities of the United States, the insurgents must use the traditional weapon of the weak to launch 'terrorist' attacks against unprotected or 'soft' civilian targets. Through terrorism, the opponents hope either to defeat the regime, extract concessions that reward their supporters and increase their popularity at home, or provoke the government into counter-reactions that, through the collateral damage from insurgents hiding in sympathetic populations, also

[26] Kuwait appears to be the exception to this rule. See Jamal, *Of Empires and Citizens: Pro-American Democracy or No Democracy at All?*

[27] On al-Qaida, see Fawaz A. Gerges, *The Far Enemy: Why Jihad Went Global*, 2nd edn (New York, Cambridge University Press, 2009).

build support for their cause.[28] In this way, terrorism is the 'natural', indeed, nearly the *only* possible response to the structural disadvantages of private opposition groups trying to change current political relations within subordinate states and with the United States.

In the Middle East today, uniquely, political opposition has been fused with religious fundamentalism. For decades, local regimes have been unable or unwilling to shut down religious institutions, leaving religious movements as virtually the only means through which opposition to the state and *Pax Americana* could mobilise. Such movements, in turn, are easily captured by religious extremists who often adhere to an idealised image of 'tradition' in their societies, and by implication are most likely to prefer policies different from the United States and its local allies. Having solved their collective action problems, moreover, religious organisations that choose to take up violence are especially effective.[29] The net effect has been to combine the motivating ideology of religion with political opposition that has little chance of success except through the use of terrorism. This has created a particularly toxic global insurgency with broad appeal across Muslim societies.

By way of comparison, the emphasis on terrorism is different in those few states that have yet to be brought within the *Pax Americana*. Here, Iran is a prime example, long classified by the United States as a 'rogue' regime for its opposition to its authority under the Shah and in the region more generally. In this case, the opposition to the United States largely takes the form of a more traditional, state-to-state military competition, though each is strong enough to deter the other except in the most extreme circumstances.[30] The United States overthrew a similarly rogue regime in Iraq largely to remove a leader that would not acknowledge its authority and who posed a continuing threat to peace and stability in the region. It also supported the Arab Spring uprisings in other rogue states, especially Libya and Syria, while not opposing the violent repression of similar movements in its subordinates, like Bahrain. In all of these rogue states, though intertwined with terrorism or the possibility of terrorism, relations with the United States take the form of more traditional 'anarchies' that, importantly, are less focused on terrorism and more

---

[28] On strategies of terrorism, see Andrew H. Kydd and Barbara F. Walter, 'The Strategies of Terrorism', *International Security*, 31/1 (2006).

[29] Eli Berman, *Radical, Religious, and Violent: The New Economics of Terroism* (Cambridge, MA, MIT Press, 2009).

[30] If Iran actually comes close to completing a nuclear weapon or the United States sees no alternative except to change the regime, the stakes may be sufficiently high that deterrence fails. Iran, of course, supports terrorist organisations elsewhere in the region opposed to the United States and its local allies.

driven by conventional military competition. Paradoxically, terrorism within the global insurgency arises primarily from within autocratic states aligned with the United States.

A final feature of the insurgency also follows from the unique nature of the *Pax Americana*. Private actors who use terror outside established political systems are always vulnerable to state prosecution and eradication. The insurgents, as a consequence, have created decentralised networks that insulate them from penetration by informers.[31] More important, they have also gone 'global', fleeing to the ungoverned spaces where they can operate more freely away from the preying eyes of effective states. This transnational structure is facilitated through the binding power of religion, creating a world-wide jihadi movement that links loosely coupled groups. Ironically, this structure is made possible by some of the key pillars of the *Pax Americana* that the insurgents seek to overthrow, including free movement of goods, people and money and a telecommunications infrastructure that allows coordination across sometimes distant borders. Although the United States can try to monitor and restrict the global activities of the insurgents, it cannot do so completely without undermining the gains from economic integration so attractive to the members of the *Pax Americana*. Thus, the United States and its allies face not just local opposition to their international order, but a Global War on Terror in which their military and economic options are limited by the very system they seek to promote.

The counter-reaction: state-building

The United States has responded in a variety of ways to the global insurgency. One prong is enhanced counter-terrorist (CT) capabilities and operations, beginning with cruise missile attacks on suspected terrorist training centres under President Bill Clinton to drone missile strikes today under President Barak Obama. A near constant under the last four US presidents, this strategy both pursues individual terrorists and seeks to decapitate terrorist organisations. A second prong has been regime change, adopted in both Afghanistan in 2001 and Iraq in 2003. Following the terrorist attacks of 9/11, the Bush administration responded aggressively by overthrowing regimes that aided or

---

[31] Miles Kahler, 'Collective Action and Clandestine Networks: The Case of Al Qaeda', in *Networked Politics: Agency, Power, and Governance*, ed. Miles Kahler (Ithaca, NY, Cornell University Press, 2009).

might aid terrorist organisations.[32] In both Afghanistan and Iraq, however, the comparatively simple ambition to remove obstructionist regimes and leaders quickly morphed into the third strategy.

In many ways, the primary prong of the US response to the global insurgency has been state-building, both in countries where it has intervened militarily and in other ungoverned spaces that can potentially serve as havens for the transnational terrorists. The goal of the United States and its allies in state-building is to rehabilitate and expand the capacity of states to control their own territories and suppress mobile insurgents who might inhabit otherwise ungoverned spaces. This is a conservative response, in the more general sense of that word as a commitment to tradition. State-building attempts to bolster states so that they can abide by the norm of state responsibility for private violence projected across their borders.[33] Rather than contemplating alternatives to state sovereignty – perhaps an international force to fight terrorists – the preferred solution is limited to strengthening state capacity wherever it may be lacking. In this way, state-building is security policy of the highest order, but one well within historical patterns and, indeed, similar to the US role in Central America in the early twentieth century.

The central task of all state-building is to create a state that is regarded as legitimate by the people over whom it exercises authority. In recent decades, state-builders have gained new appreciation of the critical importance of legitimacy for state success. A key problem in all international state-building attempts, however, is that states sufficiently motivated to bear the costs of building a state in some distant land are likely to have interests in the future course of that regime, and will therefore seek to promote leaders who are at least sympathetic to their interests, if not active proponents, and willing to implement their preferred policies. This is identical to the problem of promoting 'loyal' leaders in hierarchy, discussed above.[34] Except in rare cases where the policy preferences of the state-builder and the population of the country whose state is to be built coincide, as in West Germany and Japan after 1945, promoting a leader loyal to the state-builder undermines that leader's legitimacy at home. The greater the interests of the state-builder in the target state,

---

[32] On the origins of the Iraq war, including the botched intelligence on ties to terrorism, see Frank P. Harvey, *Explaining the Iraq War: Counterfactual Theory, Logic and Evidence* (New York, Cambridge University Press, 2012); David A. Lake, 'Two Cheers for Bargaining Theory: Rationalist Explanations of the Iraq War', *International Security*, 35/3 (2010–11); Alexandre Debs and Nuno P. Monteiro, 'Known Unknowns: Power Shifts, Uncertainty, and War', *International Organization*, 68/1 (2014).

[33] On the origins of this norm, see Janice E. Thomson, *Mercenaries, Pirates, and Sovereigns: State-Building and Extraterritorial Violence in Early Modern Europe* (Princeton, NJ, Princeton University Press, 1994).

[34] Lake, 'Legitimating Power: The Domestic Politics of U.S. International Hierarchy'.

the more likely it is to intervene, the greater the costs it is willing to bear, the more likely it is to install a loyal leader and the less likely that leader will be to govern legitimately. Ironically, as is true of the United States in Iraq since 2003, the greater the interests of the state-builder in the target, the less likely state-building is to succeed over the long term, as evidenced in the collapse of the Iraqi state in the summer of 2014 in the face of militant attacks from Islamic State of Iraq and Syria.[35]

States have sought to manage the state-builder's dilemma in different ways at different times.[36] As practised by many states prior to 1990 and exemplified by the role of the United States in Central America in the early twentieth century, state-builders evinced little concern for the legitimacy of the externally supported state. Even in their informal empires characterised by indirect rule, state-builders privileged their own interests and policies by supporting loyal leaders willing to do their bidding. For the United States, as described above, this led to support for pro-American autocratic and even despotic rulers. The cost of this support, however, was that the political opposition inevitably became anti-American.

Current practice increasingly recognises the importance of building legitimate states but in doing so makes the tradeoff between loyalty and legitimacy more acute. Liberal state-building, beginning with the end of the Cold War, elevated the goal of building legitimate states but premised strategy on a belief that democracy and free markets would be sufficient to legitimate a government in the eyes of its people. Pursued in virtually all state-building attempts of the 1990s and early 2000s, this assumption turned out to be tragically wrong and was eventually abandoned, although not before there were shocking levels of human suffering.[37] Replacing liberal theory in Iraq and Afghanistan after 2007, a new theory of state-building based on counterinsurgency warfare (COIN) also highlights the need for state legitimacy but bases this on a social contract view of the state. Rather than relying on popular participation to legitimate the state, COIN focuses on providing security and other public goods to win the 'hearts and minds' of the people. In my view, and as experience in Iraq and Afghanistan suggests, this is an important step in the right direction.

[35] David A. Lake, *The Statebuilder's Dilemma: Legitimacy, Loyalty, and the Limits of External Intervention* (Ithaca, NY, Cornell University Press, 2016).
[36] David A. Lake, 'The Practice and Theory of U.S. Statebuilding', *Journal and Intervention and Statebuilding* 4, no. 3 (2010).
[37] Roland Paris, *At War's End: Building Peace after Civil Conflict* (New York, Cambridge University Press, 2004).

Yet, regardless of strategy, the tradeoff between the legitimacy and loyalty of newly installed leaders cannot be obviated simply by reforms or improved practice. The larger the state-building effort required, the more acute the dilemma becomes. The greater the costs of state-building, the more the state-builder will insist upon a return on investment through the installation of a leader likely to be more loyal to its interests. As in hierarchy more generally, supporting loyal leaders will stimulate opposition that, once again, has little choice but to take up arms against the state and its external supporter – the United States. Overall, state-building is not a solution to the global insurgency but, in fact, a catalyst for further opposition.

The way forward

There is likely no total or permanent solution to the global insurgency. The United States is unlikely to withdraw entirely from the Middle East – nor should it – and it will inevitably favour pro-Western regimes. Nor can it build effective states in all corners of the globe where insurgents might seek sanctuary. The United States has basically two options, portrayed here in extreme form to highlight the differences.

The United States could go 'all in' and seek to fight the global insurgency with a global counter-insurgency. The new COIN strategy aims to provide the local population the public services they need, and ultimately earn their loyalty. One alternative in the Middle East today is to generalise this counter-insurgency strategy to the regional or global level. To succeed, the United States would have to expand security efforts in the region, assist local states in suppressing the insurgents that might target civilian populations, and make credible its commitment to stabilise the region with pro-Western governments. By demonstrating the will to bear any cost, the United States might be able to convince the insurgents that they cannot win. This was, in part, the strategy adopted by the United States in Central America, and it required twenty military interventions in the region over many decades before it succeeded. In the contemporary Middle East, the United States would have to be prepared for perhaps an even greater number of military interventions in the years ahead.

To help win hearts and minds, the United States would also have to transfer a larger share of its gains from cooperation to societies in the region, most likely expanding efforts at political and economic development much as it did in Europe after the Second World War. Simultaneously, it would need to ensure that these benefits are distributed broadly and not simply appropriated by existing collaborators. In this alternative, the United States would try to buy the support of the average citizen in its Middle Eastern subordinates, not just the small autocratic elite that it has already paid for. This would entail significant increases in foreign aid, expanded support for entrepreneurship and economic openness in Arab societies, and new limits on the deadening hand of state power and corruption. This 'Marshall Plan' for the Middle East will not be cheap; nor is it likely to have a dramatic impact in the short term. But with time, with a security strategy for protecting the population against any actions likely to be undertaken by the insurgents and an economic strategy that dramatically improves the lives of moderates in the Arab world, the United States might build broader legitimacy for its hierarchies in the region and, in turn, democracy.

Yet, as Robert Jervis has written about the strategy of primacy more generally, expanding the *Pax Americana* into new regions may not be 'worth the candle'.[38] Although the potential gains from fully integrating the Middle East into the *Pax Americana* may be greater than those realised now – imagine a future Middle East as prosperous and economically integrated as Europe, or perhaps on the same trajectory as Central America – the costs of pacifying the opposition and building states able to reach this point are likely insurmountable, or at least far beyond anything American taxpayers are willing to support. As British economic historian Niall Ferguson has written, Americans simply 'lack the imperial cast of mind'.[39] Even though the United States was willing to pay the cost in Central America a century ago, the Middle East promises to be a much tougher case.

Alternatively, the United States could retrench and withdraw from the Middle East much as Britain, the last imperial power, did after 1968. To the extent the global insurgency is driven at least in part by the US strategy of expanding the *Pax Americana*, retrenchment might relieve some of the pressure on the United States and local regimes. While the insurgents might still aim to topple apostate regimes, without the United States supporting those regimes and seeking to impose its preferred order on the Middle East much of the ire now directed at Washington might eventually dissipate and be directed 'inwards'.[40] This would, of course, likely spell the end of some US-supported

---

[38] Robert Jervis, 'International Primacy: Is the Game Worth the Candle?', *International Security*, 17/4 (1993).

[39] Niall Ferguson, *Colossus: The Price of America's Empire* (New York, Penguin Press, 2004), 29.

[40] Gerges, *The Far Enemy: Why Jihad Went Global*. See also Jamal, *Of Empires and Citizens: Pro-American Democracy or No Democracy at All?*

regimes and set off new rounds of domestic instability in these now weak-ened states, such as those already seen after the Arab Spring in Libya. But the United States does not get to select the ideal world it wants. It can only choose how to deal with the world it confronts.

Most importantly, the assumption that the United States actually has vital interests in the Middle East is often taken as an article of faith in Washington, but it is an assumption that should be critically examined. The Middle East's primary resource, oil, is readily available from other countries in other regions. The region accounted for only 31% of world petroleum output in 2011, and is steadily declining as new energy sources come online.[41] Although Americans worry about security of supply, it is as much in the interests of oil producers to sell their output as it is in the interests of consumers to buy it. Price manipu-lation by OPEC is a possibility, albeit a declining threat, as OPEC's control over new entrants in the oil market is steadily receding and alternative energy sources are developed. Moreover, with what we now know about global cli-mate change, countries everywhere ought to be imposing carbon taxes to both reduce emissions and break the backs of petro-states who use their proceeds to exploit their own people, fight foreign wars and support terrorists. Finally, as oil and gas extracted from shale rock formations increases, the United States is likely to surpass Saudi Arabia as the world's largest oil producer by 2017 and may become energy independent by 2030.[42] What happens in the Middle East is likely to become increasingly irrelevant to the United States in the decades ahead. The expansion of the *Pax Americana* into the Middle East is a choice, not a requirement, for future prosperity. Current leaders in Washington from across the political spectrum appear to take the need for a presence in the Middle East for granted. Retrenchment from the Middle East is both possible and prudent – and would take at least some of the wind out of the sails of the global insurgency.

This will be the key foreign policy debate in the United States in the near term. Double-down and succeed in extending the *Pax Americana* in the face of resistance, or retrench from the Middle East and allow the region to implode on its own. Neither is attractive – and the United States today is not able to make tough choices in its highly partisan political atmosphere. We will likely muddle through, oscillating between the two extremes. This may well be worse than acting decisively in either direction: keeping the United

---

[41] US Department of Energy, US Energy Information Administration, available at: http://www.eia.gov/cfapps/ipdbproject/IEDIndex3.cfm?tid=5&pid=53&aid=1 [accessed 9 February 2013].

[42] Benjamin Alter and Edward Fishman, 'The Dark Side of Energy Independence', *New York Times*, 28 April 2013.

States involved in the region without actually creating the international order that could attract moderates to its leadership. My own view is that the United States, as a country, has far less at stake than normally averred, and thus should favour a strategy of retrenchment. But this is a debate the United States and its allies, who will inevitably be affected by either choice, should have soon.

Index